सूत्रधारमण्डनकृतम्

वास्तुमण्डनम्

VĀSTUMAṆḌANAM

OF

SŪTRADHĀRA MAṆḌANA

कलामूलशास्त्र-ग्रन्थमाला
KALĀMŪLAŚĀSTRA SERIES

इ.गा.रा.क.के.*क.मू.शा.*-६७
I.G.N.C.A. *K.M.S.*-67

सूत्रधारमण्डनकृतम्

वास्तुमण्डनम्

VĀSTUMAṆḌANAM

OF

SŪTRADHĀRA MAṆḌANA

Critically Edited Text with Critical Notes,
Translation, Appendices and Plates by

DR. ANASUYA BHOWMICK

INDIRA GANDHI NATIONAL CENTRE FOR THE ARTS,
NEW DELHI
and
MOTILAL BANARSIDASS PUBLISHERS PVT. LTD.,
DELHI

First Edition : Delhi, 2017

Managing Editor : Dr. Sudhir Lall

Published by
INDIRA GANDHI NATIONAL CENTRE FOR THE ARTS
Central Vista Mess, Janpath, New Delhi-110001

in association with
MOTILAL BANARSIDASS PUBLISHERS PVT. LTD.
Bungalow Road, Jawahar Nagar, Delhi - 110007

ISBN : 978-81-208-4019-5

Price : Rs. 1350/-

Typeset by
Amar Printing Press
8/25, Vijay Nagar, Delhi-110009
e-mail : amarprintingpress@gmail.com

Printed in India by
Thomson Press (India) Ltd.
18.35, Delhi Mathura Road,
Faridabad (Haryana)

CONTENTS

FOREWORD

The *Kalāmūlaśāstra* series of Indira Gandhi National Centre for the Arts (IGNCA) is aimed at bringing to light the primary textual source material hitherto unknown, unpublished or inaccessible both in original language as also in translation. Under the aegis of this ongoing and long term research programme, the publication of the fundamental texts of Indian arts is undertaken along with annotations and translations. The critical edition of each text is prepared on the basis of several manuscripts, those being collated, transcribed, etc. along with the commentary of the source material, if any.

So far in this series, along with other works on different aspects of Indian arts, three seminal works on Indian architecture have been brought to light, namely, *Mayamatam* (edited and translated by Bruno Dagens), *Śilparatnakośa* of Śthāpaka Nirañjana Mahāpātra (edited and translated by Bettina Baumer and Rajendra Prasad Dash) and *Śilpa Prakāśa* of Rāmacandra Mahāpātra Kaula Bhaṭṭāraka (edited and translated by Bettina Baumer, Rajendra Prasad Das and Sadanana Das). The present volume titled the *Vāstumaṇḍana* of Sūtradhāra Maṇḍana is another value addition and it is a matter of immense pleasure for us at IGNCA to publish this significant work on medieval Indian architecture from western India under the *Kalāmūlaśāstra* series. Sūtradhāra Maṇḍana is believed to be the chief architect of Mahārāṇa of Kumbhalgarh and his fundamental writings were used as manuals by the practicing architects. Thus the *Vāstumaṇḍana* is a critical landmark in the development of Indian architecture.

Dr. (Smt.) Anasuya Bhowmick is a noted modern scholar and is an authority in the field of Indian architecture. She has painstakingly prepared the critical edition by surveying all the available manuscript material and has given a suitable English translation to it. She has also given various indices, charts and illustrations to make the concepts embedded in the text more intelligible to readers. The edition paves the way for a better comprehension of Indian architecture. This publication is another example of Dr. (Smt.) Anasuya Bhowmick's scholarly contribution to the field of Indian architecture in particular and to Indian Arts in general. Dr. Sudhir Lall of the Kalākośa division is the managing editor of this volume, who contributed tirelessly, in bringing the output submitted by Dr. (Smt.) Bhowmick to the stage of publication.

We fervently hope that the academic fraternity will welcome this significant contribution by IGNCA and will benefit from it. The IGNCA looks forward to receiving feedback from the readers of this publication. We would appreciate your suggestions or comments for incorporation in the future editions of *Vāstumaṇḍana*.

Dr. Sachchidanand Joshi
Member-Secretary,
IGNCA

October, 2016

INTRODUCTION

In *The Indian Encyclopedia*, architecture has been depicted as the rudimentary art of India and almost all other forms of art have emerged as accessories to it. We find similar tune in the article written by K.R. Pisharoti, who writes, 'Architecture is one of the most important forms in which the Indian culture has found expression from ancient times.' The *New Encyclopedia Britannica* explicates architecture along with some other arts, the practice of architecture embraces both aesthetic and utilitarian aspects. In this context Pisharoti says, 'Architecture is primarily utilitarian, both in conception and in practice, and at the same time it is expected to satisfy aesthetic sense. A structure which has any pretence to architectural quality must satisfy both these aspects of utility and of beauty.'

Architecture has a sprawling history in our country. We find references of various architectural forms specially altars of multifarious shapes and sizes for sacrifices in the Vedic literature.

Some of the major Purāṇas like *Matsya, Agni, Garuḍa* and others, expatiate and explain various aspects of architecture. In the later period we find a number of texts from different regions of India, which deal extensively with different forms of architecture; religious as well as secular. To name a few they are *Mānasāra, Mayamata, Viśvakarmā Vāstuśāstra, Samarāṅgaṇasūtradhāra, Aparājitapṛchhā* and so on.

The *Vāstumaṇḍana,* a treatise on architecture of medieval age, shows close acquaintance with the *vāstu* works from Gujarat. Basically it is a compilation from other *vāstu* texts, in some places it shows its inherent exclusivity.

MANUSCRIPTS OF THE *VĀSTUMAṆḌANA*

To prepare the critical text of the *Vāstumaṇḍana*, five manuscripts have been consulted. These are collected from different parts of India.

Manusript A

The mother one (A) was collected from BORI. Pune. Its record no. is 123. It is written in Devanāgarī script, and complete with 35 folios, each consisting of 12/13 lines. The size of this manuscript is 9. 5/9 inches x 41/8 in. The material is country made paper. The date is saṁvat 1675 i.e., 1618 A.D.

The manuscript has some peculiarities. The scribe writes ष्, and घ् in stead of थ and ष instead of ख; such as मुष instead of मुख in Ch. 1 verse no 48, 51 and in many other places. In many places, we find श instead of स such as नाशिका (नासिका), माश (मास) and sometimes स्मशान instead of श्मशान (20.a.ll).

The scribe used पृष्ठमात्रा instead of the normal one, such as he writes सुलग्ने च सुभे दिने in the first chapter. Again in the same chapter we find दित्रोन्तशषाटाधनिष्ठो। In the 10th folio we find वोर instead of वौर.

He has the tendency of interchanging the syllables, e.g., चम्पक instead of पञ्चक (f20bl.2) प्रवि instead of विप्र, (2nd Ch. v 57), स्यते instead of तस्ये (f23bl.6) and so on.

In case of रेफ् he writes रेफ् and रफला together. For example दुर्ग for दुर्ग्र् or दुर्ग्रन्धा for दुर्गन्धा (Śl. 74, 2nd Ch.).

Some times he writes छ like (31a, 11, b13, 33b, 4.67, etc.). In the colphon and post colophon the scribe did not mention his name or other particulars, but he mentions the number of *ślokas* of each chapter which does not tally always with the actual *ślokas* found herein. He has mentioned only the year of writing but not the place and other materials which are generally found in the colophon or post colophon portions of the manuscripts.

We find contradiction in his own counting. He writes, प्रकीर्णकाध्यायोऽष्टम:, श्लोक – 109, just after that when he is giving account of different chapters, he writes सादित्ये शतमष्ठते, i.e., 112.

He writes

वास्तुमण्डनश्च सम्पूर्ण: स हये द्वेशते आद्ये 207, सप्ताशीति द्वितीयके 87। तृतीये पञ्चनवति 95, रुपाग्येकास्तुरीयके 131 द्वात्रिंशत्पञ्चमे श्लोका 32 भूद्वयेकारससंमिते 121 सप्तमे पञ्चनवति सादित्य शतमष्टमे 112

श्री वास्तुमण्डने तन्त्रे अध्यायेतु प्रकीर्णके एक्ये पुन:शतान्यष्टश्लोकाश्चाशीतिसन्मिता: 882

Here also we find difference in indicating verse numbers. Once he is giving verse number 800, next he writes verse number 882.

Manuscript B

The second manuscript (B) is collected from the Asiatic Society. Its record no. is G 5505. It is written on country-made paper and the size is 10 x 4.5 inches. It is complete in fifty-two folios containing ten lines generally, but sometimes we find nine lines also. The script is Devanāgarī. The condition of the manuscript is good. It is dated *saṁvat* 1797, i.e., 1730 A.D.

Here also we find a few peculiarities of the scribe. He has a tendency of writing same consonants one after another. Such as मानसलोल्लास् (lbsl8) or भर्भु instead of भर्तुः (ld3sl3) or ललं instead of तलं (28b.5) and many more.

He writes 'राम' on each 'B' folio and after folio 28th it seems the handwriting has been changed.

Here, in the post-colophon entry the scribe writes

सुतेन देवसिंहेण प्रार्थितः श्रेनन्दनः /

Then he indexed the *ślokas* with numbers in each chapter and at the end he gives his own short details संवत् 1897 माधवदिगरौश्री उदयपुरत्राधान्या श्रीपुराणा श्रीजगत्सिंह विजयराज्ये भट्टभाइ रामसुतोभट्टनीलकंठोहम लेखि श्रीरामोजयति /

It seems the scribe is a devotee of Rāma. In the descriptive catalogue, it is written that extent in *ślokas* are 900 but actually we find lesser numbers.

Manuscript C

The third Manuscript (C) is collected form the Oriental Institute, M.S. University of Baroda. Its accession no. is 5317. This is a complete manuscript with 49 folia, but 8 folia are missing in between. These are 1, 2, 7, 10, 28, 29, 32,43 folio. The lines per folio are inconsistent. There are 8, 9, 10 or 11 lines in different folia. Script is nāgari and the date is saṁvat 1811, i.e., 1754 A.D. The name of the scribe is not mentioned in the post colophon. Only the date of copying is given as follows:-

सम्वत् १८११ मितिमाघवदि २ मंगलवासरायां लिपिकृतम् //

Manuscripts D and E

The fourth (D) and fifth (E) were collected from Saraswati Bhawan, Benaras (Record No. 33876 and 4330). Manuscripts D is incomplete in 18 folios, and the numbers of lines vary from 15 to 19. The script is Nāgarī and the date is not mentioned – size is 12.8 x 6.3 inches.

Manuscript E is complete in 25 folios. Numbers of lines are different in different folios varying from 11 to 13 lines. Script is *Nāgarī* and the size is 13.2 x 4 inches. In this manuscript, we find some marginal notes and a few graphs. It seems that the scribe was proficient in *jyotiṣa*, so wherever he felt, he did some graph or calculation and made a few comments on the border. In the beginning he writes :-

ग्राम नाम अधिष्ठाता कर नक्षत्रमध्यदैकर लिखव/ शुक्रेचन्द्रे जलाधारौ देवता वसते गुरौ// रवौ चतुष्पदस्थानम् मेडिका निश्चयावधः/ भौमेऽग्निधकं चैव शनौ राहौ क्षयंकरः //१//

Date is 1890 *saṁvat,* 1755 *śaka,* i.e., 1833 A.D.

In the post-colophon it is written:

ग्रंथसंख्या ८८०/ सम्वत् १८९० शके १७५५ फाल्गुनशुक्ल ३ वृहस्पतौ / श्रीरामो

He also writes श्रीराम on each folio.

For nasal consonants – ङ्, ञ्, ण, न, म all the scribes write.

This is in short the description of five manuscripts used in editing the *Vāstumaṇḍana.*

MAṆḌANA SŪTRADHĀRA AND HIS DATE

In the 15th century, a brief but glorious period existed for the late medieval style of western Indian Architecture. The prevailing environment provided Maṇḍana Sūtradhāra with the opportunity of evincing his flair, potency, conceptual acuity and functional brilliance on architecture as well as on sculpture. Maṇḍana, who was endowed with scholastic erudition, enjoyed the royal patronage of Rāṇā Kuṁbhā of Chitor in whose court flourished several men of literary prowess. This royal architect wrote and compiled a number of treatises on architecture and iconography.

Being an author of that period, he had an exposure to the previous authoritative *Vāstuśāstras* and the Purāṇas from which he elicited his inspiration.

Maṇḍana's father Kṣetra was also an architect. In the concluding *śloka* of *Vāstumaṇḍana,* he writes –

सुतेन दैवसिंहेन प्रार्थित: क्षेत्रमण्डन:
स्थपति: सृजति स्मेदं मण्डनो वास्तुमण्डनम्

There has been lot of confusion regarding his origin. According to one tradition Maṇḍana hails from Gujarat and was invited by Mahārāṇā Kuṁbha in his court to compose treatise on *Vāstuśāstras.* According to other tradition and a few colophons of Maṇḍana's works – Kṣetra and his son Maṇḍana belonged to proper Mewar but their forefather hailed from Gujarat.

Whatever the origin may be, Maṇḍana's work evidently show close acquaintance with the vāstu works from Gujarat. In this book, i.e., the Vāstumaṇḍana he followed the technology of *Aparājitapṛchhā* and *Śamarāṅgaṇasūtradhāra* to a great extent.

In his works *Rūpamaṇḍana* and *Rājavallabhamaṇḍana* Maṇḍana specifically mentions that, he is the eldest son of the eminent architect Kṣetra.

श्रीमद्देशे मेदपाटाभिधाने क्षेत्राख्योऽयुत सूत्रधारो वरिष्ठ
पुत्रो ज्येष्ठोओ डनस्तस्य प्रौक्तं शास्त्रं मण्डनं रूपवुर्पम् //40//

In the 14th chapter of *Rājavallabhamaṇḍana* he says-

श्री मेदपाटे नृपकुम्भकर्णस्तदङ्घ्रिशजीव परागसेवी
स मण्डनास्यो भुवि सुत्रधरस्तेनोद्धृतो भ्तपतिर्वल्लभोऽयम् //43//

R.C. Agarwala in his article 'Some famous sculptors and architects of Mewar', writes, 'It is interesting to learn from the concluding portion of the Jāvar inscription of Ramā bāī (Rāṇā Kuṁbhā's daughter) dated V.S. 1554, i.e, 1497 A.D. that Sūtradhara Maṇḍana had another son named Iśvara' –

श्री मेद्पाटे वरे देशे कुंभकर्णनृपगूहे क्षेत्रांक सूत्रधारस्य पुत्तो मण्डण त्मवान् //92//
सूत्रधारमण्डण स्तन ईशर् र कमठाणु विरचित्

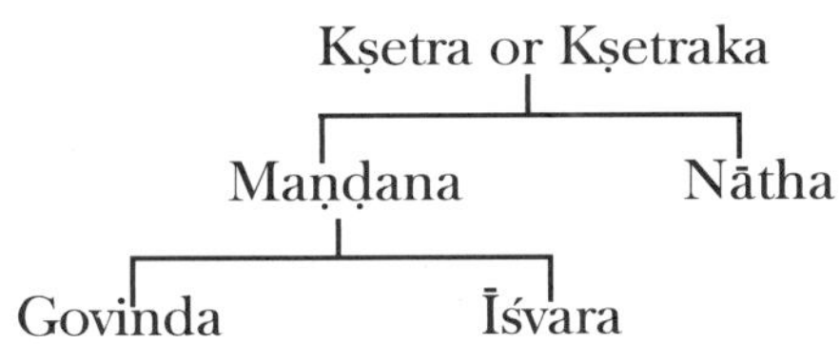

During Rāṇā Kuṁbhā's regime, *Sthāpatyaśāstra* received attention of celebrated eminent architects. Among them Maṇḍana Sūtradhāra was one of the most famous and glorious architect judged by the references in and from authorship of magnificent and widely used treatise on architecture and sculputre, *Rūpamaṇḍana*, *Rājavallabhamaṇḍana* and *Vāstumaṇḍana* were always in the forefront.

Rāṇā Kuṁbhā was the ruler of Mewar from 1433 to 1468 AD. More or less same period can be predicted for Maṇḍana also.

In the book *Saṅgītarāja* by Rāṇā Kuṁbhā which was edited by Smt. Premlata Sharma, we find her salutary remarks in the introduction: 'Kumbhalgarh' the famous fort, which has the distinction that in all the wars against the enemies of Mewar it remained unconquered (except for once). Its architect was Sūtradhāra Maṇḍana. It is a marvellous feat of military engineering.

Again a Viṣṇu temple, erected within the precincts of Ekaliṅga temple, is modelled on the principles enunciated in *Rūpamaṇḍana*. It is therefore assumed that it might have been built during Kuṁbhā's regime and, may be, by Maṇḍana Sūtradhāra himself.

From the above statements, we can conclude that *Vāstumaṇḍana* certainly had few examples of tangible construction made at the time of author's period.

HIS WORKS

'At least 8 works of Maṇḍana are well reputed. These are by name *Prāsāda Maṇḍana, Vāstumaṇḍana, Vāsturājavallabha, Vāstuśāstra, Vāstusāra, Rūpamaṇḍana, Rūpāvatāra* and *Devatāmūrtiprakaraṇa.* The exact date of none of these works is so far known, but a relative chronological position of a few can be ascertained by a comparative appraisal. The *Vāsturājavallabha* for instance, seems a recast and an abridged one, of the *Vāstumaṇḍana;* the *Vāstusāra* is just a summary of either *Vāsturājavallabha* or the *Vāstumaṇḍana*' writes M.A. Dhaky in his article, The Vāstuśāstras of Western India. Maṇḍana Sūtradhāra was a connoisseur in architecture as well as in sculpture. He was said to have had been entrusted with the assignment of designing and building the fort of Kumbhalgarh. In *Vāstumaṇḍana,* we find references of similar forts.

In the unique library of Kavindracarya (17th century AD.) some manuscripts on architecture were stored. Among them we find

1. *Rājavallabhamaṇḍana* (2146)
2. *Vāstumaṇḍana* (2849)
3. *Prāsādamaṇḍana* (2150)
4. *Rūpamaṇḍana* (2151), etc. (GOS No XVII, 1921).

The *Rājavallabhamaṇḍana* and some other texts of Maṇḍana Sūtradhāra fetched tremendous popularity within two centuries. Copies of his work reached Benaras the unanimously revered nerve centre of Indian culture.

From Benaras, Maṇḍana's works probably promulgated to other places. His works are now available in Kashmir as well as in Madras, in Baroda and in West Bengal. He must have been looked upon as an authority on this subject in his period. It is evident that his handbooks on architecture and sculpture earned unstinted popularity with artists and craftsmen of the time.

Out of his works many have been published and are available, but these books are not critically edited. From his writings it seems that the author is well-versed in a variety of subjects, e.g., principles of architecture, town planning, location of different buildings, tanks etc. environmental science, soil technology, astrology, rituals connected with the starting of the construction, etc.

He was not only endowed with unprecedented expertise over the science of architecture and allied branches of learning but also had unplumbed poetic talent. However, his Sanskrit was rather abstruse and esoteric. It appears that sometimes he has jumbled up local terms with Sanskrit language. Since many words are not found in any lexicon of the time hence it is very difficult to execute translation. Words like *Sandhipāla, Priyamukha, Viṁśopa, Puradvīpa, Kuḍyadvāra, Gavāṅgāyadi kaṇapāli* (p. 47). *Jādyakumbha* (p. 87), *Dhiñkuli* (Ch. 3) are not traceable in the lexicons.

Sometimes the descriptions are not vivid, and legible, some verses in between the lines are missing also. This book appears to be a compilation from other Vāstuśāstra books especially from *Aparājitapṛchhā* and *Samarāṅgaṇasūtradhāra*, but it has its own ingenuity in some chapters. Specially in the third chapter the portrayal of different types of yantras, is unique, though the picture is not legible in some places. The topic is not available in other recognized *Vaśtusastras.*

Again, in the description of *gavākṣa, siṁhāsana, śivikā,* he leaves marks of his originality. Descriptions of *śāla* houses are extremely analytical, elaborate and praiseworthy from which one can learn about his stupendous expertise over this technical aspect of architecture.

CONTENTS

Vāstumaṇḍana is a treatise on architecture of 15th century A.D. epitomizing secular architecture of that period. This book primarily reflects the architectural pattern and its technology prevalent in Rajasthan, by which the date and time can be easily ascertained. The author was the chief architect of the ruler Rāṇā Kuṁbhā, whose history is known from other literary sources. The very name *Vāstumaṇḍana* suggests either a treatise written by Śrī Maṇḍana or a sheer ornamentation of Vāstu.

If this book is compared with other *Vāstu* texts like *Aparājitapṛchhā, Samarāṅgaṇasūtradhāra, Mayamata* and *Mānasāra*, it is found to be different from all of these. At first glance, this book seems to be a compilation from other Vāstu texts specially *Aparājitapṛchhā* and *Samarāṅgaṇasūtradhāra*. But deeper readings reveal its uniqueness and speciality. The book mentions few other Vāstu texts, Purāṇas and names of few authors of similar texts. These are *Mānasollāsa, Sārasāgara, Mātsyapurāṇa*, and Maya, Bhoja, Viśvakarmā, Varāha, etc.

Unlike other *Vāstu* texts, this book contains only about 880 *ślokas*, divided into 8 chapters. Among these chapters, the first one *Miśrakādhyāya* embraces highest number of *ślokas* (207) and the fifth chapter *Gṛhavinyāsa adhyāya* is having only 32 *ślokas*.

This book may be referred best as a guidebook or a handbook for an architect. The book must have been very popular in its period as manuscripts of it are found almost all over India. *Rājavallabhamaṇḍana* another treatise of the same author seemed to be very popular also, as large number of manuscripts of it could also be located. Few similar verses in both the books could be noticed, but *Vāstumaṇḍana* deals with each topic more elaborately. For example, in *Rājavallabhamaṇḍana* twenty-three *ślokas* describe one particular topic *āyādi ṣaḍvarga*, whereas in *Vāstumaṇḍana* eighty-five *ślokas* are written to describe the same topic. Although *Rājavallabhamaṇḍana* contains more chapters (14), yet the number of *ślokas* is found to be more in *Vāstumaṇḍana.*

Uniqueness of this book lies in a particular field; that is, on the fort architecture. This is probably the only book where the description of a fort, the remains of which still exist near Udaipur, could be located. This book gives original blueprint of the planning of that particular fort. It is traced from other references that Maṇḍana himself, during the rule of Rāṇā Kumbhā, built this fort. The remains of the boundary wall of the fort, even today, look like that of the great China wall.

Vāstumaṇḍana provides the detailed description of the fort as well as those of palace and its inside.

BASIC TOPICS

Topics of the book can be divided into four main groups;

1) Astrology, astronomy, and ecology.
2) Fort and palace architecture.
3) Building architecture – śālā houses, etc.
4) Different components of the house.

CHAPTERS ON ASTROLOGY, ASTRONOMY & ECOLOGY

Vāstumaṇḍana clearly indicates ardent passion of Rāṇā Kuṁbhā towards astronomy and astrology. In his time, astrologers were hired to execute activities and works within the ambit of the entire kingdom. Astronomy was closely related to astrology and Rāṇā Kuṁbhā being the astronomer himself, observed intently the movements of the planets based on which important decisions were taken. Every step of construction activities, from the onset to the conclusion was governed by the decisive and instrumental influence of astronomy and astrology.

The very first chapter starts with the description of good and evil *yogas*, position of the stars, solar and lunar zodiacs, etc. All these were incisively scrutinized at the outset of any new construction. In all sorts of construction the book categorically mentions of the *lagna, tithi, vāra*, auspicious for the owner as well as that of the influence of lunar zodiacs.

With the help of astrology or owner's zodiac sign, the author tried to determine the direction of one's house plan. According to him a person having zodiac signs of pisces, scorpio or leo shall have his house facing toward East and so on (Ch1. Śl 41–42).

In this connection the book *The Royal Palaces of India,* may be referred which says the plan of Jaipur was based on a *maṇḍala* with the royal residence in the middle. Its rectangular grid plan is tilted at an angle of 12 degree East to North to coincide with Leo, the astrological sign of Kacchwaha dynasty. Thus it is distinctly evident that Vidyādhara Bhaṭṭācārya, the planner of Jaipur city kept in mind the verdict of Maṇḍana Sūtradhāra and acted accordingly.

Consideration of omen was considered to be another important aspect for construction activities. These are known as *śakunalakṣaṇaṁ* and with their help one could determine the auspiciousness of the place.

Direction is another important part for designing any type of building plan. For this reason, the author took the help of the pole star and the gnomon to determine proper direction. On a sunny day with the help of a gnomon one used to find out east-west direction, and at night with the help of pole star one used to find north-south direction. The author mentioned of specific timing for the purpose of deciding on the direction. When the sun is in *tulā* or *meṣa* and in between *citrā* and *svāti nakṣatra* then it is the right time to determine the direction.

To find out *śalya* in a land, the author took help of astronomical chart. A chart having 28 chambers with 28 *nakṣatras*, is divided between solar and lunar system. Knowing the position of the sun, moon and the stars, one could determine the presence of *śalya* in a land and rectify.

The second chapter deals with a specific formula known as *āyādi ṣaḍvarga*. The *Āyādi* is a cluster of six elements – *āya, vyaya, rṁśa, ṛkṣa, yoni, vāra-tithi*.

The conformity to the perimeter of structure has been nicely covered in this formula. There are six basic components of a building comprising *adhisthāna* (base), *pada* or *stambha* (column), *prastara* (entablature), *karṇa* (ear, wings) *śikhara* (roof) and *stupa* (dome).

The *āya* represents the group of eight elements beginning with *dhvaja, dhuma, siṁha, śva, vṛṣa, khara, kuñjara* and *dhāṁkṣa*. According to Stella Kramrisch these are eight *Vāstupuruṣas* placed in the eight direction of a plot of the land. However this *āya* formula is slightly different from that of *Vāstumaṇḍana*.

Vyaya represents the group of three parts, i.e., *yakṣa, piśāca* and *rākṣasa*. *Yakṣa* is less than *āya*, *Piśāca* is equal to *āya* and *rākṣasa* is more than *āya*. Again *vyaya* is divided into eight varieties. These are *śānta, paura, pradyota, śrīnanda, Manohara, śrivatsa, vibhava, cintātmaka*.

Aṁśa are also of three types – Indra, Yama and Nṛpa.

Ṛkṣa, (tārā) are distributed in three groups of nine elements each–*suragaṇa, rākṣasagaṇa* and *manuṣyagana*. These twenty-seven *tārās* are known commonly.

Whether the orientation of a building is correct or not and whether the measurements as laid down with regard to the different structures are correct and auspicious conforming to the orientation, are all tested by this formula.

Yoni constitutes the length and breadth of a structure, particularly that of a house. A proper and auspicious *Yoni* is therefore required to be chosen for the structure.

Stella Kramrisch in her book *The Hindu Temple* writes, 'The *yoni* formula is but one of the six formulae, of the *āyādi-ṣaḍvarga*, in which the remainder determines the gain or loss which will accrue to the builder, and the *nakṣatra (Ṛkṣa)*, the lunar day (*tithi*) and the solar day (*vāra*), on which it is good to build that particular building. These formulae belong to astrology in general. These are applied to the building as if it is a living entity whose destiny is to be determined. However it is only the cumulative bad effect that makes any perimeter inauspicious even if the *Yoni* formula is satisfied. (V.K.R. Menon, "Six Canons Of Indian Architecture", Bulletin of the Sri Rama Varma Research Institute,1934, pp. 66-67). The formulae are not canons. The *yoni* and the other five formulae are considered when no other definite injunction is given where the temple of a specified divinity has to face, etc (part VII). The power of the specific divinity and its appropriate orientation outweigh the *āyadi ṣaḍvarga*.'(Footnote, p. 34).

Though this is the opinion of Stella Kramrisch, yet almost all *Vāstu* texts discuss *āyādi ṣaḍvarga* in details. The author of *Vāstumaṇḍana* was not only an ardent proponent of this formula but also added on some more to it. These are *candra, rāśimaitrī, grahamaitrī, pañcatattva, vargaprīti, viṁśopā,* etc.

After astronomy and astrology the author expressed concern with the surrounding environment of a house also. Plants and trees have significant relation with *Vāstu*. Almost all *Vāstu* texts refer to different types of trees and their respective utility in a habitation. The author of *Vāstumaṇḍana* is no exception. He carefully chose the plants telling where to plant those. In the first chapter, he has enumerated forty-five types of trees and plants, which were to be planted or not to be planted near one's house, their suitability or unsuitability for a new construction. In addition to this, the author suggested the determination of the shading time of a tree and creeper recommending astute discards of those, which provide shades more than three hours.

The fourth chapter recommends wood as the material for construction. At first one must appraise the type and nature of the wood, circumvent specific places from where one not to collect wood, selection of the places from where one should derive woods or so. Condition of the wood must also be taken care of. Author mentioned fifty-eight types of trees which are regarded auspicious for human dwelling and forty types of trees which are most apposite – suitable for temples but malicious for human dwellings.

Not only the types of trees are important, but their joinery is also equally important too. Here in this book the author categorically mentioned the principles of joinery, which established his peerless expertise in the craft of wooden structure. Two similar parts of a tree should neither be joined together; nor the new and old parts of a tree be joined. Pillars and *Brahmasthānas* will be free from any joint. Again in the eighth chapter, while giving description of types of beds, he mentioned twenty types of trees, which are best, suited for beds, seats and vehicles.

CHAPTERS ON FORT AND PALACE ARCHITECTURE

Fort occupies a major and very important place in this text. In the middle of 15th century, warfare was regular phenomenon in the western region and a strong secured fort with a palace was inevitable. Rāṇā Kuṁbhā (1433-68) built numerous forts in his domain the prime one of which was the Kumbhalgarh. From two references, we infer that *Maṇḍana Sūtradhāra* was the chief architect of Kumbhalgarh. These are: –

a) *Saṅgitarāja* by Rāṇā Kuṁbhā, which is edited by Premlata Sharma. In the introduction she writes 'Kumbhalgarh the famous fort of which has the distinction that in all the wars against the enemies of Mewar it remained unconquered (except for once). Its architect was Sūtradhāra Maṇḍana. It is a marvellous feat of military Engineering.'

b) In 'Some famous Sculptures and Architects of Mewar (15th century A.D.),' I.H.Q.1957, Vol. xxxiii Sri R.C. Agarwal writes, 'there where is contemporary artists like light and Maṇḍana had attained perfection in the sphere of carrying out stone sculptures and constructing monumental structures like the Kirtistambha at Chittor and the fort at Kumbhalgarh.'

Maṇḍana Sūtradhāra in his book *Vāstumaṇḍana* gave detailed description of fort and its inside, the palace and its elaborate planning. He described Kumbhalgarh fort as built by him. In the beginning he advises that one must built a strong fort even if he has to demolish the existing structure. Interestingly the fort Kumbhalgarh was built on the location of another old fort. In the Encyclopaedia of India (Rajasthan), pp. 107-8, it is written that Kumbhalgarh was built by Maharana Kumbha in 1448 on a rock plateau and in a site of an earlier ancient fortress. The rampart of the fort is very strong and can be compared with the Great Wall of China. Inside the fort there is a palace, which is self-contained and complete in all respects. The text provides detailed planning of the palace and fort. Original blueprints of the two could be located and in that aspect this book has great documentary importance. Four corners of the fort were specially prescribed for the artisans, wine sellers, hunters etc but those corners were not recommended suitable for others. Brahmins were allocated to reside in the East, *Kṣatriyas* in the South and *Vaiśyas* in the North. Water reservoirs were all in the West. The Sun god was placed in the North-East corner, *Gaṇādhipa* in the South-East, *Sahasrākṣa* in the South-West, and *Janārdana* in the North-West. Gods were either facing the East or the west. City inside the fort was complete being adorned with palace, garden, ramparts, main entrance (huge) gates, water reservoirs, gardens, tower of fame, etc.

Next the book provides an insufficient description of machineries, which were used to protect the fort. Though the description is not very lucid yet it makes the readers apprised with the name of machineries that were developed in those days.

It is the only *Vāstuśāstra* so far, which deals with weapons, a few other books such as *Samarāṅgaṇasūtradhāra* or *Aparājitapṛchhā* mentions merely the names only. Here the author describes eighty-four machineries, out of which nine each are the air and water machineries. There are six varieties of firearms and sixty varieties of war machineries. In this book we get different descriptions of war and fire machineries. Here he enumerates names and measurement of eight types of rods/shafts used in the warfare. Next one is probably the description of a bow, which is not very legible. This bow is named as *Markaṭī*, which was to be made very firm with the help of leather strips and iron.

After this we find a description of *Gophanā*, which in succinct version is still used to drive away birds in the paddy fields. It appears that this simple device was used to throw stones at the enemy from far distance. In one word it seems to be stone or dart thrower.

Subsequently we have noticed the illustration of another machinery known as *Markaṭi*. Probably it was made of iron nets, looking like a cage or drum and was used to carry stones and arrows. It has few rotating discs, which has made it highly resilient and facilitated easy hassle free movements of that machine. This drum like thing has two supporting rods, a few holes and in the center a place for light etc. We find also the measurement of the cage and the discs. There will be two wings for easy movement. Author gave elaborate description of this item and it seemed that it was an inevitable device in the warfare. This machine is named as *Dhinkuli* or *Gauriyantra*.

In the seventy-second chapter of *Aparājitapṛchhā* similar names could be found out.

This is the uniqueness of this book that tried to describe the local war machineries. We find fairly a vivid description of firearms, used in the warfare during that period. Small cannons, which were easily moved and carried, were well known to people. There is detailed description and measurement of a cannon, the silhouette of which resembled a *Dhatura* flower. It was made of brass or bell metal with a pointer to help aiming cardinally the target. The measurement of the weapon is three to six times of a *Dhatura* flower. It may be noted that the size of a *Dhatura* flower available in Rajasthan is rather large approximately of 8-10 inches in length. Along with the cannons we find references of cannon balls and the ingredients with which the balls were manufactured.

Eighth chapter of this book describes six types of king's palaces. These are *Śrīdhara*, *Śrīnivāsa*, *Lakṣmīvilāsa*, *Pṛthvījaya*, *Pratāpavardhana*, and *Kṣiṇaibhūṣaṇa* compared to *Aparājitapṛchhā* mentioning twenty types of king's palaces. While describing these palaces the author mentions of *six chhandas* or characteristics. These are *Māḍa*, *Mauḍa*, *Śuddha*, *Śekhara*, *Tuṅgāra* and *Simhakarṇa*. Previously he mentioned of another *chhandas* for the aerial view of a construction. These are *Meru, Khaṇḍameru, Patākā, Sūci, Neṣṭa* and *Uddiṣṭta.* Mostly palaces are of *Māḍa* type and they come under *Meru chhanda.* Another peculiarity of these palaces is that most of the palaces are either three and half or five and half or seven and half storied and the ground plan of these palaces are either 8 x 8, 9 x 9 or 10 x 10 square as required.

Śrīdhara type of palace is five storied with sixteen pillars in the centre. The projected part of the palace is two and half storied. While there are four pillars in one part, there are four pillars each for all the four doors with lattice. Platforms were fitted with glittering silver seats adorned with *Mattavāraṇa* (A.P. Ch. 87, Ś16-17). *Aparājitapṛchhā* mentions of three *chadyas* adorned with platforms and bells, which are the decoration of this palace.

The palace *Pratāpavardhana* has four doors in four directions. There the projected part will be one third of the breadth of the palace and the front portico constitutes another part. No other information on this type of palace are found in the book whereas *Aparājitapṛchhā* describes the land to be twenty-five hands in measurement with four pillars in the center, twelve more pillars on the *alindas,* totaling thirty-two pillars in outside and inside. *Māḍa* type of construction is described to have two stories and above going up to three and half stories.

The palace *Lakṣmīvīlāsa* is found to be similar to *Pratāpavardhana* to certain extent. *Vāstumaṇḍana* adds that out of ten pillars in the *mukhabhadra,* six will be inside and four will be on the outside. *Māḍa* type of construction is done two stories and above on *bhadra* and for a house it will be upto five and a half storey. This type of palace is best suited for a king. Compared to this, *Aparājitapṛchhā* writes, the *Bhadra* for *Pratāpavardhana* palace is divided into three parts breadth wise and one of the part is regarded as *mukhabhadra,* which is adorned with ten pillars is known as *Lakṣmīvīlāsa* palace. Here the *Māḍa* is done above two storey can go unto five and half storey.

For *Śrīnivāvsa* palace similar description was noticed in both the books. This palace is having thirty-six pillars on twenty-five parts of the land. Wall will be equal to one-tenth part of the construction in length and four doors are also erected. *Bhadra* is divided into nine parts with three *mukhabhadras* in one part. This palace will be three and half storied with hundred and four pillars. *Māḍa* type of construction is done above three or five storeys.

Kṣīṇabhūṣaṇa type of palace is constructed on a square land measuring eight by eight squares and the foundation is on the seventh segment. Partition wall will be within half of the squares. There will be four doors and twenty-five small pillars. *bhadra* is divided into three parts and three *Pratibhadras* will be raised on one part of *bhadra.* The number of pillars in a *bhadra* may be four or five but total number of pillars may vary from eighty to two hundred. *Māḍa* is constructed above three stories in a *bhadra* and in a house it will be above sixth stories.

Aparājitapṛchhā differs to certain extent on this type of palace. The wall is one-eighth part of the construction and there will be four doors. *Bhadra* will have twenty-five small pillars and thirty-six large pillars. There will be three *pratibhadras* in a *bhadra* and six pillars in each *pratibhadra.* Altogether there will be seventy-two pillars and sixty-four small pillars. *Māḍa* type of construction will be above three stories and may go upto six stories.

The last one known as *prithvījaya,* is mentioned in *Vāstumaṇḍana* where the land is divided into ten by ten squares and walls are erected proportionately. The center of the palace is adorned with hundred pillars and the construction goes up to seven and half stories. There will be fifty-two pillars in a three and half storey construction. We find general measurement of the palaces also. The area of a palace can start from twenty-five hands and can go upto hundred and eight hands. Palaces are decorated with various ornamental materials.

Sūtradhāra Maṇḍana deals with this topic elaborately. From his description it is clear that expertise on the architectural design and the construction were very much available at that period. With the help of a *chhanda* named as *prastara,* an architect could design varieties of houses. *Prastara* or permutation is regarded as an important mathematical model by which a graphic representation of different arrangement of a building could be done.

D. N. Shukla in his *Vāstuśāstra* writes--, 'Thus this *(prastara)* is all mathematical gymnastic. Its practical value is only to avoid wrong orientation and misplacement of any of the component parts in the building of *śālā* in order to provide the maximum comfort and the fullest of space together with conformity to the mystic ideas of the doctrine of orientation.' (p. 320)

Here *Prastara* means a combination of *guru* and *laghu* in accordance with certain rules. In *Vāstu, guru* implies wall and *laghu* insinuate *alinda.* With various combinations of *guru* and *laghu* one can design thousand varieties of houses.

Vivid illustration of different types of dwelling houses has been found in different chapters of *Vāstumaṇḍana.* Sometimes it is a description of the abode of a king or landlord, whereas sometimes it is for common man.

Chhanda is the seminal aspect of a building, which is applicable to an ordinary house as well as to a king's palace. It is a rudimentary characteristic of *Nāgarī* style of architecture and discussed elaborately in *Aparājitapṛchhā* as well as *Samarāṅgaṇasūtradhāra. Chhanda* of *Vāstu* meant 'disposition of a structure,' says Mr. Mankad in the introduction of *Aparājitapṛchhā.*

These rhythmic patterns are of six types, which again have sixteen varieties. These patterns have been planned mainly for designing common people's residence. These are *tṛṇa, paṭṭa, vāji, khaṇḍa, parṇa* or *pūrṇa* and *pāṇḍu.* These are the names of the type of houses which indicate the material by which these houses are to be constructed. For example: - *Tṛṇa* type of houses have thatched roof, *vāji* is made of stone, *pāṇḍu* is storied mansion and so on.

Here the author gives another pragmatic suggestion for six types of *chhandas* starting with *meru.* These are *meru, khaṇḍameru, sūci, patākā, uddiṣṭa* and *naṣṭa. Uddiṣṭa* and *naṣṭa* are not independent *chhandas.*

With the *laghu* and *guru* placement, a *meru* structure will look like a Meru mountain. The central part rising considerably above the ground will have side sloping step by step all around till it reaches the ground surface. It is mentioned that in *meru, khaṇḍameru* and *sūci* the construction will start with *guru* that means wall and at the end there will be *laghu,* i.e., *alinda,* and the lines will be drawn before hand. In *meru* and *khaṇḍameru* the section will increase downwards.

In *patākā* or *khaṇḍaprastāra, guru* will follow *laghu* and at the end there will be one *laghu.* Here the multitude of *laghu* numerals has been shown in the different manner. Ground plan of a house is regarded as the quintessence of the structure. *Vāstumaṇḍana* states that the ground plan can start from one square and can go up to thousand squares. According to the shape of a land, ground plan may be of thirty-two types. The best and commonly known ground plans are with sixty-four square or eighty-one squares. These are known as *chandita* and *paramaśāyika.* There is a *Vāstupuruṣa* in every site and a chart is drawn accordingly which is known as '*Vāstupuruṣamaṇḍala.*' Here forty-five deities reside also on different parts of *Vāstupuruṣa.* Again we find positions of gods in sixty-four, eighty-one and hundred square plans.

Marmavāstu is another type of ground plan, which according to the author should be kept in mind during any type of construction. *Marma,* the orthogonal is very important in site plan with '*Vāstupuruṣamaṇḍala.*' *Marma* indicates the particular places, where there will be no structure. It not only states that a percentage of the plot should remain unused but also insinuates the location of the open places in the general plan. Moreover, *Vāstumarma* is co-extensive with the *prāsāda* and these *marmas* affect the position of pillars in a construction.

[Ninety-third chapter of *Agnipurāṇa* describes twelve *marmas* in a *Vāstu.* This orientation of structure is the practical application of the general principle of *Vāstupadavinyāsa*].

With the given description in *Vāstumaṇḍana* one can easily draw a chart of *Marmavāstu* and can get a legible and perspicacious picture where construction should be done or not to be done.

In the fourth chapter he gave general height of houses. It can be of three types. The half of the width is to be multiplied by four, three and two, and one will get the prescribed height of a house. Calculation can be started from the floor of the house. These three types of houses can again be divided into nine (three each) by dint of permutation combination. Here we find illustration of multi-storied houses meant for different class of people.

Minimum diameter of a house will be eight hands and it can go up to ten and half hands similarly. For common people there will be one or two storied house Eleventh storey is the highest number, which are designed for a king with top and bottom floor construction.

Each upper floor will be one twelfth part less than the lower one.

Lime powder, limestone, gravel and brick powder were deployed for plastering.

About the shape, the author mentioned that the land could be square or rectangular, hexagonal or octagonal, round or oval. Thus one could have wide options for selecting a land.

The book also describes a type of house, known as *śālā* house. These types of houses are mentioned in the *Purāṇas* as well as in some other *Vāstu* texts such as *Mānasāra, Mayamata, Aparājitapṛchhā*, etc. This text discusses the *śālā* houses very systematically catering to the need of everybody starting from common man to the king. One to four *śālā* houses are meant for common people of four *varṇas*, and five to ten *śālā* houses are meant for king or people of similar category. Here the author quotes sometimes from *Mayamata* and *Aparājitapṛchhā* mentioning that the width of a *śālā* house could start from four hands and can go upto twenty to twenty-four hands. The length will be one and half times of the breadth for a king's house, but may be more for a religious establishment.

Prescribed measurement and location of the corridor are also mentioned. Here we find the use of *guru* and *laghu* for the design of different types of *śālā* houses.

At first a religious establishment known as *paṭhaṣālā* has been described. It is adorned with latticed window, altar, porticos, specific type of gates, etc. This may be a double storied building furnished with granary, treasury, kitchen, etc.

While constructing a house, the author places special emphasis upon the foundation details, walls and pegs. Himself being an architect, he has attached importance to each and every minute intricacy of a construction and judicious placing of the components.

In the sixth and eighth chapters we notice elaborate discussion of houses with different number of *śālā*. The *śālā* houses may be of ten varieties, but five to ten *śālā* houses are of different types combining the result of one to four *śālā* houses.

According to the various position of *Prastarachhanda* each *śālā* house has many sub varieties. For example:- *Ekaśālā* houses primarily have only sixteen varieties each of which have again sub varieties and so on. Likewise we get several thousand forms of *ekaśālā* houses.

Dviśālā houses start with fifty varieties, each of these has two thousand forms and again each of two thousand has eight forms and so on.

Triśālā and *catusśālā* houses have several thousand forms.

Viśvakarmā writes 'by this way the number of total varieties of houses is one crore fifteen lakhs four thousand and eight.'

First four types of *śālā* houses are formed by means of *prastara,* i.e. the arrangement of *guru laghu saṁsthāna,* but the remaining six types of *śālā* houses, i.e. *pañcaśālā* to *daśaśālā* are from the combination of first four types of houses.

Through this method the author provides six combinations of *Pancaśālā.*

1) One *catusśālā* house + one *ekaśālā* house.

2) One *triśālā* house + one *dviśālā* house.

3) One *triśālā* house + two *ekaśālā* house.

4) Two *Dviśālā* house +one *ekaśālā* house.

5) Three *ekaśālā* house + one *dviśālā* house.

6) Five *ekaśālā* houses.

Likewise we found mentioning of nine combinations of *śaṣṭaśālā,* eleven combinations of *saptaśālā,* fifteen combinations of *aṣṭaśālā,* eighteen combinations of *navaśālā* and twenty-three combinations of *daśaśālā.* [These combinations are clearly explained by Sri Mankad in the introduction of *Aparājitapṛchhā.]*

This book provided various names of *ekasālā* houses. At first these are sixteen in number, each of these having more varieties.

Next is the description of *dviśālā* houses. While describing these varieties, author tells us about another variety of *śālā* house, that is *yugmaśālā* or twin halled house. In a square land, nine chambers of equal size are to be erected. Leaving the central chamber, there will be four twin chambers on four sides. These are known as *hastinī, mahiṣī, gāvī* and *chhāgalī,* and serially they will face towards North, East, South and West. These are also known as *dvihaṁsa, dvikokila, dvisārasa,* and *dvicakravaka.*

There may be thirty-two types of *yugmaśālā* according to the author.

There are fifty-two types of *dviśālās* mentioned in this book. This rhythmical disposition varies according to the position of porticos and ventilation. *dviśālās* are six in number to start with and the first four numbers have eleven varieties each and the rest two have four varieties each. All the *dviśālās* have their own name and some of them have prescribed place of *alindas*, such as *roga* type of *dviśālā* has *alindas* on the Eastern and Western direction. Again it is stated that *dviśālā* facing East or North are always auspicious.

Next are the *triśālā* houses. According to the location of doors it may have seventy-two varieties. Four *gurus* will dominate the form of *Prastaras* in this variety. Seventeenth form will have two *laghus* on all four sides and eighteenth form of *triśālā* will be adorned with *ṣaḍḍāruka* in the centre.

Absence of *śālā* on the North or East of a *triśālā* house brings in prosperity, longevity etc to the residents. At the same time a *triśālā* house without a *śālā* on the South or West, is regarded inauspicious.

Author did not give elaborate description of *catusśālā* houses, thinking that by studying previous *śālā* houses, it would not be difficult to find the varieties of *catusśālā* houses. He only indicated that there would be eight *gurus* in this form and varieties may go up to two hundred fifty six in number.

DIFFERENT COMPONENTS OF A HOUSE AND OTHERS

Kaṁvikā – *Kamvi* originally means *kuśa*, probably it was the first measuring methodology by which one used to measure. The book used *kaṁvikā* as measuring scale. The code of discipline in measurement is a very important aspect for any type of architecture. Without accurate measurement a construction will be faulty.

The first chapter of *Vāstumaṇḍana*, discusses elaborately the measurement aspect. Similar descriptions are also available in *Samarāṅgaṇasūtradhāra* (Ch.11), and in *Aparājitapṛchhā* (Ch. 41).

Aṅgula is regarded as the standard measurement, which is three fourth of an inch. *Aṅgulas* are of three variety – *uttama, madhyama* and *kaniṣṭha.* These formed the first three units of *hasta* measurement. In general the scale will be of twenty-four *aṅgulas* in length, one and half *aṅgula* in breadth or circumference. Scale is to be made of special type of wood, such as *madhuka, khadira, añjana, candana, dhātuka* or of bamboo.

This rod will be divided into eight *parvas* – three *aṅgulas* each, and this will be decorated with flower pigments marks. Nine gods starting from Rudra, Anila, Viśvakarmā, Vahni, Brahmā, Yama, Aṁbupa, Dhanada, Viṣṇu will occupy one *parva* each. Again these *parvas* may have sub divisions.

Superior yardstick will be used to measure village, city, *krośa*, land, etc. Middle type is to be used to measure palace, idol, phallus, temple, reservoir, well and water tank, etc.

Smallest type of measuring scale is used to measure *yantras*, weapons, seats, umbrella, bed, chariots and others.

Before starting any construction, one has to be very careful not to deviate from prescribed measurement to ensure entire fabrication devoid of defects.

Water reservoirs – Water body plays an extremely pivotal role in habitation. At initial stage civilizations started by the river banks only. In the later period people started finding out other sources of water by digging well, tank, ponds, *jheels,* etc. It was regarded very auspicious to dig a water reservoir and deemed as part of the essential duty of a king or landlord of that locality.

In this book, we find Śrīkṛṣṇa advising Yudhiṣṭhira regarding the beneficial impact of digging water reservoirs. Here we find description of different types of water reservoirs with various numbers of projections. Dimensions and shapes of different types of *kuṇḍas* and wells are also provided.

Garden – As is said earlier, the author of this book was much concerned on the ecological balance and as an architect he took extreme and overall solicitude on this noteworthy and momentous issue while designing a city or township. Even in palaces and forts, he felt the necessity of gardens everywhere.

In the third chapter, author advised creating a pleasure garden/park either inside or outside of a city. For a house, the garden will be either on right or on left side. Prescribed measurements are also provided. These gardens will be bedecked with varied and specific trees and creepers, playgrounds, water reservoirs, bathing places with showers, etc.

Doors – Any construction entails proper placing of the entrance door. Here in this book, while describing different arrangements of a house, the author writes thirty *ślokas* (46-76) in the fourth chapter. Here he writes about different types and parts of the door, their measurements, and types of doors whether they are auspicious or inauspicious, etc.

According to him there may be three types of doors in a house as per the height. Particular measurement is given for each and every component of a door and there is definite instruction as to which part is to be bejeweled or not.

There is a fixed position of the door for different types of houses, stables etc. If it is done otherwise there will be disorder in the construction.

In addition to door, we find description of the location of side doors, a door adorned with latticed window as well as revolving door.

In this book, author has enumerated the measurement of a main gate, which may be of three types and will be well decorated. There are different doorways of *pratoli* (main entrance gate), which are known as *utsaṅga, pūrṇavāhu, hinavāhu,* and *pratikāya.* These are mentioned in *Samarāṅgaṇasūtradhāra* as well as in *Aparājitapṛchhā.* Among these four types of doors the first two types are regarded auspicious.

Doors should not be bent, projected outside, too low or too high or curved inwardly.

Proper material is to be used for a door so that it becomes strong, elegant and fixed properly.

Door primarily protects the owner from external peril, and keeping this in mind a builder will erect the door in prescribed location making it as strong as possible.

Gavākṣa – For a house, temple, palace and so on, proper ventilation is the fundamental requirement. Being the Vāstu text of the Rajasthan belt, *gavākṣas* known as windows, are speciality of Rajasthan and Gujarat architecture. Due to the hot and dry climatic condition, this type of window is different from those in other parts of India. Latticed window gives proper ventilation and at the same time functions as a buffer protecting one from heat, dust and cold. They may be of five types according to the different types of *lumvika* and we find mention of another five types according to the number of *chhādyas.*

Alinda – *Alinda* plays an instrumental role in designing of a house. Here the design of a house is created with the help of a device known as *prastara,* which is a combination of *guru* and *laghu,* i.e., wall and *alinda.* Placing *alindas* in the proper place and right direction is very crucial for a palace or a house. For a normal house there must be at least two, three or four *alindas.* According to this book, wall and *alindas* are to be juxtaposed side by side, and the author is very much particular about proper placing of the *alinda.* Here he writes that one can design myriad number of houses by placing those two items in different pattern.

In the glossary-index of *Mayamatam, alinda* is described as aisle, gallery, portico, and verandah, etc.

Robert Chitham in the book, *The Classical Orders of Architecture,* writes, 'portico is the columned logjam in front of the entrance to a temple or other building, frequently surmounted by a pediment.'

Transport – In the eighth chapter we find scanty description of palanquin, and its measurement, which seems to be very small in size.

Other household materials – In the eighth chapter of this book we find description and measurement of umbrella or pedestal for worshipping as well as for bed-stead. All of these are described precisely.

The author is specific about the measurement of the bed. According to him, bed is to be made according to one's own height and special woods are to be used. Quality of woods should not be mingled with one another.

This book seems to be a handbook of an architect who was a *sūtradhara* by himself. We find this book to be of unprecedented popularity in the mediaeval period as manuscripts of this text have been found in many parts of India. In this book architects can derive an original blueprint of a fort, which was constructed during that time, and the remains of the fort are still existing in the 21st century even after withstanding the seasonal vagaries of tropical climate and the passage of time. Along with the systematic planning of *śālā* houses and their varieties, the vivid illustration of various types of war machineries have also been mentioned over here. Analyzing the contents of the book it can be averred that this stupendous composition, formulated by a stalwart of magnificent erudition, will be immensely beneficial for researchers in future.

Acknowledgements

First of all, let me acknowledge my gratitude to Prof. Devavrata Sen Sarma, who motivated me to edit the *Vāstumaṇḍana* text. Dr. Kapila Vatsyayana, the founder Member-Secretary of IGNCA and eminent art-historian and Pt. Satkari Mukhopadhyaya, former Coordinator of Kalākośa division of IGNCA were very kind and affectionate to bestow me with the responsibility of editing and translating the above text for IGNCA. I would also like to place on record my sincere thanks to Dr. Sudhir Lall of IGNCA, the managing editor of the volume. The team of scholars of Kalākośa comprising Dr. N.D. Sharma and Dr. Sushma Jatoo also deserve to be thanked for their kind support. My best wishes are for Dr. Arvind Sharma, the young scholar of Kalākośa, who saw through the proofs and charts, etc.

(Late) Prof. Manabendu Banerjee, the supervisor and philosopher from my doctoral stage was always there to guide and help me, wherever necessary.

Sri Priyadarsan Sen Sarma and Dr. A.K. Bag helped me and tried their best to clarify ideas on all war weapons and mathematical calculations described in the first chapter, which appeared corrupted.

Prof. Dilip Kanjilal and (late) Dr. Kripamoyi Kanjilal extended their co-operation to me in all aspects, and without their able guidance it would have not been possible for me to complete editing this book. Ms. Shampa Kanjilal took pains to type the text, translation; contents and verse index of this book, in spite of her ill health and her other personal difficulties.

Sri Anjan Banik prepared kindly the charts, typed ancillary parts of the book with great care.

Lastly, I acknowledge heartily the support of my family, especially my husband, Mr. Susanta Kumar Bhowmik and his active involvement without which, this book would not have taken its present shape.

—Dr. Anasuya Bhowmick

Scheme of Transliteration

Vowels		
Initial	Medial	Equivalent
अ	—	a
आ	ा	ā
इ	ि	i
ई	ी	ī
उ	ु	u
ऊ	ू	ū
ऋ	ृ	ṛ
ॠ	ॄ	ṝ
ऌ	ॢ	ḷ
ए	े	e
ऐ	ै	ai
ओ	ो	o
औ	ौ	au

Consonants

	Equivalent	
क	ka	Gutturals
ख	kha	
ग	ga	
घ	gha	
ङ	ṅ	
च	ca	Palatals
छ	cha	
ज	ja	
झ	jha	
ञ	ña	
ट	ṭa	Cerebrals
ठ	ṭha	
ड	ḍa	
ढ	ḍha	
ण	ṇa	
त	ta	Dentals
थ	tha	
द	da	
ध	dha	
न	na	

	Equivalent	
प	pa	Labials
फ	pha	
ब	ba	
भ	bha	
म	ma	
य	ya	Semivowels
र	ra	
ल	la	
व	va	
श	śa	Spirants
ष	ṣa	
स	sa	
ह	ha	
:	ḥ (Visarga)	
	ṁ (Anusvāra) & (Anunāsika)	

Abbreviations

A.P.	:	*Aparājitapṛchhā*
M.M.	:	*Mayamatam*
S.S.	:	*Samarāṅgaṇa Sūtradhāra*
B.S.	:	*Bṛhatsaṁhitā*

वास्तुमण्डनम्

VĀSTUMAṆḌANAM

(Text and Translation)

श्रीगणेशाय नमः।

वास्तुमण्डनम्

प्रथमोऽध्यायः

[मिश्रकाध्यायः]

स्रष्टारं जगतामीशमनेकाश्चर्यरूपिणम्।
पालकं [१]सर्वसत्त्वानां वन्दे शक्तिमयं शिवम्।।१।।

वास्तुवे[२]दोदधेः कश्चित्सारमादाय मण्डनः।
बालानामवबोधाय तनुते वास्तुमण्डनम्।।२।।

शस्ते मासे सिते पक्षे [३]अतीते चोत्तरायणे।
चन्द्रताराबले [४]भर्तुः सुलग्ने च [५]शुभे दिने।।३।।

पुरःप्रासादगेहानां वाप्याः कूप[६]तडागयोः।
आराममठ[७]वास्तूनां प्रारम्भः सद्भिरिष्यते।।४।।

नन्दाभद्राजयारिक्ता[८]पूर्णाः [९]प्रातिपदादिकाः।
षष्ठ्या[१०]द्येकादशी[११]सर्वास्तिथयः पञ्चधा मता।।५।।

१. सर्वा-in A
२. देदेधो-in A
३. आतीक्षे-in A अतीत इत्यनेन श्रावणमार्गयो र्ग्रहणमपि शब्दात् चकारेणोत्तरायणस्याचैत्रस्य त्यागः सूचितः। Marginal note in Ms. A.
४. कर्त्तु-in D, E
५. सुभे-in A
६. तटाक-in B
७. वास्तुनां-in A, B
८. पूर्वर्णा-in D, E
९. प्रदि-in B
१०. द्यो-in A
११. पूर्वा-in A

Salute to Lord *Gaṇeśa.*

Vāstumaṇḍanam

Chapter I

[Miśrakādhyāyaḥ]

1. I praise Lord *Śiva* the Almighty, who is the creator, lord of the world with different manifestations. He is the mentor of the whole creation.

2. For the comprehension of the young folks, *Maṇḍana* has collected some important materials from the ocean of science on building architecture, and written the *Vāstumaṇḍana.*

3-4. In an auspicious month, day and time in the bright half of the lunar month, and after the *Uttarāyaṇa*[1] is over, when the moon and the stars are in favourable positions for the master, then one should start building a town, palace, house, well, tank, pond, pleasure garden, monastery.

Starting from *Pratipadā -Nandā, Bhadrā, Jayā, Riktā, Pūrṇā,* and from

5. *Ṣaṣṭhī* to *Ekādaśī,* all *tithis* (lunar days) are of five types.

---

1. Notes: -*Uttarāyaṇa*- Northern progress of the Sun
Nandā- Pratipada, Ṣaṣṭhī, Ekādaśī, .
Bhadrā- 2nd, 7th and 12th Lunar days.
Jayā -3 rd, 8th and 13th Lunar days.
Riktā -4th, 9th, 14th Lunar days.
Pūrṇā - 5th, 10th, full moon and *Amāvasyā.*

शुक्रे नन्दा बुधे भद्रा जया भौमे तथा तिथिः।
शनौ रिक्ता गुरौ पूर्णास्तिथयः सर्व[१२]सिद्धिदाः।।६।।

एकादशी गुरौ षष्ठी भौमे शुक्र [१३]त्रयोदशी।
सिद्धयेर्केष्ट [१४]नन्देकाश्चन्द्रे नवदशद्विकाः।।७।।

[१५]सिद्धिदार्के शनौ रिक्ता[१६]भद्रा चन्द्रे बुधेऽपि च।
इत्याह मान[१७]सोल्लासे ग्रन्थे सोममहीपतिः।।८।। (मानसोल्लासः)

मुशलः [१८]सप्तमी [१९]भानौ संर्वतः प्रतिपद्बुधे।
कर्कस्त्रयोद[२०]शाङ्के स्या[२०]द्वार [२२]तिथ्य स्त्रयं त्यजेत्।।९।।

मघाविशाखाद्रार्मूलं [२३]कृत्तिका रोहिणीकरः।
अ[२४]शुभेऽर्कादिवारेषु यमघण्टः प्रजायते।।१०।।

विशाखादिचतुष्केषु चत्वारोऽर्कादिषु क्रमात्।
उत्पातमृत्युकाणाख्या सिद्धियोगाः शुभोऽन्तिमः।।११।।

हस्तो मृगोऽश्विनी[२५]मैत्रं पुष्यं [२६]पौष्णं च रोहिणी।
स्याद्योगेमृतसिद्धाख्यः सूर्यादौ सर्वसिद्धिदः।।१२।।

१२. कामदा-in A
१३. क्रयो-in A
१४. नादे-in A
१५. सिद्धदाअर्के-in A
१६. भुद्राचान्द्र-in A
१७. सोलोल्ला-in A
१८. सप्तमी-in B
१९. भानुं-in A
२०. शांवो-in B
२१. द्वारि-in B
२२. तिथौ-in A
२३. कृतिका-in A
२४. शुभो-in A
२५. मैत्रे-in A
२६. पुष्णं-in A

6. If *Nandā* is in *Śukra, Bhadrā* in *Budha, Jayā* in *Bhauma* (Mars, *Maṅgala*), *Riktā* in *Śani* and *Pūrṇā* in *Guru (Bṛhaspati)* then the lunar days bring success in all spheres.

7. If *Ekādaśī,* falls in *Guru* (Jupiter) *Ṣaṣṭhī* in *Bhauma* (Mars), *Trayodaśī* in *Śukra, Aṣṭamī* in *Arka* (Sun) *Eka* (*Pratipada*) in *Nandā, Navamī, Daśamī, Dvitīyā* in *Candra* (Moon) - these bring success.

8. There will be fulfillment of desire if *Riktā yoga* falls in *Ravi* (Sun) and *Śani* (Saturn) and *Bhadrā* fall in *Candra* and *Budha* (Mercury). King Soma has said this in the book named *Mānasollāsa.*

9. If *Saptamī* falls in the Sun then there will be *Muśala Yoga,* and *Saṁvarta Yoga* will occur if *Pratipada* falls in Mercury. If *Karka* (Cancer) falls in the 13th position then the three solar and lunar days are to be discarded.

10. *Maghā, Viśākhā, Ārdrā, Mūlā, Rohiṇī* produce *Yamaghaṇṭa yoga* on an inauspicious Sunday and other days.

11. If the four stars *Viśākhā* etc fall serially in the Sun and others then there will be *Utpāta, Mṛtyu, Kāṇa, Siddhiyoga*[2] and the last one is auspicious.

12. If *Hastā, Mṛga, Aśvinī, Maitra, Puṣyā, Pauṣṇa,* and *Rohiṇī* stars enter into the Sun, the result will be *Amṛta* and *Siddha,* it brings success in all spheres.

2. *Siddhiyoga-* If *Nandā* falls on Friday, *Bhadrā* on Wednesday, *Pūrṇā* on Thursday, *Riktā* on Saturday and *Jayā* on Tuesday — then it is known as Siddhiyoga.

[२७]याम्यं चित्रोत्तराषाढा धनिष्ठोत्तरफाल्गुनी।
ज्येष्ठा पौष्णं च सूर्यादे[२८]स्त्यजेत्सर्वत्र जन्मभम्।।१३।।

अश्विनी मृगशीर्ष च सार्प्यं हस्तोऽथ मित्रभम्।
ऊषाढा शतभसूर्यादानन्दः स्यात् [२९]ततःपरे।।१४।।

आनन्दः कालधूम्रो च ब्रह्मासौम्यो[३०]ऽथवा यमः।
[३१]ध्वजः श्री[३२]वत्सवज्राख्यौ मुद्गरश्छत्रमित्रकौ।।१५।।

मानसः पद्मको [३३]लम्बः उत्पातमृत्युकाणकाः।
सिद्धिः [३४]शुभोऽमृतोज्ञेयोमुशलोऽथ गदो गजः।।१६।।

रक्षश्चरः स्थिरो वर्द्धमानयोगक्रमेण हि।
अष्टाविंशतिभौरुक्ताः कुर्युर्नामसमं फलम्।।१७।।

[३५]त्रिद्व्येकखेन्दुपक्षाग्नि युगेषु षठ्शरायुगाः।
क्रमान्मेषादिराशिनां [३६]मध्यपादाः प्रकीर्त्तिताः।।१८।।

[३७]सप्तांश शंकोछायोना[३८] मध्यांकै षड्भिरन्विताः।
तैर्भजेतद्दिनं[३९]त्रिघ्नं लब्धा[४०]पद्यदूनोदयात्।।१९।।

---

२७. यामि-in A
२८. सूर्यास्तजेशर्वत्र-in A
२९. तस्मात्परे कालदंडादि-marginal note in E
३०. च वा-in A, B
३१. ध्वजं-in E
३२. वशवज्राक्षौ-in A
३३. लम्भ-in A
३४. मूलां मृतौ ज्ञेयौ मुशलौ यं गदा जगे-in A
३५. त्रिध्येक-in A
क्रिध्यकं खोन्दु-in B
त्रि-३ द्वे-२ क-१ खे-० इंदु-१ पक्षा-२ ग्नि-३ युगे-४ षु-५ षट्-६ शरा-५ युगा-४-in D-E We find numerals along with wordings
३६. रंध्य-in A
३७. शप्त-in A
३८. मध्यमा-in D,E
३९. त्रेघ्नं-in A
४०. धद्व्य-in D, E

13. If *Yāmya* (*Bharaṇī*), *Citrā*, *Uttarāṣāḍhā*, *Dhaniṣṭhā*, *Uttaraphālgunī*, *Jyeṣṭhā*, *Pauṣṇa* (*Apabharaṇī*, *Revatī*) fall in the Sun, then one's *Janmabha* (Zodiac sign) should be discarded.

14. *Aśvinī*, *Mṛgaśirā*, *Sārpya* (*Āśleṣā*), *Hastā*, are *Mitrabha* (congenial stars), *Uttarāṣāḍhā*, *Śatabhiṣā* will be counted from *Sūrya* and after that the auspicious conjunction will start.

15-17. *Ānanda*, *Kāla*, *Dhūmra*, *Brahmā*, *Saumya*, *Yama*, *Dhvaja*, *Śrīvatsa*, *Vajra*, *Mudgara*, *Chatra*, *Mitra*, *Mānasa*, *Padmaka*, *Lamba*, *Utpāta*, *Mṛtyu*, *Kāṇa*, *Siddhi*, *Śubha*, *Amṛta*, *Muśala*, *Gada*, *Gaja*, *Rakṣas*, *Cara*, *Sthira*, *Vardhamāna*, are serially the *Yogas*, — which are known as 28 stars and their results are equal to their names.

18. 3, 2, 1, 0, 1, 2, 3, 4, 5, 6, 5, 4 – are serially the middle part of the *Meṣa* and other Zodiac signs.

19 If one seventh part of the shadow of the gnomon, less than the median (*aṅka*), is added by six and the total then be divided by three, this would result in day time from the time of sunrise.

(Note: Verses 18 and 19 indicate the measurement of day and night. Comp Rājavallabha maṇḍana ch 12 v7)

[४१]रवावेक[४२]द्विषठ्शुद्धाश्चन्द्रेत्वष्टैक[४३]पञ्चमाः।
[४४]वेदसप्ताष्टमा भौमे बुधेऽष्टत्रिरसोन्मिताः।। २०।।

गुरौ [४५]द्विपञ्चमुनयः शुक्रेष्टैकषडब्धयः।
शनौ त्रिपञ्चसप्ताष्टः दिवाष्टांशाः शुभावहाः।। २१।।

सर्वकार्ये बुधैर्ग्राह्यं सदा चान्द्रमसं बलम्।
यस्माच्छतगुणं तेन विना [४६]कार्यं न सिध्यति।। २२।।

[४७]दशैकादशषट् त्र्येकसप्तमः पक्षयोर्द्वयोः।
चन्द्रमाः [४८]शोभनः प्रोक्तः शुक्ले पञ्चनवद्विगः।। २३।।

क्षीणः कृष्णदशम्यूर्ध्वं दशाहं चन्द्रमास्तदा।
तारया फलदः सोऽपि त्रिपञ्चाद्रिविहीनया।। २४।।

हिमांशोर्द्वादशावस्था राशौ राशौ स्वव[४९]त्फलाः।
प्रवासाद्याक्रमेणैव मेषादिषु यथाक्रमम्।। २५।।

प्रवासनाशिनीमृत्युर्जयाहास्यारतिस्तथा।
क्रीडिता [५०]निद्रिता भुक्ता ज्वरिता कम्पिता [५१]स्थिता।। २६।।

---

४१. रैवेक - In A
४२. E writes wordings and numerals
४३. मंचमा - In A
४४. वेद ४ ७ ८ रसो-६
४५. द्वि-२ पञ्च-५ ष्टै-८ क-१ षड्-६ ब्ध-४ त्रि-३ पञ्च-५ सप्त-७ ष्ट-८ ....ष्टांशाः- ८ - note in D, E
४६. कार्यं न सिद्ध्यते - In A
४७. गोचरपरत्वं विषयम्, दश-१० एकादश-११, षट्-६, त्र्ये-३ क-१, षट्-६, त्र्येक-३, १, सप्तमः-७ notes in - DE
४८. शोभनः प्रक्ताः - In A, B, C
४९. फलाम् - In A
५०. निद्रेता - In A
५१. स्विता - In D

20 *Prathamā, Dvitīyā, Ṣaṣṭhī* is auspicious in the Sun, as are *Aṣṭamī, Prathamā, Pañcamī,* in the Moon. *Caturthī* (Veda), *Saptamī, Aṣṭamī* are auspicious in *Maṅgala* (*Bhauma*) and *Aṣṭamī, Tṛtīyā* and *Ṣaṣṭhī* (*Rasa*) are auspicious in *Budha.*

21. *Dvitīyā, Pañcamī, Saptamī* in *Bṛhaspati, Aṣṭamī, Prathamā, Ṣaṣṭhī, Saptamī (Abdhi)* in *Śukra* and *Tṛtīyā, Pañcamī, Saptamī* and *Aṣṭamī* in Saturn and the 8th part of the day; these all are regarded as auspicious.

22. In all sorts of constructions, the learned men prefer the strength of lunar zodiac, because it has a hundred times more strength and without the influence of the moon, no work can be done.

23. *Daśamī, Ekādaśī, Ṣaṣṭhī, Tṛtīyā, Prathamā, Saptamī,* in both the *Pakṣa* (bright and dark fortnights) of the moon are said to be beneficial, and for the bright fortnight *(śukla), Pañcamī, Navamī, Dvitīyā* (are beneficial).

24. In the dark fortnight after *Daśamī* the power of the moon decreases for the next ten days but, in conjunction with favourable stars, the same yields good result except in *Tṛtīyā, Pañcamī* and *Saptamī.*

25. The twelfth position of the moon in the twelve zodiac signs yields results according to the respective positions like *Pravāsa* etc, in the *Meṣa* and others, serially in each zodiac sign.

26. They are *Pravāsa, Nāśinī, Mṛtyu, Jayā, Hāsyā, Rati, Krīḍitā, Nidritā, Bhuktā, Jvaritā, Kampitā, Sthitā.*

सार्धद्विघटिका होरा [५२]स्ववारा द्वारवत्फला।
रविशुक्रज्ञचन्द्राणां शनिजीवकुजन्मनाम्।। २७।।

मुहूर्तं प्रथमं त्याज्यं वेदतिथ्यर्कदिग्मनुः।
शेषा नवमुहूर्ताश्च गृहकार्ये शुभामताः।। २८।।

मृगाश्विरेवतीमैत्र[४३]ज्येष्ठादित्यकरत्रयम्।
तिर्यग्वक्त्रं हितं याने हले यन्त्रे चतुष्पदे।। २९।।

पुष्योत्तरार्द्रा[४४] रोहिण्यामूर्ध्ववक्त्रं श्रुतित्रयम्।
[४५]गृहच्छत्रध्वजारामप्रसादेष्वभिषेचने।। ३०।।

[४६]विशाखाकृत्तिकामूलं [४७]पूर्वयाम्यं [४८]मघा हि भम्।
अधोमुखानि खातेषु [४९]गृहादीनां जलाशये॥ ३१॥

भौमार्कौ तिथयो रिक्ता दग्धमुत्पातभं [५०]दिनम्।
ज्योतिःशास्त्रानुसारेण [५१]दुष्टमन्यमपि त्यजेत्॥ ३२॥

[५२]चैत्रादौ द्विगुणा मासा गताभिस्तिथिभिर्युताः।
सप्तभिस्तु [५३]हृते भागे [५४]यच्छेषं तद्दिनं भवेत्॥ ३३॥

---

५२. वत्यला - In B, D
४३. .....येष्टा - In A
४४. रोहिण्य ऊर्द्ध - In B, C D
क्रुद्ध - In A
४५. गढछत्र - In A
गच्छत्र - In B
४६. यात्रायां राज्याभिषे इष्ट दिनम् - In D, marginal note
४७. पूर्वायाम्यां - In A
४८. मथा - In A
४९. आदिशव्दाद्देवमन्दिरादि - In E marginal note
५०. ४।९।२४ दिवसे न तु रात्रौ - - In D, E marginal note
५१. दुष्ट मन्यदपि - In A
५२. चैत्रादि - In B
५३. हतेभागं - In A
५४. ये- In A

27.AB *Horā* is of two and half hours duration; its result is counted from one's own day (beginning from the very start of the day and giving results according to the results of the day)

27CD-28. For Sunday, Friday, Wednesday, Monday, Saturday, Thursday and Tuesday--- the 1st *Muhūrta* should be discarded, as well as the 4th, 15th, 12th, 10th, and 14th. The remaining nine *Muhūrtas* are regarded as auspicious in the construction of a house.

29. *Mṛgaśirā, Aśvinī, Revatī, Maitra, Jyesṭhā, Krittikā, Uttarāṣāḍhā, Uttarabhādra, (āditya karatrayam)* with their faces in slanting positions are auspicious for transport *(Yāna),* plough *(hala)* machinery and for quadruples.

30. *Puṣyā, Uttarā, Ārdrā, Rohiṇī* and three *śrutis* with their faces in up- ward positions are auspicious for the sanctification of a house, umbrella, flag, pleasure garden and palaces.

31. *Viśākhā, Kṛttikā, Mūlā, Pūrvā (Bhadrā), Yāmya (Bharaṇī) Maghā*–if facing downwards are good for houses and water-reservoirs.

32. Sunday, Tuesday, *Riktā* and *Dagdhā Tithis* and *Utpāta yogas* and other inauspicious things according to the *śāstra* of astrology, should be discarded.

33. The number of *Caitra* and other months are to be multiplied by 2, and to be added by15. Then it will be divided by 7, and the remainder is the number of days of the construction.

श्रीवत्सः कलिकर्त्ता च नन्दीशः कालकर्णकः।
[५५]धर्मदिनं क्षयश्चैव विजयी दिवसाः क्रमात्॥ ३४॥

इति दिनशुद्धिः॥

गृहारम्भे तिथिर्नन्दा जया पूर्णा च शोभना।
भौमार्कवर्जिता वारा योगा [५६]शोभननामकाः॥ ३५॥

[५७]हस्तत्रयोत्तरा पुष्ये धनिष्ठा शतभे मृगे।
मैत्रे मूलेऽश्विनी पौष्णे ब्राह्मे प्रारम्भणं श्रिये॥ ३६॥

सूर्यभान्मस्तके त्रीणि चत्वारि चाग्रपादयोः।
चत्वारि [५८]पश्चात्पादयोः पुच्छे त्रीणि प्रदापयेत्॥ ३७॥

वामे कुक्षौ तु चत्वारि पुनश्चत्वारि दक्षिणे।
[५९]पृष्ठे च त्रीणि [६०]धिष्ण्यानि [६१]नासिकायां द्वयं न्यसेत्॥ ३८॥

[६२]मस्तके स्वामिनो मृत्यु[६३]रुद्वसं [६४]चाग्रपादयोः।
स्थिरं स्यात् पश्चिमे पादे पुच्छे क्लेशनिवेशने॥ ३९॥

कुक्षौ धनक्षयं वामे दक्षिणे तु [६५]धनागमम्।
पृष्ठे धनागमं [६६]विद्यान्नासिकायां पतिक्षयम्॥ ४०॥

इति वृषचक्रम्॥

---

५५. धमं धर्मादनं - In D
५६. शुभनः - In A
५७. हस्ते - In B
५८. पादयोः पश्चात्पुच्छे– In ABCD
५९. प्रष्टे - In A
६०. धिष्मानि - In A
६१. नाशिकायां - In A
६२. मस्तिके - In A
६३. रुद्वशं - In A
रुद्वासं - In D, E
६४. चाधपाद - In A
श्चाग्रपाद - In D, E
६५. धनागमः - In B C, D, E
६६. विद्यानाशिकायां - In A
विंद्यान्नासिकायां - In D, E

34. Serially the days are known as *Śrīvatsa*, *Kalikarttā*, *Nandīśa*, *Kālakarṇaka*, *Dharmadina*, *Kṣaya* and *Vijaya*.

Thus ends the purification of the days.

35. In the beginning of the construction of a house, *Nandā*, *Jayā*, *Pūrṇā Tithis* are suitable. The days, except Tuesday and Sunday, the *Yogas* called *Śobhana*.

36. It is auspicious for starting a construction when the Sun is in the constellations, Hasta, three uttarās *(uttarāṣāḍā, uttrabhādrapada, uttaraphālgunī), Puṣyā, Dhaniṣthā, Śatabhiṣā, Mṛga, Mitra (Anurādhā), Mūlā, Aśvinī, Pauṣṇa (Revatī)* and *Brāhma (Rohiṇī).*

37. In a *Vṛṣa cakra* three solar dominated stars will be placed on the head, four on both the front feet, four on both the back feet and three on the tail.

38. Four stars are to be placed on the left lap and four on the right. Three stars are to be placed on the back side and two on the nose.

39. If the construction is done on the head there will be death of the owner, while construction done on the front part will lead to emptiness of the house. It will be permanent on the Western leg and there will be trouble in entering the house if the construction is done on the tail.

40. There will be loss of wealth if construction is done on the left lap, but gain of wealth on the right side as well as on the back. There will be loss of oneés husband if constructed on the nose.

Thus ends the circle of Vṛṣa.

मीनवृश्चिकसिंहानां [६७]पत्युः [६८]पूर्वामुखं गृहम्।
कन्यामकरकर्काणां गृहं याम्याननं मतम्॥ ४१ ॥

तुलामिथुनचापानां [६९]पश्चिमास्यं गृहं भवेत्।
कुम्भमेषवृषे शस्यः पुंसः सौम्याननं शुभम्॥ ४२ ॥

[७०]श्रावणे धनवृद्धिः स्यात् प्रारम्भे मन्दिरादिषु।
शून्यं भाद्रपदे मासे आश्विने कलहः [७१]सदा॥ ४३ ॥

कार्तिके भृत्यनाशः स्यात् कैश्चिद्धान्यागमः स्मृतः।
मार्गशीर्षे धनं पौषे लक्ष्मीश्चौरभयं [७२]क्वचित्॥ ४४ ॥

माघे वह्निभयं विद्यात् फाल्गुने श्रीगृहे कृते।
चैत्रे [७३]शोकागमो भर्तु[७४]र्वैशाखे तु धनागमः॥ ४५ ॥

ज्येष्ठे मृत्युः तथाऽऽषाढे पशुनाशः प्रजायते।

सारसागरः॥

तृणपर्णगृहारम्भे मासदोषं न चिन्तयेत्॥ ४६ ॥

तन्निषिद्धेऽपि काले हि [७५]स्वानुकूले दिने हितम्।
न कुर्याद्युग्मगे[७६] सूर्ये कन्यामीनधनुःस्थिते॥ ४७ ॥

---

६७. पुरुषस्य नाम राशिः - In E
६८. सर्वां - In A
६९. पश्यमांस्य - In A
७०. श्रवने In A. Similar verses are found in the Matsya purāṇa ch 253 v 3-5.
७१. रदा - In A
७२. कश्चित् - In A
७३. कर्तु - In D, E
७४. वैशाके - In A
७५. स्वानकुले - In A
स्वानकुले - In C
७६. गेहे for गे - In A

41. The house owner having the zodiac signs of Pisces, Scorpio, and Leo will have his house facing towards the East. The houses of people having the zodiac signs of Virgo, Capricorn, and Cancer will face towards the South.

42. Owners having the zodiac signs of Libra, Gemini, Sagittarius will have houses facing towards the West. (Those having) Aquarius, Aries and Taurus will have houses facing towards the North and it is regarded as auspicious.

43. If the construction of a temple and others start in the month of *Śrāvaṇa* then there will be increase of wealth but there will be void if done in *Bhādra* and eternal quarrels if in *Āśvina*.

44. If construction is started in the month of *Kārtika* then there will be loss of servants, but some people say there may be gain of grain. A construction in the month of *Mārgaśirṣa* brings in wealth, and *Lakṣmī* in the month of *Pauṣa*, but in some cases there may be fear from thieves.

45-46a. There will be fear of fire if a construction starts in the month of *Māgha* and prosperity if in *Phālguna* . There will be sorrow for the master in *Caitra* and wealth in *Vaiśākha*,, death in *Jyeṣṭhā*, loss of animals in *Āṣāḍha*.

Sārasāgaraḥ.

46b. One should not think of faulty months if a house is built with grass or leaves.

If the timing is inauspicious, but the days are favourable, the construction will be beneficial.

47. One should not start construction if the Sun is in Gemini (*Yugmaga*), Virgo, Pisces and Sagittarius.

पूर्वापरमुखं सूर्ये कर्कसिंहमृगे घटे।
[७७]तुलालिवृषमेषस्थे कुर्याद्याम्योत्तरं गृहम्॥ ४८॥

[७८]मतिभ्रंशेन यः कुर्यादन्यथा भवनादिकम्।
व्याधिशोकमवाप्नोति धननाशं [७९]मृतिं पुनः॥ ४९॥

वत्सः पूर्वा[८०]दिगः सृष्ट्या कन्यादित्रित्रिगे रवौ।
द्वाराधं तन्मुखे मृत्युकरं [८१]पार्श्वद्वये शुभम्॥ ५०॥

॥ इति [८२]माससंक्रान्तिफलम्॥

[८३]द्विस्वभावे स्थिरे लग्ने [८४]शुभैर्युतिविलोकिते।
निर्माणं भवनस्याहुः शस्तं कर्म स्थितैः शुभैः॥ ५१॥

त्रिषडायगतैः क्रूरैः शुभैः [८५]केन्द्रत्रिकोणगैः।
शुभं गृहस्य निर्माणं क्रूरो मृत्युप्रदोऽष्टमः॥ ५२॥

पञ्च[८६]ग्रहबले लग्ने प्रासादोद्वाहमन्दिरम्।
कुर्याच्छाकुनवीर्येण नान्यज्जालं विचिन्तयेत्॥ ५३॥

---

७७. वास्तु तूपी वृषभः सर्पो वा २ marginal notes in E
७८. ६।७।८ – पू.
९।१०।१२ – द
१२।१।२ – प
३।४।५ – उ these are marginal notes in E
७९. मृतं – in A
८०. दिन – in C
८१. याश्वद्वयै – in A
८२. माशक्रांतिवत्सफलम् - A
८३. द्विस्थवै २।३।५।६।८।९।११।१२ – – in A
८४. शुभेयुक्ते – in A
८५. ७।८।७।१०
८६. गृहै – in A

48. If the Sun is in Cancer (*Karka*), Leo *(Siṁha)*, Capricorn(*Mṛga*) and Aquarius(*Ghaṭa*), one can start construction of a house facing the East and West, and if the Sun is in Libra, Scorpio, Aries and Taurus, one can construct a house facing the South and North.

49. Due to mistakes, if anybody builds a house in other than the prescribed form, he will have disease, affliction, loss of wealth and death.

50. In a year, when the Sun moves towards the East, and rests in Virgo[3] and in two other zodiac signs, the lower and forepart of a door should not be constructed as it brings death, but the construction of the sides(of the door) is auspicious.

Thus ends the result of months and the passage of the Sun from one sign to the next.

51. In the dual nature of the zodiacs and in the fixed *Lagna* and auspicious auguries it is said that the construction of a house would be favourable.

52. With 3, 6, 12, *Krūra*, centres and with three favourable corners, the building of the house is auspicious, but the 8th position brings in death.

53. According to the good signs of five planets and in the auspicious *Lagna*- palaces, marriage centers and temples should be constructed according to the science of the omens and one should not think otherwise.

3. Three Zodiac signs are Virgo, Libra, and Scorpio.

[८७]शकुने भवनारम्भे प्रथमं [८८]धुवजः शुभः ।
[८९]तयोर्याम्ये पुनः [९०]सौम्ये शान्तः [९१]स्वस्थानसंस्थितः ॥ ५४ ॥

स्वानस्य दक्षिणे चेष्टा शान्ताः सर्वार्थकारिणी ।
वामे चेष्टा [९२]न विहिता[९३] दुष्टं [९४]जृम्भांगधूननम् ॥ ५५ ॥

शुभस्थाने गृहारम्भे मधुरं रौति वायसः ।
स्थाने तस्मिन्भवेद्द्रव्यं शल्यं दीप्ते खरस्वरे ॥ ५६ ॥

प्रधानं शकुने [९५]दुर्ग तद्बले [९६]नगरं गृहम् ।
वाणिज्यकृषिसेवादिकर्म सिध्यति निश्चितम् ॥ ५७ ॥

[९७]दिशारात्र्यन्त यामार्धदिवार्धप्रहरावधिः ।
स्यात्पूर्वज्वलितान्याश्च भवन्त्येवं रवेर्वशात् ॥ ५८ ॥

[९८]दिशायामष्टकेनाष्टौ दीप्ताः शान्ता भवन्ति ताः ।
यस्यां सूर्योदयः सा दिग्ज्वलिता धूमिताग्रगाः ॥ ५९ ॥

अङ्गार[९९] भस्मवात्यौः चतस्त्रोऽन्याः शुभा[१००]वहाः ।
वामस्वरोगतिस्तारा शान्ते [१०१]कार्ये प्रशस्यते ॥ ६० ॥

दीप्ते तु दक्षिणः शब्दो [१०२]गतिर्वामा प्रवेशने ।
नकुलाजमयूराणां [१०३]चाषखं जनयोरपि ॥ ६१ ॥

---

८७. शकुनो - in B, C, D, E
८८. ध्रुवजनः - in C
८९. तत- in A
९०. शुम्ये- in A
९१. संस्थान - in C
९२. वामा - in B C D E
९३. चमेहिका- in A, वभिहिका - in B, C
९४. जुंजांग - in A
९५. दुर्गा - in A, B
९६. न गृहं करं - in C
९७. दिशोशत्र्यं च मार्यार्द्धा - in A
९८. दिशो - in A
९९. भस्मत्यौ - in A
१००. मृताः - in A
१०१. काये - in A
१०२. तति - in A
१०३. चाखसं - in A

54-55. At the commencement of the construction of a house following the science of prognostication the pole star is to be fixed first of all. Then, on the right side or on the left side the *Śānta* will stay in its own place. *Śānta* on the right side of the dog brings in fulfill-ment. It is not favourable if on the left side and is regarded as inauspicious if expanded/stretched or shaken.

56. If the construction of a house begins in an auspicious place, the crows will caw sweetly. If in that place there are materials, objects(*Dravya*) or splinters (*Śalya*) the crow will caw hoarsely.

57. With the effect of the principal omen a fort is erected, and with its power a city and house is to be built, and it is for certain that trade, agriculture and other types of occupations become fruitful under its influence.

58. In the direction or quarter of the compass, at the end of the night half of the *Yāma* and in the day up to half the *Prahara* in the Eastern side are known as *Jvalitā* and others are likewise under the influence of the Sun.

59-60. On the eight directions they are eight types, such as *Dīpta* (bright) *Śānta* and others. The direction where the Sun rises is known as *Jvalitā* and *Dhūmitā* on the forepart. *Aṅgāra* (fire), *Bhasma* (ash), *Vāta* (air) and another four are regarded as auspicious. If the sound comes from the left side, it is regarded as auspicious in the *Śānta* (cool) work.

If the Southern direction is bright and the motion of the sound en- ters from the left side then there will be concern for the mongoose, goat, and peacock. The sight, narration and sound will be totally beneficial for Kings.

दर्शनं [१०४]कीर्त्तनं शब्दः सर्वसिद्धिकरं नृणाम्।
शशगजाहकगोधा हि शूकराणां तु कीर्त्तनम्॥ ६२॥

ऋक्षवानरयोर्दृष्टिः शब्दौ सिध्यै न कीर्त्तनम्।
दीप्ते दीप्तादिशः शान्ताः शान्ताकार्ये शुभावहाः॥ ६३॥

धनसौख्यादिकं शान्तं दीप्ते हानिभयादिकम्॥ ६४॥

इति शकुनलक्षणम्।

[१०५]गृहभूमिः शुभाश्वेताकृष्णास्निग्धोन्नता घना।
सुगन्धा षड्[१०६]रसाश्चैकवर्णा [१०७]प्रदक्षिणप्लवा॥ ६५॥

त्रिपञ्च[१०८]सप्तरात्रेण सर्वशस्यप्ररोहिणी।
घृतगन्धा शुभास्वादे[१०९]स्वेतेष्टा ब्राह्मणस्य भूः॥ ६६॥

रक्तशोणितगन्धा च [११०]तु वरा क्षत्रियस्य सा।
[१११]पीताम्ला [११२]तैलगन्धा च[११३] वैश्यवर्णत्रयस्य च॥ ६७॥

कटुका मत्स्यगन्धाभूः कृष्णा [११४]शूद्रेऽखिलेष्वपि।
शरावे घृत[११५]पूर्णेस्मिन्नामे वर्ति[११६]चतुष्टये॥ ६८॥

---

१०४. कीर्तिनम् - in A
१०५. Similar verse are seen in M.P. ch 253 v 11-12
१०६. रस in C
१०७. प्रादक्षिणा - in D
१०८. शप्त - in A
१०९. श्वेते - in D
११०. तुर्वश - in D
१११. पीतख्रला - in B
११२. लैल - in C
११३. वैश्ये - in A, BCD omit वर्ण - शस्तवैश्यत्रय - in E
११४. शुद्धे - in A अंत्यजादि Egives note
११५. प्रर्णे -in C
११६. चतुष्टयम् - in A
१।३।५हलादिकर्मणि एकादिपंचमान्तः रेखाधराणि खनने श्रेष्ठतरान्यथा हानिकरा, notes in Eforv 66ab

The narration of the hare, goat, alligator, and pig is totally beneficial for the King, but the sight and sound alone of the bear and monkey serves the purpose, not the narration.

If the directions are bright its known bright and *Śānta* is auspicious for all *Śānta* work.

61-64. *Śānta* causes wealth and friendship, while *Dīpta* causes loss, fear and other evils.

Thus ends the topic of Omens.

65. The plot for a residence is regarded as auspicious if it is white, black, smooth, elevated and compact; it should exude a good smell and have one of the six types of *Rasas*[4] and should have the same colour all over the land. The slope of the land should be on all sides.

66. When scattered on the land, if all types of seeds germinate well within three, five, or seven nights, and the land has the smell of ghee and good taste, then the land is regarded as auspicious for Brahmins.

67. If the soil is red and emits the smell of blood, it is best suited for a *Kṣatriya* (for constructing his house) ; yellow coloured, sour tasting soil, which exudes an oily smell is regarded as auspicious for the three types of *Vaiśyas.*

Pungent tasting, black coloured soil, which has the smell of fish is universally accepted as the best suited for all *Śūdras.*

68. On the plot, in an earthen pot full of ghee, one should place wicks in the four directions.

4. Six *Rasas* are *Madhura, Kaṣāya, Tikta, Lavaṇa, Amla, Kaṭu.*

पूर्वाद्या [११७]दीप्यते वर्त्तिर्विप्रादीनां शुभा मही।
खातं हस्तमितं कृत्वा पूरयेत्तन्मृदा पुनः ॥ ६९ ॥

[११८]हीने तुल्येऽधिके[११८] तत्र हीन[११९]मध्योत्तमं फलम्।
तत्खातमम्बुनाऽऽपूर्य गच्छेच्छतपदं सुधीः ॥ ७० ॥

[११९]पादोनेऽर्धभृते खाते [१२०]मध्यहीनोत्तमा मही।
आखुमार्जारयोः[१२१] स्नेहो यस्यां [१२२]श्वानविडालयोः ॥ ७१ ॥

[१२३]क्षितौनकुलसर्पाणां तस्यां [१२४]सौख्यकरं गृहम्।
गोविप्रैः [१२५]सेविता श्रेष्ठा प्रागुदक् शङ्करप्लवा ॥ ७२ ॥

[१२६]सर्वदिक्प्रवणावापि मनोज्ञा भुः प्रशस्यते।
[१२७]वल्मीकिन्यूखरानि [१२८]निम्ना स्फुटिता शल्यसङ्कुलाः ॥ ७३ ॥

विवर्णा रूक्षवर्णा वा दुर्गन्धा बहुलोपलाः।
कीटसर्पखरोष्ट्राजैः सेविता भूः [१२९]सुदुःखदाः ॥ ७४ ॥

इति भूपरीक्षा ॥

---

११७. दाप्यते - in A
११८. हीनेधिके तुल्येधिके - in A
११९. मभ्यो - in C
११९. पादोनर्द्ध - in A
१२०. मध्या - in A, C, D, E
१२१. स्नयो - in A
१२२. स्वान - in A
१२३. कुतौ - in A
१२४. सख्यकरो - in A
१२५. शेविता - in A
१२६. सर्वादपि - in A
१२७. वल्मीके - in A
१२८. नेम्रा - in A
१२९. सुखप्रदा - in C

If the eastern wick glows brightly, then that land is auspicious for Brahmins and so on.

In the centre of the land, dig a pit up to the depth of one hand and then replace the soil. If the (filled up) soil is less than the depth of the pit, the result (compactness) is to be treated as poor; if equal, it is medium and if the soil is in excess, it is regarded as auspicious.

69-70. One can fill a pit with water, and walk a hundred steps away from it.

On return, if one sees the remaining water filling one-fourth part of the pit the land is to be considered as medium, if less than one- fourth it is bad, and if the pit is half-filled it is regarded as the best.

That house, where rats and cats or cats and dogs or mongooses and snakes live peacefully, gives happiness.

71-72. That land, which has a slope for water towards the East, and which is favoured by cows and Brahmins is regarded as the best.

73-74. That land is praiseworthy which has slopes on all sides and which has a beautiful appearance. If any land is full of ant-hills or is barren, low, covered with darts (full of *Śalyas*), faded and rough coloured, giving off a bad odour, is full of stone-chips, or is frequented by worms, serpents, asses, camels, and goats, it would give extreme sorrow to the owner of the land.

Thus ends the method of soil-testing.

गृहासन्ना कण्टकिनः फलिनः क्षीरिणो द्रुमाः ।
भयं प्रजाक्षयं हानिं क्रमात्कुर्वन्ति ते सदा ॥ ७५ ॥

मत्स्यमते ।

प्रदक्षिणे गृहमुखाद्वटोदुम्बरपिप्पलाः ।
प्लक्षश्चो[१३०]त्तरतो धन्या विपरीतास्त्वसिद्धये ॥ ७६ ॥

अश्वत्थशाकाशोकाश्च केतकीबीजपूरिकाः ।
यस्मिन्गृहे प्ररोहन्ति न समृध्यति तद्गृहम् ॥ ७७ ॥

खर्जुरी[१३१]दाडिमी रम्भा बदरी बीजपूरिका ।
केतकी चेक्षवो रूढा स्वयं गेहे न सौख्यदाः ॥ ७८ ॥

दाडिमीं च हरिद्रां च श्वेतां च गिरिकर्णिकाम् ।
य इच्छेदात्मनः श्रेयो गृह[१३२]द्वारे न रोपयेत् ॥ ७९ ॥

[१३३]अश्वथ्थोदुम्बरवट[१३४]प्लक्षाम्र[१३५]क्रमुकादिकान् ।
वर्जयेद्गृहमाश्रित्य [१३६]हर्म्यवृद्धिविघातकान् ॥ ८० ॥

करवीरमुनि[१३७]द्राक्षाजातीतगर[१३८]कुब्जिकाः ।
[१३९]अन्ये देवदुमास्तेषां न कुर्यादाश्रितं गृहम् ॥ ८१ ॥

अपि सौवर्णिकं वृक्षं स्थापयेन्न गृहाश्रये ।
भयाद्भूताश्रितो वृक्षो यदा [१४०]च्छेत्तुं न शक्यते ॥ ८२ ॥

---

१३०. त्तरतौ – in A
१३१. डाडिमी – in A
१३२. द्वारि – in B, C, D, E
१३३. अश्वच्छो in A
१३४. प्रक्षाश्च in C
१३५. कार्मुका in A, MsE gives marginal note पूगीफलम् for क्रमुका (v.80)
१३६. हर्म in A
१३७. द्राक्षाश्च in DE
१३८. कुब्जिकान् in E
१३९. अन्येदैव in B, अन्यैदैवि E
१४०. च्छतुं in A

75. There is always chance of fear, loss of subjects and damage respec- tively if thorny trees, tree with fruits, and juicy trees are planted near the house.

So says the Matsya Purāṇa.

76. If *Vaṭa, Udumbara, Pippala, and Plakṣa* trees surround a house starting with its front side from the Northern direction, these are considered as beneficial, but their being in the opposite direction produces adverse effects.

77. *Aśvattha, Śāka, Aśoka, Ketakī, Bījapūrikā (trees),* if planted near the house, brings no prosperity to the builder.

78. *Kharjura, Dāḍima, Rambhā, Badarī, Bījapūrikā, Ketakī, Ikṣava,* (trees) when planted near a house, brings no happiness to the owner of the house.

79. *Dāḍima, Haridrā,* and the white *Girikarṇikā* should not be planted on the front door of a house if one cares for one's prosperity.

80. *Aśvattha, Udumbara, Vaṭa, Plakṣa, Āmra, Kramuka* and others should be avoided near the house. These will create obstruction in carrying out the extension of a house.

81-82. *Karavīra, Muni, Drākṣā, Jātī, Tagara, Kubjikā* and other *Devadrumas*[5] should not be planted near a house. Moreover, the *Sauvarṇika* tree also should not be planted near a residence. As this tree is inhabited by ghosts, it is not possible for a person, terrified by the ghost, to cut off the tree.

5. *Devadrumas* are mentioned in the fourth chapter, *v.*121 in this book.

तत्समीपे वपेद्बिल्वी शमीबकुलचम्पकान्।
पुन्नागाशोकतिलकद्राक्षाकुसुममण्डपम्॥ ८३॥

दाडिमी पिप्पलि[१४१]चापि तज्ज दोषोपशान्तये।
[१४२]यामे गते [१४३]स्थिते छाया वृक्षप्रासाद[१४४]गुल्मजा॥ ८४॥

गृहेषु दोषदा प्रोक्ता वर्जनीया प्रयत्नतः॥ ८५॥

इति [१४५]वृक्षादिछायानिर्णयः॥

[१४६]प्राचीमुखादिनां शस्ते [१४७]भास्करे तौलिमेषयोः।।
चित्रा स्वात्यन्तरे चैवं कृत्तिका श्रवणोदये॥ ८६॥

शङ्कुं सूर्याङ्गुलं तीक्ष्णं द्विगुणे मण्डले शुभे।
[१४८]मध्ये न्यसेत्ततः छायात्रये[१४८] पूर्वपरादिशः॥ ८७॥

स्थाप्याः कुम्भास्त्रयपूर्णा धनधान्यैः क्रमेण च।
सौम्याननाः सदीपाश्च निशायां निर्मलेऽम्बरे॥ ८८॥

[१४९]ध्रुवमर्कटिकातारे [१५०]अवलम्बेन सम्मिते।
दीपाग्रैश्च यदैक्यं स्यात्तत्सूत्रे दक्षिणोत्तरा॥ ८९॥

१४१. श्चापि in A
१४२. याम्मे in E
१४३. स्तिते in E
१४४. कुल्मजा in e
१४५. वृक्षवायादिनिर्णव in A
१४६. प्राच्यीमुख्यायनां
१४७. भास्वमैच्छिमेषया in C
१४८. समेमध्ये न्यसेत्तत्रः छायात्राये in B
समेमध्ये न्यसेत्तत्र छायात्राये in C
समेमध्ये न्यसेत्तत्रद्धायाति in E
१४९. ध्रुवकर्मटिका in C.
Ms. D gives marginal note बकुलमौलसरी for बकुल (v. 84)
Ms E gives marginal note दुर्वा for शमी and नागकेशरी युन्नाग for (v. 84)
Ms. D given mariginal note प्रत्यङ्मुचाानि दौ भास्करे तौलिमेषयोः
१५०. अवलंलेभ in A

83. Therefore, one should plant *Bilva, Śamī, Bakula, Campaka, Punnāga, Aśoka, Tilaka, Drākṣā (trees)* near one's house and can have a flower garden also.

84-85. *Dāḍima* and *Pippala* should be discarded for rectifying of faults, if any. If even after three hours, the shadow of a tree or a bush continues to cast its shade on a palace, these are to be considered inauspicious; so these are to be carefully avoided.

Thus ends the section on the shady trees.

86. When the Sun is either in the *Tulā* (Libra) or *Meṣa* (Aries) and it comes in between *Citrā* and *Svāti* it is auspicious to determine the Eastern direction. Likewise, it is marked with the rise of *Kṛttikā* and *Śravaṇā* also.

87. The gnomon will be of 12 *Aṅgulas* and pointed, it is auspicious if the radius is twice its size; then, it is to be placed in the centre to determine the Eastern and Western directions with the help of the shadow measured thrice.

88. At night when the sky is clear, three pitchers full of wealth and grains with lamps on them should be serially placed facing towards the North.

89. With the help of the pole star when the light of the lamps will be in the same line, then the South and North direction can be determined with a thread[6].

6. Similar *verses* in (1) *Rājavallabha Maṇḍana* -ch 1 *Sl* 9-10. *Aparājitapṛcchā* - ch. 63, *Śl* 30-32.

[१५१]दिङ्मुखं गृहिणां वास्तु धनसौख्य[१५२]करं भवेत्।
दिङ्मुढमर्थनाशाय पुरप्रासादमन्दिरम्॥ ९०॥

नदीनां सङ्गमे तीर्थे दुर्गे सिद्धा[१५३]श्रमे गिरौ।
वास्तुस्थानवशात्कार्यं दिशादोषो न विद्यते॥ ९१॥

इति दिक्साधनम्॥

पुरान्धकवधे शम्भोर्ललाटात्पतितः क्षितौ।
स्वेदस्तस्मात्समुद्भूतं भूतमत्यन्तदुःसहम्॥ ९२॥

गृहीत्वा सहसा देवैर्न्यस्तं [१५४]भूमावधोमुखम्।
[१५५]जानुनी कोणयोः पादौ[१५६]रक्षोदिशि[१५७]शिवे शिरः॥ ९३॥

पञ्चचत्वारिंशदस्य [१५८]वास्तोर्देहे स्थिताः सुराः।
[१५९]देव्योष्टौ बाह्यगास्तेषां वसनाद्वास्तुरुच्यते॥ ९४॥

अधोमुखेन विज्ञप्तै स्त्रिदशैर्विहितो बलिः।
तेनैव बलिना शान्तिं कुरुते हानिमन्यथा॥ ९५॥

प्रासाद[१६०]भवनादीनां प्रारम्भे [१६१]परिवर्तने।
वास्तुकर्मसु सर्वेषु पूजितः सौख्यदो भवेत्॥ ९६॥

---

१५१. दिक्समुखं in A.C.
१५२. करो in A·
१५३. श्रमौ in A
१५४. भुमावेधो in A
१५५. जानुनाकोणयो: in B.CDE.
१५६. रक्रो in A
१५७. शिवेशिर: in A
१५८. पुंसो in A
१५९. देव्यौष्टौ in A
१६०. शवना in A.
१६१. परिवृर्त्तने in A

90. The house having proper directions bestows wealth and happiness to the owner. The reverse direction causes loss of wealth for a city, palace and temple.

91. In the confluence of rivers, holy places, forts, hermitages, one should construct houses according to the type of the site, as no fault of direction is counted therein.

Thus ends the rule of Orientation.

92. In ancient times, after killing the demon *Andhaka*, a drop of sweat from *Śiva's* forehead fell down on the earth and out of that an unbearable spirit was born.

93. Immediately, the Gods placed him on the earth keeping his face down. His thigh, torso, legs were placed in the corners and the head was placed in the North East.

94. Forty-five deities are presiding over the body of *Vāstu*. Among them eight deities reside outside. Because of the God's settling therein, it is known as *Vāstu*.

95. As he was made to face downwards, so thirteen offerings should be made to him, and by this there will be peace; otherwise, there will be loss and destruction.

96. During the initial start and further alterations to the palace, house etc it is auspicious if he (*Vāstudeva*) is propitiated in all *Vāstukarma*.

[१६२]**मत्स्यपुराणे ॥**

सूत्रारम्भे [१६३]शिलान्यासे द्वारवंशोच्छ्रयेऽपि च।
प्रवेशे शान्तिकार्ये च वास्तु[१६४]यज्ञस्तु पञ्चधा ॥ ९७ ॥

एकपादोदितो वास्तुर्यावत्पदसहस्रकम्।
द्वात्रिंशन्मण्डलानि[१६५] स्युः क्षेत्रतुल्याकृतीनि च ॥ ९८ ॥

एकाशीतिपदो वास्तुश्चतुःषष्टिपदोऽथवा।
सर्ववास्तुविभागेषु पूजये[१६६]न्मण्डलद्वयम् ॥ ९९ ॥

यद्वा ॥

चतुःषष्ट्या [१६७]पुरग्रामे मर्मराजगृहेषु [१६८]च।
एकाशीत्या पदैर्गेहे शतेनार्चे सुरालये ॥ १०० ॥

सर्ववास्तु[१६९]विभागेषु [१७०]विज्ञेया नवका[१७१] नव।
[१७२]प्रासादेष्वेवमेवस्याद्वापीकूपेषु चैव हि ॥ १०१ ॥

ईशो मूर्धनि [१७२]पर्जन्यो दक्षिणं कर्णमाश्रितः।
जयस्कन्धे[१७३]महेन्द्राद्याः पञ्च दक्षिणबाहुगाः ॥ १०२ ॥

---

१६२. मात्स्ये in B, D, E
१६३. शिल्पा in A
१६४. यजत्स्तुं in A
१६५. द्वाविंश- in A
१६६. न्मण्डले in DE
१६७. पुरे in E
१६८. तं in A
१६९. विभावेषु in A
१७०. विज्ञेयाकानवा in B
१७१. E gives marginal note देवगृहादि
१७२. जर्जन्यो in A
१७३. मेहेन्द्राद्या in A

(In the) Matsyapurāṇa

97. *Vāstuyajña* is of five types and this should be performed in the measurement of the thread, laying of the foundation stone, in the erection of the door beam, in the first entry of the house and for ushering peace.

98. The ground plan of a *Vāstu* starts from one square (*Pāda*) to thousand squares. According to the shape of the land, the diagram (*Maṇḍala*) ground plan can be of thirty-two types.

99. Among all the divisions of *Vāstu,* two ground plans are to be counted as the best. They are eighty-one squares or sixty-four squares(*Pāda*).

Otherwise

100. The sixty-four square plan in suitable for a town, village, royal palace made of stone, while a house is to be built on the eighty-one square plan and a temple should be erected on the hundred square plan.

101. The ground plan of *Vāstu* is to be divided nine into nine (square). The same is to be followed for the water-tank and well.

(Now the position of the Gods on *Vāstudeva* is presented).

102. *Īśa* rests on the head while *Parjanya* rests on the right ear, *Jaya* rests on the shoulder, *Mahendra* and the other five *Devas* reside on the right hand.

महेन्द्रादित्यसत्याश्च वृष आकाशमेव ते।
वह्निर्जानुनि पूषाद्याः सप्तपादतलोऽस्थिताः ॥ १०३ ॥

पूषाऽथ वितथश्चैव [१७४]गृहक्षतो यमस्तथा।
गन्धर्वो भृङ्गराजश्च मृगसप्तसुरा इति ॥ १०४ ॥

पादयोः पितरस्तस्मात्सप्त[१७५]पादतलास्थिताः।
दौवारिकोऽथसुग्रीवपुष्पदन्तो [१७६]जलाधिपः ॥ १०५ ॥

असुरः शोषयक्ष्माणौ रोगो जानुनि संस्थितः।
[१७७]नागो मुख्यश्च भल्लाट सोमः शैलश्च बाहुगाः ॥ १०६ ॥

अदितिः स्कन्धदेशेऽस्य वामकर्णे दितिः स्थिताः।
द्वात्रिंशद्बाह्यगादेवा नाभिपृष्ठे स्थितो विधिः ॥ १०७ ॥

अर्यमा दक्षिणे वामे स्तने तु [१७८]पृथिवीधरः।
विवस्वानथ [१७९]मित्रश्च दक्षवामोरुगावुभौ ॥ १०८ ॥

आपःकण्ठे स्थितो [१८०]वास्तोरापवत्सो हृदि स्थितः।
सावित्रः सविता तद्वत् करं दक्षिणमाश्रितौ ॥ १०९ ॥

इन्द्र इन्द्र[१८१]जयो [१८२]मेण्ढ्रे [१८३]रुद्रो वामेकरेऽस्य च।
रुद्र[१८४]दासोऽपि तत्रैव इति देवमयं वपुः ॥ ११० ॥

---

१७४. गृहक्षा यमः in B
१७५. पादलता in A
१७६. जनाधिपत् in A
१७७. नागा in A
१७८. पृथवी in A
१७९. मित्रस्य in A
१८०. वास्तोपेंरोवत्स्थ्यैहर्यदिगं in C
१८१. जययो in A
१८२. मेद्रे in BCDE
१८३. रुड्ये in A
१८४. दाजो in C

103. They are *Mahendra, Āditya, Satya, Vṛṣa* and *Ākāśa*. *Vahni* rests on the knee. Starting from *Pūṣā* seven other deities reside on the feet.

104. *Pūṣā, Vitatha, Gṛhakṣata* as well as *Yama, Gandharva, Bhṛṅgarāja* and *Mṛga* - these are the seven deities.

105. In between the two feet the seven *Pitṛs* take rest. *Dauvārika, Sugrīva, Puṣpadanta,* and *Jalādhipa* reside under the feet.

106. *Asura, Śoṣa, Yakṣmā and Roga* reside on the knee, *Nāga, Mukhya, Bhallāṭa, Soma, Śaila* reside on the hand.

Aditi rests on the shoulder and *Diti* resides on the left ear. There are

107. thirty-two external Gods who live in the outer periphery. The lord *Brahma* (*Vidhi*) rests on the navel part.

108. *Aryamā* rests on the right breast while *Pṛthivīdhara* rests on the left breast. Both *Vivasvān* and *Mitra* rest on the right (*Dakṣa*) and left thighs (*Uru*).

109. *Āpa* rests on the neck, and *āpavatsa* resides on the heart of the *Vāstu*. Likewise, *Sāvitra* and *Savitā* rest on the right palm.

110. *Indra* and *Indrajaya* rest on the penis(Mendhra). Also, *Rudra* and *Rudradāsa* rest on the left palm. So, the whole body of *Vāstu* is full of Gods.

भूमीं [१८५]परीक्ष्य तां पञ्चगव्यैरा[१८६]सेचयेत्सुधीः ।
पश्चाद्वास्तुं लिखेद्रन्तहेमरौप्यफलादिभिः ॥ १११ ॥

काष्ठांगारनखैः शस्त्रैर्लिखितो भयकारकः ॥ ११२ ॥

तथा चापराजिते ॥

ततो [१८७]वास्तुः सुसंपूज्य[१८८]स्तत्र [१८९]क्षेत्रे सुकल्पिते ।
पुष्पाक्षतैः समालिख्य निलयादिप्रमाणतः ॥ ११३ ॥

चतुःषष्टि पदे वास्तौ मध्ये ब्रह्मा युगांशकः ।
अर्यमाद्याश्चतुर्भागा मध्यकोणे द्विभागिकाः ॥ ११४ ॥

बाह्यकोणेषु[१९०] सार्द्धांशा शेषाः एकपदा सुराः ।
एकाशीतिपदे वास्तौ ब्रह्मा मध्ये नवांशकैः ॥ ११५ ॥

षठ्पदा अर्यमाद्याः स्युद्व्यंशः कोणेषु मध्यगाः ।
सर्वेऽपि भागिका बाह्ये [१९१]देवा अथ शतांशके ॥ ११६ ॥

ब्रह्मा तु षोडशपदो वश्वंशा अर्यमादयः ।
[१९२]बाह्यकोणेषु सार्धांशा शेषाः स्युः पूर्ववास्तुवत् ॥ ११७ ॥

[१९३]इशश्चैव तु पर्जन्यो जयन्तः शक्रभास्करौ ।
सत्यो भृशोऽम्बरं चेति देवान्पूर्वे प्रपूजयेत् ॥ ११८ ॥

---

१८५. परीक्ष्यती in A
१८६. सौच्य बुद्धिमान् in B सोच्य बुद्धिमान् in CDE
१८७. वास्तुस्तु संपूज्य in A
१८८. त्रेत्रे in A
१८९. Ms E given note गृहादि
१९०. वार्द्धाशाः in e, चार्द्धायाः in BDE
१९१. दैवा in B.C. दैव in DE
१९२. वारुणी in A
१९३. A writes इशान and omits तु

111. A wise man will examine the land first, and then sprinkle it with *Pañcagavya*[7]. Later on, he will draw the plan of *Vāstu* with a sharp stick (*Phalā*) made of gems, gold or silver.

112. If written with wood, charcoal, nails or sharp weapons it is inauspi- cious.

Likewise in the Aparājitapṛcchā.

113. Then *Vāstu* should be worshipped properly and the ground plan should be in accordance with the conception. According to the size of the house, decorations should be done with flowers and rice(*Akṣata).*

114. In the *Vāstu* plan of sixty-four squares, *Brahmā* will occupy the central four *Pādas Aryamā* and others will occupy the four *Pādas* and the corners will be divided into two sections in the middle part.

115. *Pādas* in the outer corners will be divided into half. The rest of the squares will be occupied by the deities, each having one square. In the eighty one square ground plan, *Brahmā* will occupy the central nine squares.

116. *Aryamā* and others will occupy six squares, and the inner corners will be divided into two squares each. In a hundred square plan all deities will occupy one *Pāda* each in the outer periphery.

117. *Brahmā* occupies sixteen squares, *Aryamā* and other deities occupy eight *Pādas* each. The outer corners are to be divided into half and the rest will be like the previous ground plan.

118. *Iśa, Parjanya, Jayanta, Śakra, Bhāskara, Satya, Vṛṣa, Ambara-* these deities will be worshipped on the Eastern periphery.

---

7. *Pañcagavya* - Milk, Curd, Honey, *Gomaya* (cow dung) *Gocanā*..

[१९४]अग्निः पूषाऽथ वितथो [१९५]गृहक्षतयमौ तथा।
गन्धर्वो भृङ्गराजश्च मृग[१९६]इत्यष्ट दक्षिणे॥ ११९॥

पितरोद्वास्थ सुग्रीवपुष्पदन्तजलाधिपाः।
असुरः शोषयक्ष्माणौ इत्यष्टौ पश्चिमे यजेत्॥ १२०॥

[१९७]रोगो नागश्च मुख्यश्च भल्लाटः सोम एव च।
शैलोऽदिति[१९८]र्दितिश्चेति देवानुत्तरतोऽर्चयेत्॥ १२१॥

आपापवत्सावीशाने मध्यकोणे [१९९]प्रपूजयेत्।
सावित्रः सविताग्नेये इन्द्र[२००]श्चेन्द्रजयोऽन्यतः॥ १२२॥

[२०१]रुद्रं च रुद्रराजं च[२०२] वायव्ये द्वौ समर्चयेन्।
अर्यमा पूर्वदिग्भागे [२०३]विवस्वान् इह दक्षिणे॥ १२३॥

मित्रस्तु पश्चिमे तद्वदुत्तरे [२०४]पृथिवीधरः।
ब्रह्मागर्भे सुरा एवं संपूज्या सर्ववास्तुषु॥ १२४॥

ईशाने चरकीं बाह्ये पिलिपिच्छां तु पूर्वतः।
विदारीमग्निकोणे च[२०५] जम्भां याम्यदिगाश्रितान्॥ १२५॥

---

१९४. अग्र in A
१९५. ग्रह in BCD
१९६. इष्टत्ये in C
१९७. A omits V 121
१९८. दिश्चोति in B दिश्चेति in C
१९९. प्रभुजयेत् in A
२००. श्चेन्द्रयोजन्तः in A
२०१. रुद्रांश्च in DE
२०२. वायव्यो in A, वायवे in e
२०३. विविस्वान् in B
२०४. पृथवीधरः in A
२०५. जृभं in C, जृभां in E

119. *Agni, Pūṣā, Vitatha, Gṛhakṣata, Yama, Gandharva, Bhṛṅgarāja, Mṛga*- these eight deities reside on the Southern periphery.

120. *Pitara, Udvāstha, Sugrīva, Puṣpadanta, Jalādhipa, Asura, Śoṣa, Yakṣma*,- these eight deities should be offered sacrifice (*Yajña*)on the Western periphery.

121. *Roga, Nāga, Mukhya, Bhallāṭa, Soma, Śaila, Aditi* and *Diti* - these eight deities should be paid homage on the Northern periphery.

122. *Āpa* and *Āpavatsya* should be worshiped on the central corner of the North-East direction (*Īśāna*), *Sāvitra* and *Savitā* on the South-East direction (*āgneye*). *Indra* and *Indrajaya* should be worshipped on the South-West direc- tion.

123. *Rudra* and *Rudrarāja* are to be worshipped on the North West direction (*Vāyavya*). *Aryamā* resides on the Eastern direction; like-wise *Vivasvān* on the South.

124. *Mitra* rests on the Western direction; likewise *Pṛthivīdhara* on the Northern direction. *Brahmā* resides on the central part. Thus in all ground plans will the Gods be worshipped.

125. Outside the *Maṇḍala, Carakī* rests on the North-East corner (*Īśāna*). *Pilipicchā* rests on the East. *Vidārī* rests on the South-West (*Agni*) and *Jambhā* occupies the South.

[२०६]नैऋत्ये पूतनां स्कन्दां पश्चिमेऽथ मरुद्दिशि।
तां पापराक्षसीं वास्तोः सौम्ये [२०७]यमदिशान् यजेत्॥ १२६॥

हेतुकादींश्च [२०८]तद्बाह्ये क्षेत्रेशानष्ट पूजयेत्।
हेतुकस्त्रिपुरघ्नश्च वेताल[२०९]श्चाग्निजिह्वकः॥ १२७॥

कालः कराल [२१०]एकांघ्रिर्भीमश्चेत्यष्ट भैरवाः।
देवीः क्रूरां यमादींश्च माषान्नैः सुरयामिषैः॥ १२८॥
अपरान् घृतपक्वान्नैः सर्वान् गन्धादिहेमभिः॥ १२९॥

तथा च।

कुण्डे त्रिमेखले हस्तमिते होमं समाचरेत्।
क्षीरवृक्षसमिद्भिर्वा पालाशीभिः कुशैरपि॥ १३०॥

होमधान्यैर्नवैः शुद्धैर्मधुसर्पिसमन्वितैः।
यव[२११]प्रियङ्गुगोधूमैस्तिलैर्व्रीहिभिरेव वा॥ १३१॥

बिल्वैर्वापि पृथक्कुर्याद्धोममष्टोत्तरं शतम्।
अष्टाधिकां विंशतिं वा [२१२]प्रतिदैवतमाचरेत्॥ १३२॥

ततो मण्डलं [२१३]संस्थाप्य देवताभ्यो बलिं हरेत्।
एवं संपूजिता देवाः शान्तिं कुर्वन्ति ते सदा॥ १३३॥

राक्षसानां बलिर्देयो [२१४]मांसौदनमयस्तथा।
ततः सर्वौषधिसस्नानं यजमानस्य कारयेत्॥ १३४॥

---

२०६. नैऋत्यः in A
२०७. चार्यमाणं in C
२०८. तद्बाध्येपि in A
२०९. स्थाग्निजिकक: in A
२१०. एकोहि- in BD
२११. प्रयंग in A
२१२. प्रतिदैवमता in A
२१३. संस्ताभ्यो
२१४. मासोदनयस्था in B

126. *Pūtanā* resides on the South-West (*Nairṛta*), *Skanda* rests on the West as on the North-West. *Pāparākṣasī* should be worshipped on the North and Southern side of the *Vāstu*.

On the outer periphery, starting from *Hetuka,* eight lords of the land are to be worshipped. *Hetuka, Tripuraghna, Vetāla, Agnijihva, Kāla, Karāla, Ekāṁghri, Bhīma* are the eight *Bhairavas.*

All *Devīs, Krūṛas, Yama* and others should be worshipped with meat, rice wine and other non-vegetarian items.

127-129. Others are to be offered with rice cooked in ghee, all types of per- fumes and gold.

As well as:-

130. The *Homa* should be performed in a *Kuṇḍa* which is equal to three hand strings (*Mekhalā*). The sacrificial wood is to be collected from *Kṣīravṛkṣa, Palāśa* or *Kuśa.*

131. The *Homa* should be done with fresh corn, pure honey, clarified butter (*Sarpi*), barley(*Yava*), long pepper, saffron(*Priyaṅgu*), wheat, sesamum (*Tila*), or rice.

132. Otherwise one can perform the *Homa* one hundred and eight times separately with *Vilva* or offerings can be offered to each God more than eight times or twenty times.

133. Then the diagram should be drawn and offerings are to be made to the Gods. Thus worshipped, the Gods always bestow peace.

134. *Rākṣasas* are to be worshipped with offerings of meat and rice, then the worshipper (*Yajamāna*) will take a bath in water with many types of medicinal herbs.

द्विजास्तु पूजयेद्भक्त्या ये चान्ये गृहमागताः ।
एतद्वास्तूपशमनं कृत्वा कर्म समाचरेत् ॥ १३५ ॥

प्रासादभवनोद्यानप्रारम्भपरिवर्त्तने ।
[२१५]पुरवेश्मप्रवेशे च सर्वदोषोपशान्तये ॥ १३६ ॥

अनेन विधिना यस्तु प्रतिसंवत्सरं बुधः ।
गृहे वायतने [२१६]कुर्यान्न स दुःखमवा[२१६]प्नुयात् ॥ १३७ ॥

न च व्याधिभयं तस्य न च वन्धुधनक्षयः ।
जीवेद्वर्षशतं स्वर्गे कल्पमेकं च तिष्ठति ॥ १३८ ॥

इति वास्तूत्पत्तिविन्यासपूजनविधिः ॥

अथ मर्मवास्तुः-

युगास्त्रे वा(ऽ)यते क्षेत्रे चतुःषष्टिविभाजिते ।
मध्ये रेखा स्मृता[२१७]स्तिस्रो वंशापूर्वापरायताः ॥ १३९ ॥

याम्योत्तरायतास्तिस्र उपवंशाः [२१८]प्रभिन्नगाः ।
कर्णात्कर्णगतं सूत्रं शिरासंज्ञमिह न्यसेत् ॥ १४० ॥

तत्पार्श्वयोस्तथा [२१९]रेखा भागभागान्तरे इह ।
तत्राष्टसूत्रैः पद्मानि षड्भिर्वज्राणि द्वादश ॥ १४१ ॥

चतुष्कोणेषु शूलानि विकर्णोर्ध्वे तु लाङ्गलम् ।
मर्माणि वंशसंपाता महामर्माम्बुजादिकम् ॥ १४२ ॥

२१५. Ms A omits VI36cd and V137ab
२१६. कुर्यान् रदुरकमवा- in A
२१७. स्तिस्तो in A
२१८. प्रतिन्नगाः in A
२१९. रेखो in AD रेखे in CE

135-136. At the time of alteration or at the commencement of a palace, house and a garden, as well as while entering into the city or a house for the removal of all sorts of evils, the Brahmins and other guests should be worshipped with devotion and in this manner one should start work by appeasing the *Vāstu* God.

137. Following this method, he who performs the worship of *Vāstu* every year in his house or abode will not undergo any misery.

138. Neither he has any fear of diseases, nor loss of friends and prosperity. He lives up to a hundred years and stay in heaven for one *Kalpa.*

Thus ends the origin of Vāstu, its layout and the method of worshipping.

Now the ***Marmavāstu*** **:-**

139. A square or rectangular plot of land is to be divided into sixty-four parts. Three lines of beams should be drawn in the centre which run from East to West.

140. Three minor lines of beams should be drawn from South to North. Diagonal lines known as *Śirā* are to be drawn from one corner to another corner.

141. Likewise, the side lines should be drawn here and divided accordingly. Eight measuring lines will form a lotus and six measuring lines will form twelve *Vajras.*

Śūlas will be drawn on the four corners and *Lāṅgalas* on the upper part of the *vikarṇa.*

142. The meeting points of the longer diagonals will be known as *Mahāmarma, Ambuja,* etc.

पदमध्ये चोपमर्म तानि भित्त्यादितस्त्यजेत्।
[२२०]मर्मभिर्भित्तिभिः स्तम्भैः कीलोच्छिष्टोपघातकैः ॥ १४३ ॥

पीडयेद्यदि तद्वास्तु भवनादिषु हानिकृत्।
[२२१]पदस्य षोडशांशेन द्वादशांशेन वा पुनः ॥ १४४ ॥

मर्ममानं स्मृतं कैश्चिदेकद्वित्र्यंगुलोन्मितम् ॥ १४५ ॥

इति मर्मवास्तुः ॥

सर्वदेवमयस्यापि पुंवास्तोः प्रथमं खनेत्।
कुक्षौ सौख्यं पुराघाते [२२२]शरीरे सर्वसंक्षयः ॥ १४६ ॥

इति खातविधौ पुरुषवास्तुः ॥

विप्रस्याश्वत्थजाः [२२३]कीला युगास्रा रदमात्रिकाः।
क्षत्रियस्याष्टयुग्मांशा वस्वस्राः खदिरोद्भवाः ॥ १४७ ॥

विशां जिनाङ्गुलादीर्घाः षोडशास्राः शिरीषजाः।
[२२४]शूद्रे नखाङ्गुला वृत्ता अर्जुनां जनजा दृढाः ॥ १४८ ॥

सूत्रं स्यादङ्गुल[२२५]स्थूलमष्टदण्डायतं दृढम्।
द्विजानां दर्भजं राज्ञां मौजं काशं भवं विशाम् ॥ १४९ ॥

शूद्राणां शणजं क्षौमं कार्पासं चाखिलेष्वपि।
बहिकोणादितो गेहे [२२६]सृष्ट्या कीलान्प्रविन्यसेत् ॥ १५० ॥

२२०. मर्मणितित्तिभिः in A
२२१. पदमध्ये in A
२२२. शारीरे in AB
२२३. कीलायुलायुगा in B
२२४. शुद्धे in A
२२५. राल in B
२२६. सृष्ट्वा in DE

143-144. At the inception of the foundation, *Upamarmas* should be avoided in the middle of the plot. If that *Vāstu* is afflicted by *Marma*, walls, pillars, nails or unclean things, it will be disastrous for a house.

145. Measurement of the *Marmas* is done by twelve or sixteen units but according to some it is measured by one, two or three fingers.

Thus ends Marmavāstu.

146. Though each of the *Pādas* are occupied by Gods, even then the *Puṁvāstu* is to be dug first of all. It is beneficial if dug in the cavity of the abdomen; if dug on the other parts of the body, it brings destruction.

Such is the principle of digging in the Puruṣavāstu.

147. The house of a Brahmin will have nails made out of the *Aśvattha* tree, it will be thirty-two *Aṅgulas* in measurement and quadrangular in shape. For a *Kṣatriya* it will be sixteen[8] *Aṅgulas*, made out of the *Khadira* tree and octagonal.

148. For a *Vaiśya*, it will be twenty four *Aṅgulas* in length made out of the *Śirīṣa* tree and hexagonal. For a *Śūdra*, it will be twenty *Aṅgulas* made out of the *Arjuna* tree, and it will be strong and circular in shape.

149-150. The thread will be sturdy, eight *Daṇḍas* (32 hands =48 feet) in length and one *Aṅgula* in breadth. For a Brahmin, the thread will be made out of *Darbha* (a type of grass), for a King, out of *Muñja*, for *Vaiśya*, out of *Kāśa*, for *Śūdra*, out of jute, silk, and cotton; these will be made universally. In the laying out of a house, the nails should be inserted from *Vahni* (South-East corner).

---

8 It is twenty eight *Aṅgulas* in A.P.

सूत्र[२२७]च्छेदेन [२२८]सिद्धै स्यादष्टीले विच्युते भयम्।
कीलकेऽवाङ्मुखे रोगस्ततो यत्नं समाचरेत्॥ १५१॥

समारभेत कर्माणि [२२९]अष्टसूत्रविधिक्रमात्।
विद्यादृष्टिकरं मौजं कार्पासमवलम्बकम्॥ १५२॥
काष्ठं च साधकं लेख्यमष्टसूत्राण्यनुक्रमात्॥ १५३॥

इति कीलकारोपणम्॥

नागस्य प्रथमे घाते पुच्छे [२३०]पृष्ठे मुखे भयम्।
वामकुक्षौ भवेत्सौख्यं तस्मात्कुक्षिरिहोच्यते॥ १५४॥

सिंहादि त्रित्रिगे भानौ सृष्ट्या नागमुखं दिशि।
खातं वायौ महेशेऽग्नौ नैर्ऋत्ये शोभनं क्रमात्॥ १५५॥

इति नागवास्तुविधिः।

शल्यज्ञाने फणेचक्रमष्टाविंशतिकोष्ठकम्।
तिर्यक् [२३१]पञ्चोर्ध्वगारेखाः कर्तव्या [२३२]अष्टसन्मिताः॥ १५६॥

द्वारशाखामघायाम्यं द्वारमध्ये च कृत्तिका।
पृष्ठपंक्तौ लिखे[२३३]त्स्वातेः सप्तधिष्ण्यान्यनुक्रमात्॥ १५७॥

चित्रापुनर्वसू रौद्रं मृगशीर्ष धनिष्ठिका।
[२३४]श्रवणं चाभिजित् पंक्तौ द्वितीयायामतो लिखेत्॥ १५८॥

---

२२७. च्छेदोन in A
२२८. सिद्धयै in A, सिध्य in D, सिद्धिं in E
२२९. This अष्टसूत्रविधिः is mentioned in AP ch 55 V15-17
२३०. पृष्ठमुखे in B
२३१ यंत्रोर्द्धग in A पंचोद्धूणा in B
२३२. चाष्ट- in E
२३३. त्वातः in E
२३४. ष्टवनं in A

151. If the thread is torn or the pebbles of the measuring thread are displaced, then there is a chance of fear. If the peg faces downwards, there may be disease, so one should take care in placing the nails.

One should start work according to the eightfold procedure of con- struction .

152-153. *Muñja* is conducive to the auspicious look and cotton (*Kārpāsa*) leads to support. Wood is congenial for writing according to the eightfold procedure.

Thus ends the discourse on pegs.

154. In a *Vāstu,* resting on *Nāga,* if the first digging is made on the tail, back or face it will cause fear. But if it is done on the left side of the womb it is regarded as auspicious and is known as *Kukṣi.*

155. If the Sun is on the three Zodiac signs of Leo and others and digging is done on that side where the *Nāga* faces, then it is auspicious and the digging is to be made serially from *Vāyu* (North-West), *Maheśa* (North-East), *Agni* (South-East), and *Nairṛta*(South-West).

Thus ends the rules of Nāgavāstu.

156-157. To know about *Śalya* one should draw a chart of serpents with 28 chambers (*Koṣṭha*). There will be five slanting lines drawn upwardly with eight on the other side. *Maghā* will be on the lower part of the door frame and *Kṛttikā* will be on the centre of the door. On the back row one should put the name of *Svātī* and other seven stars serially.

158. *Citrā, Punarvasū, Raudra* (*Ārdrā*), *Mṛgaśirā, Dhaniṣṭhā, Śravaṇā, Abhijit* -these stars are to be written on the second row.

हस्तः पुष्यस्तथाश्लेषा रोहिणीशततारकम्।
पूर्वभाद्रोत्तराभाद्रं तृतीयायां लिखेत्सुधीः ॥ १५९ ॥

उत्तरफाल्गुनी पूर्वफाल्गुनी पितृमाग्निभे।
भरणी चाश्विनी पौष्णं द्वारपंक्त्या भसप्तकम् ॥ १६० ॥

अश्विन्यादित्रिकं चैव आर्द्रायाश्चैव पञ्चकम्।
[२३५]पूर्वाषाढाचतुष्कं च उत्तरारेवतीद्वयम् ॥ १६१ ॥

एतानि शशीधिष्ण्यानि शेषाणि रविभानि च।
चन्द्रधिष्ण्ये स्थिते सूर्ये [२३६]सूर्य चन्द्रे [२३७]समागते ॥ १६२ ॥

तत्र शून्यं भवेत्स्थानं द्रव्यशल्यविवर्जितम्।
द्रव्यशल्यं विना ह्येवं [२३८]स्वल्पं द्रव्यादि निर्दिशेत् ॥ १६३ ॥

चन्द्रपूर्वापरो भानुस्तत्र शल्यं विनिर्दिशेत्।
भानुः पूर्वापरश्चन्द्रस्तत्र द्रव्यं विनिर्दिशेत् ॥ १६४ ॥

उदयादिगता [२३९]नाड्यः भग्नाः षष्ट्याप्तशेषके।
दिनेन्दुं [२४०]भुक्तियुक्तेऽसौ भवेत्तत्कालचन्द्रमाः ॥ १६५ ॥

चन्द्रवत साधयेत् सूर्यं नक्षत्रं [२४१]चेष्टकालिकम्।
[२४२]शल्यमभ्युध(द्ध)रेत्काष्ठ लोहाङ्गारकवास्थिकम् ॥ १६६ ॥

निखन्य गृहभूमिं तु शिलान्तं वा [२४३]जलान्तकम्।
शल्यं समुद्धरेद्धीमानित्याह स्मापराजितः ॥ १६७ ॥

---

२३५. पूर्वाषाढय in B
२३६. सूर्ये चन्द्र in E
२३७. समागमे in BDE
२३८. शिल्यं in A
२३९. नाभ्यो in A
२४०. भुक्तेयुक्तो in D भक्तयुक्तो in E
२४१. E gives marginal note परिमाणादिलक्षणम्
२४२. B omits V166 cd and 167ab.
२४३. जलांतिकम् in A

159. *Hastā, Puṣyā, Āśleṣā, Rohiṇī, Śatatāraka* (*Śatabhiṣā*), *Pūrvabhadrā, Uttarabhadrā* - these stars are to be written on the third row.

160. *Uttaraphālgunī, Purvaphālgunī, Pitṛ* (*Maghā, Mūlā*), *Agni* (*Kṛttikā*), *Bharaṇī, Aśvinī,* and *Pauṣṇa* (*Revatī*) - these seven stars are to be put on the door line.

161-163. Three stars starting from *Aśvinī*, five stars starting from *Ārdrā*, four stars starting from *Pūrvāṣāḍhā, Uttarabhādrapadā* and *Revatī* - these are under the lunar house while others are under the solar house. If the lunar stars come under the Sun, and the Sun is united with the Moon then that place will be devoid of any particles and *Śalya*. It indicates that there is no *Dravyaśalya*, only a small quantity of other particles may be there.

164. If the Sun is in the western direction and the Moon in the East, in that position one can detect *Śalya*. If the Sun is in the Eastern direction and the Moon is in the West there one can indicate (*Vinirdiśet*) the *'Dravya'*.

165. At the time of sunrise, the star of the Nāḍi is to be divided by 60. If the remainder is 17 (*dinendu*) in the daily motion of the planet (*bhuktiyukte*), it will be *candramā* at that time.

166. The position of the Sun and the stars will be counted in the manner of the Moon to get the desired time. Wood, iron, charcoal (*Aṅgāra*), bone, will be counted as *Śalya* .

167. While digging the residential land under the stone or water one should weed out all these. A wise man will uplift the *Śalya*, - so says *Aparājitā*.

ग्रन्थान्तरे-

अधः पुरुष[२४४]मात्रात्तु न शल्यं दोषदं गृहे।
जलान्तकं स्थितं शल्यं प्रासादे दोषदं नृणाम्॥ १६८॥

शल्ये नृपभयं गव्ये हयजे रोगसम्भवः।
मार्जारशल्ये नाशश्च शुनोऽस्थिनि[२४५]कलिर्भवेत्॥ १६९॥

हानिः खरोष्ट्रयोः शल्ये नराङ्गे बालकक्षयः।
छागे वह्निभयं चान्यत्सर्वं शल्यं भयावहम्॥ १७०॥

अङ्गारेषु तथोन्मादं कपालेषु स सम्भ्रमः।
काष्ठशल्ये तु जानीयात् [२४६]पौंशल्यं स्त्रीषु वास्तुवित्॥ १७१॥

इति शल्योद्धारविधिः॥

कम्बिकालक्षणं ज्ञेयं मानार्थं सर्वकर्मणाम्।
विश्वेशोऽपि जगत्स्रष्टुं यां दधार करे पुरा॥ १७२॥

परमाणुभिरष्टाभिस्त्रसरेणुरुदाहृतः।
रेण्वष्टकेन बालाग्रं लिक्षा तैरष्टभिर्मताः॥ १७३॥

लिक्षाभिरष्टभिर्युका ता अष्ट स्याद्यवोदरम्।
अष्टभिः सप्तभिः षड्भिस्तैर्मात्राङ्गुलमंशकः॥ १७४॥

त्रिविधैरङ्गुलैर्हस्तो ज्येष्ठो मध्यश्च कन्यसः।
जिनैकार्धाङ्गुलो दैर्घ्ये व्यासे पिण्डे क्रमा[२४७]न्मतः॥ १७५॥

धातुवंशमधूकोत्थः खदिराञ्जनचन्दनैः।
तत्र पर्वाष्टकं पुष्पं त्र्यङ्गुले त्र्यङ्गुले भवेत्॥ १७६॥

---

२४४. मात्रां in A
२४५. E gives Footnote २४ अंगु
२४६. पौश्चत्यं in CDE
२४७. -त्ततः in DE

In the other book

168. If the *Śalya* is under one *Puruṣa* measurement it is not regarded as faulty for a house. If a *Śalya* lies beneath the water it is faulty for a palace and human beings .

169 -171. *Śalya* causes fear of the King if it comes from a cow, and if from a horse there is fear of disease. If *Śalya* comes from a cat then there is destruction and if it is from a dog then there will be discord and quarrels. (If the *Śalya* is) from an ass or camel there will be loss, and if it is parts of a human being then there will be loss of child. There is a fear of fire if the *Śalya* comes from a goat, and all other *Śalyas* are formidable (*Bhayāvaha*). From charcoal there is a fear of insanity/ madness, from a skull bone (*Kapāla*) there will be confusion. A man proficient in *Vāstu* knows that *Śalya* from wood brings forth *Pauṁśalya* in women.

Thus ends the procedure of śalyoddhāra.

172. To measure each and everything one should know the marks of *Kambikā*[9]. To create the world, the lord of the universe held it by hand.

173. One *Tryasareṇu* is made of eight *Paramāṇus.* Eight *Reṇus* make one *Bālāgra* and one *Likṣā* is made of eight *Bālāgras.*

174. *Yukā* is made of eight *Likṣhās* and eight *Yukās* make one *Yava.* By the grouping of 8,7,6(*Yavas*), the division of *Mātrā Aṅgula* and *Aṁśaka* are formed respectively.

175. Three types of finger measurements makes three types of *Hasta*(hands), *Jyeṣṭha* (big) *Madhya*(medium) and *Kanyasa* (small). The *Kambikā* is measured in the following order. 24, 1, and 1/2 *aṅgulas* will be the length, breadth and circumference respectively.

176. The measurement rod may be made of material like, bamboo, *Madhūka, Khadira, Añjana, Candana* trees. There will be eight *Parvas* having flower marks at the interval of every third *Aṅgulas.*

9 *Kambikā* : Join of a bamboo shoot or branch *Kambi-Kuśa.*

रुद्रोऽनिलो विश्वकर्मा वह्निर्ब्रह्मायमोऽम्बुपः ।
धनदो विष्णुरित्यादौ पुष्पेष्वग्रे सुरा नव ॥ १७७ ॥

उच्चाटव्याधि[२४८]सन्तापा वह्निः प्रजाक्षयो मृतिः ।
जलधान्यक्षयौ मोहः फलं तत्पीडने क्रमात् ॥ १७८ ॥

केवलान्यत्र[२४९] पर्वाणि [२५०]चत्वार्यर्काङ्गुलै[२५१]र्भजेत् ।
मध्यात्पञ्चाष्ट सूर्यांशं द्वित्रिवेदांशकैः पुनः ॥ १७९ ॥

मूले पुष्पेषु रेखासु प्रान्ते च त्रिदशाः करे ॥
त्रयोविंशतिराद्यार्धे स धार्यः पुष्पकान्तरे ॥ १८० ॥

[२५२]ईशोऽनिलो विश्वकर्मा वह्नि ब्रह्मा रविः क्रमात् ।
रुद्रो यमो विरूपाक्षो वसवो दिग्गजाम्बुपाः ॥ १८१ ॥

[२५३]स्कन्द इच्छाक्रियाज्ञानी धनेशश्चन्द्रमाजयः ।
वासुदेवः सङ्कर्षणः प्रद्युम्नश्चानिरुद्धकः ॥ १८२ ॥

एते देवाः सदैवास्यां कम्बिकायां सुनिश्चलाः ।
आगमैर्वेदमन्त्रैश्च पूज्या सा परमाकला ॥ १८३ ॥

ॐ तत्पुरुषाय विद्महे महादेवाय धीमहि ।
तन्नो रुद्रः प्रचोदयात् ॥
इयं हि रुद्रगायत्रीपवित्रीकरणं परम् ।
चतुर्विंशत्यङ्गुलेषु वर्णानेतान् क्रमान्न्यसेत् ॥ १८४ ॥

खेटकं नगरं ग्रामं क्रोशगव्यूतियोजनम् ।
क्षेत्रादिभूमिभागांश्च ज्येष्ठहस्तेन मापयेत् ॥ १८५ ॥

---

२४८. संतापो in A
२४९. वर्षाणि in A
२५०. चत्वार्थंकां
२५१. भवेत् in DE
२५२. similar verse in AP ch 41.V16
२५३. स्कन्दरो in B

177. *Rudra, Anila, Viśvakarmā, Vahni, Brahmā, Yama, Ambupa, Dhanada, Viṣṇu,* these nine gods will be placed in front of *Puṣpa.*

178. If oppressed, there may serially be evil effects of sorcery (*Uccāṭa*), disease(*Vyādhi*), bereavement (*Santāpa*), fire (*Vahni*), loss of subjects (*Prajākṣaya*), death (*Mṛti*), loss of water and grains (*Jaladhānyakṣaya*),and dilution (*Mohaphala*)

179. Here only four *Parvas* are to be distributed within twelve *aṅgulas.* From the middle, the fifth, eighth, twelfth part may again be divided into two, three, four parts.

180. On the main line of the *Puṣpa* and on the border line and on the 13th *aṅgulas* and on the upper half of the 23rd part that should be placed in between *Puṣpaka.*

181-182. Serially the deities are *Īśa, Anila, Visvakarmā, Vahni, Brahmā, Ravi, Rudra, Yama, Virūpākṣa,* eight *Vasus, Diggaja, Ambupa, Skanda, Icchākriyā, Jñānī,* (the learned), *Dhaneśa, Candramā, Jaya, Vāsudeva, Saṅkarṣaṇa, Pradyumna, Aniruddha*

183. These deities are unalterable in the front part of the *Kambikā,* so they are to be worshipped with Tantras and Vedic rites as the best one.

Oṁ, we know the great deity and my obeisance is for *Mahādeva* and may *Rudra* lead us to salvation.

184. This is the purificatory incantation of *Rudragāyatrī.* These letters are to be marked serially in the *Aṅgulas.*

185. *A Kheṭaka* (small village), city, village will be measured in terms of *Krośa, Gavyūti, Yojanas.* Fields and other plots of land are to be measured with *Jyeṣṭhahasta.*

प्रासादप्रतिमालिङ्गं गृहं राजगृहं[२५४] तथा[२५५]।
वापीकूपादिभूखातं मिनुयान्मध्यमेन तु॥ १८६॥

यन्त्रशस्त्रासनं वाद्यं वापी[२५५]कूपेन भाजनम्।
छत्रं शय्यारथादीनि कन्यसेन करेण हि॥ १८७॥

एकविंशाङ्गुलोऽरत्निरत्निर्हस्त एव च।
चतुर्हस्तो धनुर्दण्डो वंशः पञ्चकरः स्मृतः॥ १८८॥

[२५६]गृहादिकर्म[२५७]प्रारम्भे हस्तस्य सुधृतस्य तु।
पतनं न शुभं तस्मा[२५८]त्प्रयतेतास्य धारणे॥ १८९॥

इति कम्बिकालक्षणम्।

करे करगुणे हस्ता अङ्गुलघ्ने करेऽङ्गुलाः।
अङ्गुलेष्वङ्गुलघ्नेषु फलं लब्धं [२५९]जिनैर्हृते॥ १९०॥

व्यासात्त्रिगुणितो[२६०] वृत्तः परिधिः षष्ठभागयुक्।
व्यासपादे परिधिना गुणिते वृत्तजं फलम्॥ १९१॥

२५४. गृह्वथा in A
२५५. कूपेभ in BCDE
२५६. ग्रहादि in A
२५७. -मारम्भे in A
२५८. प्रयतेत्तस्य in DE
२५९. जनैहृते in A
२६०. E writes marginal note व्यासस्य षड्भागः ब्यासैः। in A

186. Temples, idols, *Liṅgas*, houses as well as royal palaces, tanks, wells, and other dugouts are to be measured with medium hand.

187. Mechanical contrivances, weapons, seats, drums, ponds, wells, utensils, umbrellas, beds, chariots are to be measured with small hands (*Kanyasa*).

188. Twenty one *Aṅgulas* make one *Aratni* as well as one *Hasta*. *Dhanu* and *Daṇḍa* will be four hands in measurement and the *Vaṁsa* will be of five hands.

189. At the beginning of the construction, the measuring hand should be counted correctly. If anybody deviates from that, it is inauspicious, so one should be careful to count it accurately.

Thus ends the characteristies of kambikā.

Linear *Hasta* measurement can be obtained by measuring with *Kara* joined by another *Kara*. By measuring *Hasta* with *Kara*, one will get the *Karāṅgula* unit measurement (superficial contents of a figure in *hasta* and *kara*).

190. Multiplying the measurement of one finger (*Aṅgula*) by another finger and dividing the result by 24, one can get the area in *Aṅgula* units[10]

191AB. Three times the diameter of a circle, when added to one sixth part of the same diameter, obtains the circumference of the circle (*Vṛtta*) with respect to diameter [If d is the diameter of a circle, the circumference as given in the *verse* is $3d + d/6 = d(3+1/6) = d(3+0.167) = 3.167d$ say approximately to $3.141d = \pi d$ i.e. the mathematical formula of the circumference of the circle].

191CD. Multiplying the circumference by one fourth part of the diameter, one can get the *Vṛtta phala* (area of the circle).

---

10 Example:- To find the area of the plot, 5 *Kara*, 12 *Aṅgula* by 3 Kara 12 *Aṅgula*.
Solution: 1st Step:- 5 *Kara* X 3 *Kara* = 15(sq.) *Karas*,
2nd Step:- 5 *Karāṅgula* X 12 *Aṅgula* = 1440 (sq.) *Aṅgula*
3 *Kara Aṅgula* X 12 *Aṅgula* = 864 (sq.) *Aṅgula*
12 *Aṅgula* X 12 *Aṅgula* = 144 (sq.) *Aṅgula*
Total = 2448 (sq.) *Aṅgula*
2448÷24=102, 102÷24 = 4(sq) *Kara* 6(sq.) *Aṅgula*

गोले व्यासघनस्यार्धंस्वैकविंशांशयुक् फलम्।
ज्याशरैक्यार्धं शरघ्नं पुराणांशयुतं धनुः॥ १९२॥

कृत्वा प्राक्सूत्रमर्धाङ्कं दक्षिणोत्तरमत्स्ययोः।
न्यस्यसूत्रैश्चतुःकोणैरङ्कितं चतुरस्रकम्॥ १९३॥

इष्टबाहुमितैर्भागैर्वृत्तार्धं विभजेत्सुधीः।
[२६१]षडंशस्यभुजो ह्येवं वृत्तान्तः क्षेत्रसूत्रणम्॥ १९४॥

क्षेत्रार्धं स्वरसांशे [२६२]न षष्ठास्तस्य भुजो भवेत्।
रसांशः स्वरसांशेन युतो बाहुः [२६३]कलास्रके॥ १९५॥

२६१. षडंशस्याद्भुजो in B
२६२. नमष्टास्र in BCDE
२६३. कलास्रकं in A

[1/4 d x circumference = $\pi d \times d/4 = \pi d^2/4$ = mathematical formula for the area of a circle.

192ab After getting the measurement of the diameter of the circle, half of the cubic value of the diameter has to be divided into 21 parts. The remaining first half of the cube of the diameter is then to be added to one twenty first part of the previous half. The result of the summation will give the volume of the *Gola.*

[If d is the diameter of the *Gola,* cubic half of the diameter when broken into twenty-one parts and one part is then added to the remaining cubic half of the diameter, this results in a summation as $d^3/2\ (1 + 1/21) = d^3/6(3+1/7) = d^3/6(3.142)$ say $\pi d^3/6$ i.e. the mathematical formula for the volume of a sphere]

192cd Add sine (*Jyā*) to verse sine (*Śara*) and half of the summation be multiplied by verse sine again. Adding one eighteenth of it further to itself, the measurement of *dhanu* (part of a circle) would be established.

193. With the above formulae one can draw the east-west as well as the north-south line of the land with the depiction of a fish. A quadrangular square can be drawn with the same formula, by lay- ing on four corners.

194. A wise man will determine half of the circumference of a circle with one's own desired *Hasta* measurement (out of three desired types). One *Bhuja* (base) will be one-sixth of the value of half circumference by *Hasta* measurement; this formula was being used for the measurement of a plot of land.

A six cornered plot of land would have 1/6 of half circumference measured by *Hasta* and added with 1/6 of the other half circumference would give the base of the 6 cornered plot of land in *Bhuja* i.e. 2 *bhuja.*

[Let us take S = the measurement in *Hasta* of half circumference of a circle. *Bhuja* is then = S/6. The base of a six cornered plot of land according to the verse is equal to $S/6 + S/6 = 2S/6$

स्वस्वमानघ्नयोर्बाह्वोर्योगान्मूलं विकर्णजम् ॥ १९६ ॥

ग्रन्थान्तरे ॥

कर्णतो बाहिके द्वे ये त्र्यंशैकान्यायुगांशकाः ।
तत्कर्णः पञ्चभागः स्यात्करे युगगुणाङ्गुलाः ॥ १९७ ॥

इति मेयविधिः ॥

भूमिं संशोधयित्वा तु पुनर्वास्तु समर्चयेत् ।
क्षेत्रपालान्दिशाधीशान् गणेशग्रहचण्डिकाः ॥ १९८ ॥

नैवेद्यैः क्षीरखण्डाज्यैः पक्वान्नैर्विविधैरपि ।
बलिभिः पुष्पधूपैश्च यथाशास्त्रं प्रपूजयेत् ॥ १९९ ॥

which is the mathematical formula of the base of a six cornered plot of land in a circle as 2S = the total circumference of the circle.]

195. For a sixteen cornered plot of land in a circle, the value of the base in *Bhuja* (arc) is available by dividing the base of Six cornered plot by sixteen into six. [Mathematically the base of a sixteen cornered plot of land in a circle as 2S/16 where S is the measurement of half circumference of the circle. [According to the verse, base of the sixteen cornered plot of land = 2S/6 X 6/16=2S/16]. By joining the summation of the measurement of each base, one will get the measurement of *Vikarṇa* (diameter, the diagonal), generating thus the *Mūla* (centre) of the circle.

In other book:

196. Two arms (*Bāhu*) out of a right angle (*Karṇa*) inside a circle joining two ends of a diameter of the circle having measurements of 3 and 4 units will end up with a diameter of 5 units of measurement.

Thus ends the methodology of measurement.

[In a right angle triangle, having two arms of dimensions, 3 units and 4 units will result in $3^2 + 4^2 + 5^2$]*

Thus ends the definition of Kamvikā.

197. Multiply *Kara* (i. e *Hasta*=24 *Aṅgulas*) with *Kara* to get (square) *Kara*; also *Aṅgulas* with *Karā ṅgulas*, and *Aṅgula* by dividing with 24(*Jina*) twice gives the result(of the area of rectangular or square plot).

197. Multiply diameter by 3 and add 1/6 to it to get the circumference of a circular (plot). To find the area of a circular plot, multiply 1/4 of a diameter by the circumference (*Paridhina)*of the circular (plot).

198 - 199. After the purification of the land, once again the *Vāstu* is to be wor- shipped. Lord of the land (*Kṣetrapāla*), the lord of the corners, (*Diśādhīśa*), *Gaṇeśa*, *Grahacaṇḍī*, should be worshipped with offerings of *Kṣīra*, sweets, clarified butter(*Ājya*), various types of cooked food, flowers, incense and according to the rule of *Śāstra*.

* [Note :- These formulae were used to find out the measurement of plots of land, and the formula has been used by the architects of mediaeval days in western India.]

पूर्वाग्न्योरन्तरे पूजां कृत्वा पूर्वं न्यसेच्छिलाम्।
शेषाः प्रदक्षिणाः स्थाप्याः शिलाधो रत्नपञ्चकम्॥ २००॥

गर्गः॥

ततः पुण्याहघोषेण शिलान्यासं प्रकारयेत्।
ऐशानी[२६४]मादितः कृत्वा प्रादक्षिण्यक्रमेण [२६५]च॥ २०१॥

अनेनैव विधानेन स्तम्भद्वाराधिरोहणम्।
शिलान्यासस्तु रोहिण्यां श्रवणे हस्तपुष्ययोः॥ २०२॥

मृगशीर्षं च रेवत्यामुत्तरात्रितये शुभः।
गृहीतवास्तुमध्ये तु समं कृत्वा भुवःस्थलम्॥ २०३॥

जलेन [२६६]दण्डमात्रेण साध्यं तच्चतुरस्त्रकम्।
भित्तेर्मूले न्यसेद्द्रव्यं रत्न-रौप्य-सुवर्णकम्॥ २०४॥

गृहे तत्र भवेल्लक्ष्मीर्द्रव्य[२६७]हीने दरिद्रता।
लेपहीनाऽधिका भित्तिरशास्त्रा [२६८]पादवर्जिता॥ २०५॥

समसन्धिः शिरोगुर्वी षड्दोषैर्धननाशनम्।
भूमेर्धनाख्यसम्पत्तिं काष्ठादिद्रव्यनिश्चयम्॥ २०६॥

सम्यग्विचिन्त्य हृदये प्रारभेत गृहादिकम्॥ २०७॥

इति श्री सूत्रधारमण्डनविरचिते वास्तुशास्त्रे वास्तुमण्डने मिश्रकाध्यायः प्रथमः। श्लोकाः २०७॥

२६४. मादेतः in A
२६५. तु in BCDE
२६६. नंड in B, मंडमांड C.D,E writes note वंसल, वंशला,
२६७. मूले in BCDE
२६८. वादविवर्जिता in· A

200. At first, there should be worshipping in between the East and South- East (*Agnikoṇa*) corners. Then the stone is to be laid and at the end the owner should go round the site and place five types of gems under the stone.

Garga

201. Then, with the declaration of an auspicious day, the stone laying ceremony is to be done and one should start going round in a circle from the North-East (*Īśa*) corner according to order.

202-203. In the same manner, the pillars and doors are to be mounted. If the stone- laying ceremony(*Śilānyāsa*) is performed in *Rohiṇī*, *Śravaṇā*, *Hastā*, *Puṣyā*, *Mṛgaśīrṣa*, *Revatī*, and the three *Uttarā*[12] stars, it is auspicious. In that plot of land, the soil should be levelled.

It should be done with the help of water and staff (*Daṇḍa*) and the plot should be made square. At the base of the foundation wall, one should keep gems, silver and gold which brings prosperity to the house; otherwise poverty may result.

Inadequate or excessive plastering, the foundation wall not made according to the formula of the *Śāstra*, a structure without any column, whose joints are one over the other in one line, whose upper part is heavy–these six types of defects reduce wealth.

204-207. One should start the construction of the house after carefully taking into account the land, and proportionate wealth, as well as materials like wood-etc.

Thus ends the first chapter Miśrakādhyāya of Vāstumaṇḍana, written by Maṇḍana Sūtradhāra. There are 207 Ślokas.

12. *Uttarāsāḍha, Uttara Phalgunī, Uttarabhādrapadā*

द्वितीयोऽध्यायः

[आयाधिकारः]

आयधिष्ण्यव्ययांशानां चन्द्रतारादिजं बलम्।
ज्ञात्वा गृही गृहं कुर्यात्स्त्रीपुत्रादिधनाप्तये॥ १॥

[१]भित्तिमध्ये गृहेष्वायः प्रासादे भित्तिबाह्यतः।
सभासु मध्ये बाह्ये वा स्यान्मध्ये शयनासने॥ २॥

नगरेऽथ पुरे ग्रामे दण्डै[२]र्मानं विधीयते।
[३]वास्तुदण्डमितं क्षेत्रं तत्रायो [४]हस्तसंख्यया॥ ३॥

दैर्घ्येन गुणिते व्यासे ध्वजाद्यायो हृतेऽष्टभिः।
शेषो [५]वास्तुवसात्सोऽपि [६]योज्यो हस्ताङ्गुलैर्यवैः॥ ४॥

ध्वजो धूमोऽथ सिंहश्च श्वानो वृषः खरो गजः।
ध्वांक्ष आया अष्ट तेषां [७]सृष्ट्वा पूर्वादिषु स्थितिः॥ ५॥

सर्वे नरकराः पक्षिचरणाः सिंहकन्धराः।
स्वनामवदनाः [८]धूमो मार्जारः [९]पुरुष ध्वजः॥ ६॥

१. E gives marginal note भीत्यन्तर्गृहे,
२. माने - in D, E
३. वसु - in A
४. E gives marginal note - समक्षेत्रभूमिषु
५. वस्तु - in ABC
६. योगां in A याज्यो in BC
७. वै सृष्ट्वा in A
८. धूम्रो - in D
९. पुरुषो धूनः in A

Chapter II

[Aāyādhikārah̩]

Now is described the command of Āya.

1. One should have proper knowledge about the place of *Āya, Vyaya,* and the power of lunar asterism; then the householder will build a house in order to obtain wife, children and wealth.

2. The *Āya* formula should be counted from the inner part of the foundation wall for a house; it should be counted from the outer part of the foundation wall for a palace. For a hall it is to be counted from inside, as well as from outside, and for beds and seats it should be counted from inside.

3. A city, town or village should be measured with the help of a *Daṇḍa* (rod). A plot of land would be measured with the *Vāstudaṇḍa* and the *Āya* will be counted by the number of hands.

4. The breadth, if multiplied by the length and divided by eight, is known as *Dhvaja* etc. The remainder will be according to the foundation of *Vāstu* and should be added by the hands, finger, *Yava* (1/8th part of an *Aṅgula*).

5. *Dhvaja, Dhūma, Siṁha, Śvā, Vṛṣa, Khara, Gaja, Dhvāṁkṣa,* – these are eight *Āyas,* their position starts from the eastern side of the construction.

6-7. All types of human hands, claws of the bird, necks of lions , faces according to their name. *Dhūma, Mārjāra* (*Dhūma* and cat are on the *S.E* corner) *Puruṣa, Dhvaja* (Eastern direction), very strong

महोत्कटा दिशां नाथाः वसन्त्यन्योन्यसंमुखाः ।
पूजिताः पूजयन्त्येते घातयन्त्यपदस्थिताः ॥ ७ ॥

ध्वजः सिंहो [१०]वृषो हस्ती स्वपदे वामदक्षिणे ।
कर्णगाः स्वपदे देया आयद्वारे [११]विदिग्गते ॥ ८ ॥

ध्वजसिंहवृषे भास्तु देवतायतने हिताः ।
विप्रादिनां क्रमाद्गेहे सर्ववर्णे गजो हितः ॥ ९ ॥

[१२]अधमानां गृहे धूमो श्वान रासभवायसः ।
वृषस्थाने गजं दद्यात् सिंहवृषभहस्तिनोः ॥ १० ॥

ध्वजः सर्वेषु दातव्यो नान्यत्र स्वपदाद्वृषः ।
नवकोष्ठीकृते भूमिमध्येऽस्याः कुलदेवता ॥ ११ ॥

स्थापयेच्छकुनार्थेषु ध्वजाद्येषु फलं क्रमात् ।
अर्थलाभश्च सन्तापो भोगः कलह एव च ॥ १२ ॥

धान्यं स्त्रीदूषणं सौख्यं मरणं च विनिर्दिशेत् ।
ध्वजः सर्वमुखः प्रत्यङ्मुखः पूर्वाननो वृषः ॥ १३ ॥

सिंह सौम्यमुखो हस्ती दक्षिणाभिमुखः शुभः ।
खण्डितं स्फुटितं दग्धं भिन्नं निपतितं तथा ॥ १४ ॥

तेषां न मन्त्रसंस्कारो गतास्ता आयदेवताः ॥ १५ ॥

देवयज्ञगृहच्छत्रध्वजवेदीषु तोरणे ।
वस्त्रालङ्कारदैवेषु दद्यात्तोयाशये ध्वजम् ॥ १६ ॥

होमकुण्डेऽग्निसंस्थाने होमशाला महानसे ।
धूमं युज्याद्विशेषेण वह्निकर्मोपजीविनाम् ॥ १७ ॥

---

१० पृष्ठो in A
११. विदिग्जजे in A
१२. अधूमानां in B

lords of all directions reside facing one another. If properly placed they bring prosperity, and if placed otherwise they destroy everything.

8. *Dhvaja, Simha, Vṛṣa, Hastī* will reside in their own position towards the left and right. The cornered one will be kept in their own place, but if placed otherwise, they are to be brought to their own position.

9. If the stars are in *Dhvaja* (East) *Simha* (South) and *Vṛṣa*, it is auspicious for temples. *Gaja* (North) is auspicious for the house of *Vipra* and all other *Varṇas.*

10. For the lower caste people the houses should be in *Dhūma* (*S.E.*) *Śvā* (*S.W*), *Rāsabha* (*N.W*) and *Vāyasa* (*N.E*) direction. *Gaja* can be put in the place of *Vṛṣa* and *Simha* and *Vṛṣa* in the place of *Hastī.*

11. *Dhvaja* can be placed everywhere but *Vṛṣa* should not be shifted from its own position. If the chart is drawn for 9x9 squares, the central plot will be reserved for one's tutelary deity (*Kuladevatā*)

He should be consecrated therein for good and bad omens. Now, the results of the *Dhvaja* and others are described serially. They indicate gain of wealth, affliction (*Santāpa*), enjoyment, as well as quarrel, grains, fault of women, friendship and death.

12-13. *Dhvaja,* can face all directions as well as westwards, *Vṛṣa* stands in the eastern direction.

14-15. It is auspicious if *Simha* faces towards the North and *Hastī* faces the South. If the directions are violated then there will be explosions, burns, separation as well as falls. They do not have any consecration of *Mantras* and *Āyadeva* is lost therein.

16. *Dhvaja* can be placed in sacrifice for God's, houses, umbrellas, flags, altars, gates, divine clothing, ornaments and water reservoirs.

17. *Dhūma* is suitable for the sacrificial pit, fireplace, sacrificial hall, kitchen, and especially for the houses of people who work with fire.

सिंहासने शुभः सिंहः सिंहद्वारे नृपालये।
यन्त्रे युद्धगृहे शस्त्रे कवचे बन्धनालये॥ १८॥

श्वानोपजीविनां [१३]स्थाने वेश्याम्लेच्छांत्यजालये।
भण्डमातङ्ग[१४]चण्डाल[१५]मलस्थानेषु शस्यते॥ १९॥

वृषो हट्टेषु संयोज्यो धान्यभोजनमन्दिरे।
वणिग्गृहेऽश्वशालायां भाजने भोजनस्य च॥ २०॥

चतुर्विधेषु वाद्येषु नट[१६]प्रेरणकादिषु।
वेश्याकुलालरजके खरस्तज्जीविनां हितः॥ २१॥

गजं दद्यात् गजस्थाने तत्र सिंहं तु वर्जयेत्।
[१७]राजक्रीडास्पदारामराजपत्नीनिकेतने॥ २२॥

आसने शयने याने गजो योज्योऽङ्गनागृहे।
ध्वांक्षो न शोभनोऽप्यायः कम्बिकायां शुभो मतः॥ २३॥

मठशिल्पपतिस्थाने [१८]शस्यते पक्षिणां गृहे।
मूर्त्तौ लिङ्गे ध्वजे छत्रे दैर्घ्य आयादिकल्पना॥ २४॥

[१९]विस्तारायामगणना तामन्यत्र प्रकल्पयेत्।
रुद्रभागायते चक्रे कृते पञ्चाशविस्तरे॥ २५॥

ऊर्ध्वपंक्तौ क्रमात् कोष्ठेष्विन्द्रे(१४) धिष्ण्य(२७) द्वि(२)भास्करान्।
तिथ्य(१४)ष्ट(८) वेद(४) रामे(३) षू राग(६) नन्दा(९)न्समालिखेत्॥२६॥

---

१३. श्वानो - in B
१४. चांडाल - C, D, E
१५. DE give note खातागाड
१६. प्रेक्ष - in C
१७. E gives note राजगद्दी
१८. दास्यते - in A
१९. A omits V 25 ab.

18. *Siṁha* is auspicious for a royal throne, main doors, kingés palaces, machineries, battle houses, weapons, armour, and prisons.

19. *Śvā* (South-West) is suitable for the houses of working class people, prostitutes, *Mlecchas,* untouchables, hypocrites, the place for elephants, *Caṇḍālas* and toilets.

20. *Vṛṣa* (West) is appropriate for markets, granary, and dining places, houses of the businessmen, stables, *Bhājana*[1] of eating places.

21. Among four types of musical instruments, actors and directors, for the prostitutes, potters, and washermen, *Khara* (N.W) is suitable for those following these occupations.

22-23a. *Gaja* should be placed on the North, and *Siṁha* (South) is to be dis- carded there. In the pleasure garden for a kingés sport, in the house of a kingés wife, seats, beds, transports, and for the house of women *Gaja* should be added.

23b-24. Though *Dhvāṁkṣa* (N.E) is not beneficial but *Āya* is regarded as auspicious for *Kambikā* (measurement). It is appropriate for a monastery business house and in the aviary. Length of the statue, phallus, flag, umbrella, can be measured with the help of *Āya* .

25. In other places, the calculation of length and breadth should be fixed. A plan of 11 divisions in length and 50 division in breadth is to be drawn.

26. In the upper chambers serially the members - 14, 27, 2, 12, 14, 8, 4, 3, 5, 6, 9 should be written.

१४	२७	२	१२	१४	८	४	३	५	६	९
अ	आ	इ	ई	उ	ऊ	ए	ऐ	ओ	औ	क
ख	ग	घ	ङ	च	छ	ज	झ	ञ	ट	ठ
ड	ढ	ण	त	थ	द	ध	न	प	फ	ब
भ	म	य	र	ल	व	श	ष	स	ह	क्ष

1. This moulding called *Bhājana* is treated as the topmost or crowning moulding of pedestals and basement. It is rectangular in form.

तदधो मातृकावर्णानका[२०]राद्यान् समालिखेत्।
ऋ ॠ लृ लॄ विसर्गान्तः संयोगाक्षरवर्जितान्॥ २७॥

नामाक्षराङ्कसन्धातान् वसुभिर्विभजेत्सुधीः।
शेषमायो मनुष्यस्य ध्वजाद्यो गेहगो भवेत्॥ २८॥

नक्षत्रं तारकां शौचव्ययाद्यं चापि गेहगम्।
ध्वजादीनां चतुर्णां तु चत्वारो वृषभादयः॥ २९॥

भक्ष्यास्ते भवने वर्ज्या गृहस्वाम्यायभक्षकाः॥ ३०॥

इति आयाधिकारः॥

[२१]गणनाद्विस्तरायात्पौर्यदैक्यं तत्फलं पुनः।
तस्मिन्नष्टगुणे धिष्ण्यैर्भक्ते शेषं तु भं भवेत्॥ ३१॥

नक्षत्रं त्रिविधं दैवं मानुषं राक्षसं तथा।
राक्षसं मृत्युदं गेहे नक्षत्रं योनिवैरवत्॥ ३२॥

Graph from MsD

ग देव	पु	ह	अ	मृ	अ	रे	श्र	स्वा	पु.	
ग मानुष	से	भ	आ	पू	पू	पु	उ	उ	उ	
ग राक्षस	म	मु	चि	ज्ये	श्ले	ध	कृ	स	चि	

Graph from Ms E

पु	ह	अ	मृ	अ	रे	श्र	स्वा	पु		देव
रो	भ	आ	पू	चू	पू	उ	उ	उ		मनुष्य
म	यू	वि	ज्ये	रले	ध	कृ	श	चि		राक्षस

Graph from Ms E

अ	छा	कृ	रो	मृ	आ	पु	पु	श्ले	म	पू	उ	ह
अ श्व	ग ज	छा ग	स र्प	स र्प	श्वा न	मा र्जा र	छा ग	मा र्जा र	मुष	क	गौः	म हि ष

चि	अ	ज्ये	भु	पू	उ	अ	अ	ध	श	पू	पु	उ	रे
व्या घ्र	मृ ग	मृ ग	श्वा न	वा न र	नकु	ल	वा न र	सिं ह	अ श्व	सिं ह	गौ	ग-	ज

२०. आद्यान् क्षतान् समा - - in B
२१. गुणना - in B

27. Under these numbers 'A' and other *Mātṛkā, Varṇas* are to be written, but Ṛ, long Ṛ, Li, long Li, *Visarga* and joint words are to be avoided.

28. The alphabets in the name are to be divided by eight. Rest is the *āya* of man and becomes *gehaga* due to *dhvaja.*

29-30. Four types of *Vṛṣabha* etc. belong to four types of *dhvajas* etc. These stars and planets are also known as *gehagas* due to *śauca* and *vyaya.* These in buildings ate called *bhakṣyas* as they eat away into the *āya* of the owner and hence they are to be discarded.

31. Again, to get the result from the *Āya,* multiply the length by eight and then it is to be divided by the lunar constellation (27); the remainder is called *Nakṣatra.*

32. *Nakṣatras* are of three types, Divine (*Daiva*), human (*Mānuṣa*) and *Rākṣasa. Rākṣasa* brings destruction to a house, like the enmity of *Yoni* pertaining to *Nakṣatras.*

नवदेवगणः पुष्यो हस्तो मैत्रमृगोऽश्विनी।
रेवती श्रवणः स्वाती पुनर्वसुरपि स्मृतः॥ ३३॥

रोहिणी भरणी चार्द्रा तथा पूर्वोत्तरात्रयम्।
मानुषाणि नवैतानि राक्षसैः सह मृत्यवे॥ ३४॥

मघामूलं विशाखा च ज्येष्ठाश्लेषाधनिष्ठिकाः।
कृत्तिका शतभं चित्रा नवमी राक्षसो गणः॥ ३५॥

स्वकुले चोत्तमाप्रीतिर्मध्यमा देवमानुषे।
देवराक्षसयोर्वैरं मृत्युर्मानवरक्षसोः॥ ३६॥

अश्वोऽश्विनी शतभयोर्भरणीपौष्णयोर्गजः।
कृत्तिकापुष्ययोः छागो रोहिणी मृगयोरहिः॥ ३७॥

श्वानोमूलार्द्रयोर्योनिः सर्पादित्ये बिडालकः।
पूर्वफा मघयोराखुरुफो (प)त्तरभयोस्तु गौः॥ ३८॥

हस्तस्वात्योस्तु महिषी व्याघ्रश्चित्राविशाखयोः।
ज्येष्ठानुराधयोरेणः पूषाढाश्रवणे कपिः॥ ३९॥

उषाढाभिजितोर्बभ्रुः सिंहः [२२]पूभाधानिष्ठयोः।
मेषमर्कटयोर्वैरं गोव्याघ्रगजसिंहयोः॥ ४०॥

श्वानैणं सर्पनकुलं बिडालोन्दुरुकं महत्।
महिषाश्वमिति त्याज्यं भृत्यस्त्रीप्रभुवेश्मसु॥ ४१॥

इति नक्षत्राधिकारः।।

नक्षत्रे वसुभिर्भक्ते यच्छेषं स व्ययो भवेत्।
आयाद्धीनः स पक्षाख्यो धनधान्यकरः स्मृतः॥ ४२॥

---

२२. पूजा - in A

33. *Puṣyā, Hastā, Maitra, Mṛgaśirā, Aśvinī, Revatī, Śravaṇā, Svātī, Punarvasu* - these nine belong to the divine group.

34. *Rohiṇī, Bharaṇī, Ārdrā* as well as three *Pūrvas* (*Pūrvāṣāḍhā Pūrvaphālgunī, Pūrvabhādrapadā*) three *Uttaras* (*Uttarāṣāḍhā, Uttaraphalgunī, Uttarabhādrapadā*) - these nine belong to the human group and if combined with *Rākṣasas,* they cause death.

35. *Maghā, Mūlā, Viśākhā, Jyeṣṭhā, Aśleṣā, Dhaniṣṭhikā, Kṛttikā, Śatabhiṣā, Citrā* - these nine belong to the *Rākṣasa* variety.

36. These are best matched if it is from the same class. The combination of Divine and Human class is of medium character. The combination between Divine and *Rākṣasas* causes hostility and the combination between the human and *Rākṣas* variety causes death.

37. According to the principle of origin, *Aśvinī* and *Śatabhiṣā* belong to the group of horse; likewise the elephant for *Bharaṇī* and *Pauṣṇa* (*Revatī*), goat for *Kṛttikā* and *Puṣyā*, snake (*Ahi*) for *Rohiṇī* and *Mṛga.*

(Śvā) dog for *Mūlā* and *Ārdrā,* cat for *Sarpa and Āditya, rat* (*Ākhu*) for *Pūrvaphālgunī* and *Maghā,* cow for two *Uttarās* (*Uttaraphālgunī* and *Uttarabhādrapadā*), buffalo (*Mahiṣī*) for *Hastā* and *Śvātī,* tiger for *Citrā* and *Viśākhā,* black antelope (*Eṇa*) for *Jyeṣṭhā* and *Anurādhā,* monkey (*Kapi*) for *Pūrvāṣāḍhā,* and *Śravaṇā* mongoose (*Babhru*) for *Uttaraṣāḍhā* and *Abhijit,* lion (*Siṁha)* for *Pūrvabhādrapadā* and *Dhaniṣṭhā.*

38-40. There is enmity between *Meṣa* (sheep) and *Markaṭa* (monkey) *Go* (cow) and *Vyāghra* (tiger), *Gaja* (elephant) and *Siṁha* (lion).

41. *Śvā* (Dog) and *Eṇa*(black antelope), *Sarpa* (snake) and *Nakula* (mongoose) *Viḍāla* (cat) and *Indura* (rat), *Mahiṣa* (buffalo) and *Aśva* (Horse) are to be discarded up in the buildings of servant, wife and master.

Thus ends the command of constellation of the stars.

42. If the constellation of the stars is to be divided by 8, the remainder is known as *Vyaya.* If it is less than *Āya* and congenial, it is known to usher grain and wealth.

आयतुल्यं पिशाचः स्यादायाधिकस्तु राक्षसः।
[२३]चिन्तात्मको व्ययः प्राज्ञैरष्टस्वायेषु वर्जितः॥ ४३॥

शान्तोऽथ पौरः प्रद्योतः श्रियानन्दो मनोहरः।
श्रीवत्सो विभवश्चैव [२४]चिन्तात्मको व्ययाष्टकम्॥ ४४॥

ध्वजे शान्तः शुभो गेहे नित्यं कल्याणकारकः।
भोगपूजाबलिर्नृत्यगीतवाद्यं सुरालये॥ ४५॥

इति [२५]व्ययाः॥

मूले व्ययान्विते वेश्म नामाक्षरविमिश्रिते।
त्रिभिर्भक्ते भवेदंश शेष इन्द्रो यमो नृपः॥ ४६॥

प्रासादप्रतिमालिङ्गे वेद्यामिन्द्रो ध्वजो हितः।
सर्वत्र शोभनो राजा पुरराजगृहादिषु॥ ४७॥

यमो मातृगणेशादि मद्यमांसादिविक्रये।
भैरवे क्रूरदेवे च हितो मृत्युकरो गृहे॥ ४८॥

इत्यंशकाः॥

[२६]गणयेत्स्वामिनक्षत्रात् यावदृक्षं गृहस्य च।
नवभिस्तु हरेद्भागं शेषा तारा प्रकीर्तिताः॥ ४९॥

शान्ता मनोहरा क्रूरा विजया कलहावहा।
पद्मिनी राक्षसी वीरा आनन्दा नवमी स्मृताः॥ ५०॥

तृतीया विपदं कुर्यात्पञ्चमी तेजसः क्षयम्।
सप्तमी धननाशं च तेन तारात्रयं त्यजेत्॥ ५१॥

इति तारा॥

२३. चित्रा - in B
२४. चिन्तात्मेति - in B, C, D, E
२५. क्षेत्रफलम् in E
२६. Similar verses in Aparājitā pṛchhā ch 66 v 32-33

43. If *Āya* and *Vyaya* are the same it is known as *Piśāca* and if it (*Vyaya*) is more than *Āya* it is known as *Rākṣasa*. The variety of *Vyaya* designated as *Cintātmaka* is to be discarded among eight types of *āya*.

44. The eight types of *Vyaya* are *Śānta*, *Paura*, *Pradyota*, *Śriyānanda*, *Manohara*, *Śrīvatsa*, *Vibhava* and *Chintātmaka*.

45. *Śānta* in *Dhvaja* is always beneficial in a house. There will be enjoy- ment prayer oblation, dance, song and instrumental music if the same com- bination happens to be in a temple.

Thus ends the Vyaya.

46. In the source connected to *Vyaya*, an addition is to be done with the letters of the name of the house. They are to be divided by three, and known as *Aṁśa*. The remainder is *Indra*, *Yama* and *Nṛpa*.

47. *Indra* and *Dhvaja* are auspicious for a palace, idol and phallus. *Rāja* is always good for a city and a royal palace.

48. *Yama* brings in death for a house but is auspicious for Mother (*Tantra*) *Gaṇeśa*, and others selling wine and meat, *Bhairava* and other cruel *Devas*.

Thus ends the Aṁśaka.

49. From the star of the owner, count the number of the presiding star of the house, then divide it by nine, the remainder is called *Tārā*.

50. *Śāntā, Manoharā, Krūrā, Vijayā, Kalahāvahā, Padminī, Rākṣasī, Vīrā, Ānandā* - these are the nine varieties .

51. The third one causes danger while fifth one reduces strength, the seventh one causes loss of wealth, so these three stars should be discarded.

Thus ends Tārā .

ईशानात्कृत्तिकादीनि सप्त सप्त प्रदक्षिणे।
धिष्ण्यानि यत्र गेहर्क्षं ज्ञेयस्तत्रैव चन्द्रमाः ॥ ५२ ॥

अग्रतः स हरेदायुः पृष्ठतस्तु धनं हरेत्।
वामदक्षिणतश्चन्द्रो धनधान्यकरो गृहे ॥ ५३ ॥

इति चन्द्रः ॥

प्रीतिस्तु षड्विधाः तासामुत्तमा समसप्तमी।
तृतीयैकादशी वृद्धयै पुष्ट्यै दशचतुर्थिका ॥ ५४ ॥

[२७]षड्वाष्टकम् त्रिकोणञ्च गृहं द्विद्वादशं त्यजेत्।
मरणं कलहो हानिस्तस्मात्प्रीतित्रयं त्यजेत् ॥ ५५ ॥

राशेर्मैत्री हरेद्वैरं [२८]ग्रहजं ग्रहजा पुनः।
मैत्री राशेर्विरुद्धत्वं नाडिवेधं त्यजेत्सदा ॥ ५६ ॥

विप्र-क्षत्रिय-विटशूद्रा मीनाद्या राशयः क्रमात्।
स्वामिनोऽधिकवर्णं हि गृहं सौख्यकरं न हि ॥ ५७ ॥

ब्राह्मणे सकला राज्ञि प्रशस्ता [२९]नवराशयः।
षठ् वैश्येऽथ त्रयः शूद्रे स्वामिराशेः क्रमोऽप्ययम् ॥ ५८ ॥

गृहस्थः गृहयोः स्वामिवैरं मैत्रीं विलोकयेत्।
दुष्टे प्रीतिर्विलोक्या सा सुप्रीतौ तां न चिन्तयेत् ॥ ५९ ॥

षष्ठिघ्नं भवनस्य र्क्षं पञ्चत्रितनुभिर्भजेत्।
शेषे मेषादिको राशिः प्रोक्तः कैश्चिन्नवांशके (कैः ?) ॥ ६० ॥

अश्विन्याद्यं त्रिकं मेषे सिंहे ज्ञेयम् मघात्रयम्।
मूलादित्रितयं चाये शेषाणि नवराशिषु ॥ ६१ ॥

इति राशिमैत्री ॥

२७. षट्का In B, D, E षद्धा In C
२८. गृहजं In A
२९. E gives note - ५ ।६ ।७ ।९ ।१० ।१२ ।१ ।२ ।३ ।६ ।२ । १० ।७ ।९ ।३ ।३ ।७ ।१२

52-53. From the North-East corner *Krittikā* and the other seven stars circu- mambulate seven houses; the part of the house where it settles is known as the house of the Moon. If placed in front, it causes loss of longevity, if placed at the back it causes loss of wealth. For a house, if placed on the left or right side, it increases wealth and prosperity.

Thus ends Candra.

54. *Prītiyoga* is of six types. Among them the best one is *Samasaptamī. Tṛtīyā* and *Ekādasī* are known by *Vṛddhā and Daśamī, Caturthī as Puṣyā.*

55. In the chart of a house one should avoid *Ṣaḍāṣṭaka, Trikoṇa* and *Dvi-dvādaśa.* Death, quarrels and loss will occur from those combinations. So, these three *Prītiyogas* should be avoided.

56. If there is parity among the zodiac signs then there will be no enmity; again the vices arising from the combination of planets are removed by the planets themselves. One should not go against the favourable zodiac sign and should avoid *Nāḍīvedha.*

57. Brahmins, *Kṣatriya, Vaiśya, Śūdra* occupy Pisces and three other zodiac signs. In a house where the *Varṇas* are higher than the *Varṇa* of the house-owner, then it is not regarded as congenial.

58. All zodiac signs are auspicious for Brahmins. Nine zodiac signs for King, six for *Vaiśyas,* and three for *Śūdras*- these are the orders of the lordship of the zodiac signs.

59. A householder will count the zodiac signs of the house and the signs of the householder and consider the enmity or *Maitrī.* If it does not match, then one should consider *Prīti.* In case *Prīti* is favourable then other factors are to be ignored.

60. The sixth place in the chart of the house destroys its star. The fifth and third zodiacs are to be considered with the *Lagna* and others are of the opinion that the *Meṣa* and other zodiacs come at the end with *Navāṁśa* .

61. *Aśvinī* group of triple stars belong to Aries (*Meṣa*), *Maghā* group of three belong to Leo (*Siṁha*), *Mūla* group of three belong to Sagittarius (*Dhanu*) and rest belong to the (other) nine zodiac signs.

Thus ends the amity of the zodiac signs

[३०]सिंहस्याधिपतिः सूर्यश्चन्द्रमाः कर्कटाधिपः ।
मेषवृश्चिकयोर्भौमः कन्यामिथुनयोर्बुधः ॥ ६२ ॥

धनुर्मीनपति[३१]र्जीवः शुक्रो वृषतुलाधिपः ।
शनिर्मकरकुम्भेशः कन्या राहुगृहं भवेत् ॥ ६३ ॥

चन्द्रार्कभौमजीवाश्च शुक्रज्ञशनिराहवः ।
चत्वारोऽन्योन्यमित्राणि शत्रवस्ते परस्परम् ॥ ६४ ॥

रविमन्दे भवेद्वैरं तथैव कूजमन्दयोः ।
सोमस्य सूर्यपुत्रस्य महद्वैरं परस्परम् ॥ ६५ ॥

इति ग्रहमैत्री ॥

भवनस्योदयं क्षेत्रफलेन गणयेत्सुधीः ।
वसुभिर्विभजेच्छेषोऽधिपतिः ससमः शुभः ॥ ६६ ॥

यद्वा [३२]व्ययाय संयोगे यदैक्यं वसुभिर्भजेत् ।
शेषस्त्वधिपतिः कैश्चिद्विषमः स भयावहः ॥ ६७ ॥

विकृतः कर्णकश्चैव धूम्रदो वितथेश्वरः ।
बिडालो दुन्दुभिश्चैव दन्तः कान्तोऽधिनायकाः ॥ ६८ ॥
इति अधिनायकाः ॥

फलमष्टगुणं कृत्वा षष्ट्या भक्तेऽवशिष्टकम् ।
पञ्चभिर्विभजेच्छेषं तत्वं स्यात्पार्थिवादिकम् ॥ ६९ ॥

पृथिव्यापोऽनलो वायुराकाशमिति पञ्चभिः ।
गृहस्यायुषि सम्पूर्णे विनाशो भवति ध्रुवम् ॥ ७० ॥

३०. Similar verses in Aparājita pṛchhā ch 65 v. 26.
३१. जीवि in B
३२. भयाम – in D, E

62. The Sun is the lord of Leo, Moon is the lord of Cancer. Mars is the lord of Aries and Scorpio, Mercury is the lord of Virgo and Gemini.

63. Jupiter (*Jīva*) is the lord of Sagittarius and Pisces. Venus is the ruler of Taurus and Libra. Saturn is the lord of Capricorn and Aquarius, Virgo is in the house of *Rāhu*.

64. Moon, Sun Mars, Jupiter and Venus, Mercury, Saturn, Rahu-they are friendly with each other, but the first four have enmity with the last four[2].

65. There is enmity between Sun and Saturn and likewise between Mars and Saturn. Moon and Saturn have great enmity with each other.

Thus ends the amity of the planets.

66. The height of a house will be multiplied by the perimeter of the plot. The measured number will be divided by 8 and the remainder will be the lord of the house. It is regarded as auspicious if it is *Sama* (even).

67. Or with the addition of the *Vyaya*, the total number is divided by 8 (*Vasu*), the remainder will be the lord. If it is *Viṣama* (uneven), it is dangerous.

68. *Vikṛta, Karṇaka, Dhūmrada, Vitatheśvara, Viḍāla, Dundubhi, Danta, Kānta* are the lord of the house.

Thus ends the topic of the lord of the house.

69. Multiply the perimeter of the land by 8, and then divide it by 6, the remainder will again be divided by 5. The residue is the fact of the primary element, starting from Earth.

70. After completion of the duration of the house, it certainly gets destructed by the five elements- earth, water, fire, air and sky.

---

2. Enemy: Sun- Venus, Saturn Mars- Mercury Mercury- Moon Jupiter -Mercury, Venus Venus- Sun, Moon Saturn -Sun, Moon, Mars Rahu- Sun, Moon, Mars Ketu- Venus, Saturn.

जीर्णं [३३]भवति भूतत्वे तोयाग्न्योस्तद्भवं भयम्।
वायौ रोगस्तथाकाशे शून्यतामेति मन्दिरम्॥ ७१॥
इति पञ्चतत्वानि॥

प्रभुः पण्याङ्गना मित्रं देशो ग्रामः पुरं गृहम्।
नाडि[३४]वेधमतं श्रेष्ठं शुभं वेधविवर्जितम्॥ ७२॥

एकनाडिगता यत्र गुरूमन्त्राश्च देवताः।
तत्रोद्वेगं रुजं मृत्युं क्रमेण फलमादिशेत्॥ ७३॥

सेव्यसेवकयोश्चैव गृहं तत्स्वामिनोरपि।
परस्परं मित्रयोश्च एकनाडिः प्रशस्यते॥ ७४॥

आद्यांशेन तुरीये स्याद्द्वितीयेन तृतीयके।
तृतीयेन द्वितीये च चतुर्थेनादिमे वेधः॥ ७५॥

इति नाडीवेधविधिः॥

आयर्क्ष व्यय तारांशाधिपं क्षेत्रफले क्षिपेत्।
अर्के भक्ते भवेल्लग्नमथ लग्नेऽष्टसंगुणे॥ ७६॥

हृते शरैकैः शेषं तु तिथिर्नाम समं फलम्।
तिथौ नवघ्ने वारः स्यादर्काद्यो मुनिभिर्हृते॥ ७७॥

इति लग्नतिथिवाराः॥

सुपर्ण ओतुः सिंहः श्वा सर्पाखुमृगमेढकाः।
वर्गाधिपः क्रमादष्टौ भक्ष्यो यः पञ्चमो मतः॥ ७८॥

इति वर्गप्रीतिः॥

३३. पतति – A, B, D, E
३४. तदद्दितं – in B C, तदादितं – in D, तददितं – in E

71. After the destruction of the earthy elements, there is a fear from water, fire, and disease from air as well as from the sky and the abode becomes desolate.

Thus ends the theory of five elements

72. The owner of the house, commodities, women or (prostitute), friends, country, village, city and houses - for them it is best to consider the theory of *nāḍivedha*, as it is auspicious and to be without any obstruction.

73. Where there is one period of time, and the lord is *Gurumantra*, serially the result of anxiety, pain, and death are in order.

74. The same period of time is praiseworthy for a master, his dependent, as well as for the landlord and mutual friends.

75. There may be obstruction by the first part to the fourth part, by the second to the third, by the third to the second and by the fourth to the first part.

Thus ends the rule of Nāḍivedha.

76-77. *Āya*[3] *Ṛkṣa, Vyaya, Tārā, Aṁśa, Adhipa*, their numbers are to be added to find out the area of a land. By dividing this number by twelve, the reminder will be the *Lagna*, then the *Lagna* is to be multiplied with eight and divided by eight. The remainder will be *Tithi* and the result will be synonymous with their name. If the *Tithi* is multiplied by nine and divided by seven, then the *Vāra* starting from Sunday is available.

Thus ends Lagna Tithi and Vāra.

78. *Suparṇa*[4] (*Garuḍa*), *Otu* (Cat), *Siṁha* (Lion), *Śvā* (Dog), *Sarpa* (Snake), *Ākhu* (Rat), *Mṛga* (Deer), *Meḍha* (Ram), these eight are serially the lords of their place but they are enemies of their fifth place.

Thus ends the amity of Varga.

---

3. *Ṣaḍvarga*-a group of six formula or proportions, six main component parts of a building, *Adhiṣṭhāna* (base), *Pada* or *Stambha* (column), *Prastara* (entablature), *Karṇa* (ear), *Śīkhara* (spire), and *Stupi* (dome) According to *Mānasāra* the *Āyādi Ṣaḍ varga* represents a set of six formulas with which any particular measurement must conform before it can be accepted.

4. *Suparṇa* -enemy to *Sarpa*, its 5th house, *otu* to *Ākhu* likewise.

स्ववर्गं परवर्गं च क्रमेण क्रमतो लिखेत्।
एकवर्गे च वर्गाङ्कमष्टभिर्भाजिते स्थितम्॥ ७९॥

[३५]तदर्धे तं विंशोपाः स्युर्देयास्ते प्रथमेन हि।
स्व सम्बन्धे गृहे ग्रामे लाभालाभे विचिन्तयेत्॥ ८०॥

इति विंशोपाः॥

मयस्य च मतांद्वारतिथ्यानयनमुच्यते।
[३६]दैर्घ्यैकघ्ने पृथग्भागैः सप्तभिस्त्रिंशता हृते॥ ८१॥

शेषाः सूर्यादयो वारास्तिथयो युग्मपक्षजाः।
भौमार्कौ च तिथी रिक्ता यमो[३७]त्पातौ मृतिं त्यजेत्॥ ८२॥

आयादिकल्पना सप्तदशाङ्के सर्वसौख्यदा।
सा तु प्राज्ञैर्विना नाल्पैर्दिवसैर्युज्यते गृहे॥ ८३॥

[३८]ततस्त्रिपञ्चसप्ताङ्कैरङ्कै कार्यं गृहं बुधैः।
श्रीविश्वकर्मणाप्युक्तं हीनदोषं गुणाधिकम्॥ ८४॥

आयार्क्षव्ययतारांशेन्दुशशिग्रहं सौहृदम्।
आयुस्तैस्त्रिशराद्यंकैः फलमङ्कैः यथोत्तरम्॥ ८५॥

इति सूत्रधारमण्डनविरचिते वास्तुमण्डने वास्तुशास्त्रे आयाधिकारो द्वितीयोऽध्यायः॥

---

३५. नाडिविद्धं मतं श्रेष्ठं न शुभं वैद्यवर्जितम् – in B
३६. दैर्ध्यं कुर्घ्न In D, E
३७. सान्तं in B, त्पातं in CDE
३८. एतात्रिपञ्चे – In D, E

79-80. One should draw oneés own *Varga* and other *Vargas* serially. In one *Varga*, the sum of the *Varga* divided by eight remains static. On the half part of that, *Viṁśopā* is to be placed at first. It should be considered for their own sake, house, village, in gain and loss.

Thus ends Viṁśopā.

81-82. According to Maya it is said to bring or (consider) *Vāra* and *Tithi*, separately. The height or length(?) is to be multiplied by seven and then take away thirty; the remainder is the *Vāra* and *Tithis* at the time of sun rise in both the *Pakṣas*. *Bhauma* (Tuesday), *Arka* days (Sunday) and *Rikta*, *Yama*, *Utpāta*, *Mṛti Yogas* are to be discarded.

83. *Āya* and other plans give happiness in all respects if they are made of seventeenth parts. Without a learned person this plan cannot be applied in a house within a short time.

84. So a wise person will plan his house by three, five, seven, nine parts; it is said by Śrī Viśvakarmā that faults should be less and good qualities should be more.

85. There will be amity among *Āya*, *Rkṣa*, *Vyaya*, *Tārā*, *Aṁśa*, moon, zodiac signs and planets. Life span will be determined by three, five, nine and results will accordingly follow.

Thus ends the Second Chapter titled Command of Āya, in the Vāstumaṇḍana, the Science of Architecture, written by Sūtradhāra Maṇḍana.

तृतीयोऽध्यायः

[दुर्गादिलक्षणम्]

बलिनाल्पबलेनापि दुर्गं कार्यं महीभुजा।
रक्षणार्थं हि लोकानां तस्मात्पुण्यं महत्तरम्॥ १॥

जलदेव[१]गृहारामतीर्थदानव्रतादिभिः।
यत्पुण्यमाप्नुयाद्राजा दुर्गे दुर्गं करोति यः॥ २॥

अन्यवास्तुस्थितं भित्वा कुर्याद्दुर्गं दृढोन्नतम्।
तत्राखिलानामाधारोऽन्यथा वित्तायुषोः क्षयः॥ ३॥

सिंहोऽपि सर्वसत्त्वानां बलवान् गिरिगह्वरे।
स्थितिं कृत्वा जयत्याशु वैरिवर्गं सुदारुणम्॥ ४॥

गजानां तु सहस्रेण न च लक्षेण वाजिनाम्।
यत्कृत्यं साध्यते राज्ञां दुर्गेणैकेन सिध्यति॥ ५॥

शतमेकोऽपि संधत्ते प्राकारस्थो धनुर्धरः।
तस्माद्दुर्गं प्रशंसन्ति नीतिशास्त्रविचक्षणाः॥ ६॥

शिलादिभिस्तु प्राकारो विशालः प्रोन्नतो दृढः।
शुद्धेष्टकाभिः कर्त्तव्यः परेषां दुर्गमो यथा॥ ७॥

प्राकारे कोष्ठका वृताः विद्याधर्यो युगास्रकाः।
तन्मध्ये बाहिका बाह्ये कपिशीर्षैरलङ्कृताः॥ ८॥

दशार्कमनुहस्तैश्च विद्याधर्योऽपि कोष्ठकाः।
तन्मध्ये बाहिका दैर्घ्ये [२]त्रिगुणा कोष्ठतो भवेत्॥ ९॥

---

१. ग्रहा - In A
२. त्रिकोणा - In B, C, D, E

Chapter III

[Durgādilakṣaṇam]

Now the characteristics of the forts are being described.

1. A king, whether he is powerful or weak , should construct a fort for the protection of his subjects and by this act he will attain great merit.
2. If a king builds the fort, he attains equal merit as is achieved by one who constructs water-reservoirs, temples, pleasure-gardens, holy spots bestows wealth and performs various *Vratas* .
3. Even after demolishing other residences, a fort[1] should be built high and strong, and after that all the people should be accommodated in that fort, otherwise there will be loss of wealth and life.
4. A lion is the strongest of all animals when he lives in his own mountain cave; likewise one can win over one's notorious enemies easily (if he resides in a well constructed fort).
5. Thousands of elephants and Lakhs of horses cannot perform for a King what a fort alone can fulfill.
6. An archer standing on a rampart of a fort can fight with hundreds of people, so the experts in political science eulogize the utility of the fort.
7. The rampart (of a fort) should be huge, lofty and sturdy; it should be built of stone or pure bricks, so that it cannot be easily accessible by others .
8. The ramparts should be adorned with *Koṣṭha*, and on the four sides of the ramparts four chambers are to be constructed; therein idols of *Vidyādharīs* should be installed. Outside the chambers, *Bāhikās* ornamented with *Kapiśīrṣas* are to be built.
9. *Koṣṭhas* of the *Vidyādharas* will be 10, 12, or 14 hands in measure- ment. In between there will be *Bāhikā* which is thrice in height than the *Koṣṭhaka*.

1. After Chittor, Kumbhalgarh is the most famous fortress of Mewar. It is nearly inaccessible even today and can be approached only by a Jeepable road. It was built by Maharana Kumbha in 1448 on a rock plateau which was the site of an earlier ancient fortress.

तदूर्ध्वे कपिशीर्षाणि वसुमात्रान्तराणि च।
दैर्घ्ये सार्धं द्विहस्तानि पिण्डे हस्तमितानि च॥ १०॥

कन्यसं नगरं राज्ञां हस्तैर्वेद सहस्त्रकैः।
मध्यमं द्विगुणं तस्मान्मध्याद्द्विगुणमुत्तमम्॥ ११॥

तुल्यं [३]वाष्टांश पादांश सार्धांशैर्दैर्घ्यतोऽधिकम्।
चतुर्विधं भवेदेकं सर्वाणि द्वादशैव हि॥ १२॥

षट्त्रिंशत्प्रथमे दुर्गे देवस्थानानि चत्वरे।
षण्णां वृद्ध्या क्रमेणैव द्वादशैर्द्व्यधिकं शतम्॥ १३॥

मध्ये राजगृहं कार्यं वामदक्षिणतोऽग्रतः।
चत्वराः शोभिता हट्टैः पृष्ठभागे जलाशयाः॥ १४॥

फलानि नानाविधदेशजानि क्रयाणकानीह विचित्रकाणि।
ताम्बुलपुष्पाम्बरमौक्तिकादि राज्ञो गृहाग्रेऽथ सुरस्य कुर्यात्॥ १५॥

पुरं प्रतोलीखटकीकपाटैर्दृढं विधेयं धनधान्यपूर्णम्।
संग्रामयन्त्रैर्विविधैर्भटैश्च सुरक्षकैः सर्वसमृद्धियुक्तम्॥ १६॥

व्यासायामे कनिष्ठं तु नगरं वसुभिर्भजेत्।
मध्यमं सूर्यभागैस्तु षोडशांशैस्तथोत्तमम्॥ १७॥

रेखासु ते प्रतिदिशं मार्गास्तत्र नवावरे।
त्रयोदश पुरे मध्ये ज्येष्ठे सप्तदशै[४]वहिः॥ १८॥

हट्टमार्गस्त्रिधा प्रोक्तो विंशत्यर्ककलाकरैः।
हीनाधिकस्तु कर्त्तव्यो भूमिभागविशेषतः॥ १९॥

---

३. चा - In A
४. चहि - In A

10. Two *Kapisīrṣas*[2] will be on the top, and there will be a gap of eight hands (in between the *Kapiśīrṣas* !). The height will be 21/ hands and the diameter will be one hand.

11. The smallest city of a king will be 1000 hands in measurement, the medium one will be double in size and the best one will be double the size of *Madhyama*.

12. The breadth will be respectively equal to $^{1}/_{8}{}^{th}$, $^{1}/_{4}{}^{th}$ or $^{1}/_{2}$ of the length . Each of the above mentioned cities will have four varieties, and therefore there will be altogether 12 types of cities.

13. In the first type of fort 36 *Pādas* will be marked for temples and courtyards, and this figure will be gradually increased by 12. In the way the number will go up to 102 pādas.

14. The king's palace will be in the centre and on the left, right and front sides there will be courtyards annexed with market places. The water reser- voir will be at the back side.

15. Varieties of fruits from different places, different types of sellable items, betel nuts, flowers, garments, pearls, etc should be displayed in the front side of the palace of the King as well as of the temple.

16. The city will be strengthened with *Pratolī* , *Khaṭakī*, *Kapāṭa* and it will be full of grains and wealth. The place will be well protected with different types of war equipments, well protected warriors; thus the city will be associated with all prosperity.

17. The city which is smallest in length and breadth will be divided by 8, the medium one by 12, and the best one by 16.

18. Along the measure of lines, roads will be drawn on all directions, 9 for the smallest one, 13 for the medium and 17 for the largest type of city from outside.

19. The market roads will be of three types. They are in number 20, 12 or 16. According to the availability of space, they may be more or less in number.

---

2. These parapets were decorated with the battlements like the *Kapiśīrṣakas-Kaṅgooras*. Their height should be of one *hasta*. Another element of beautification and defence was *Kāṇḍavāriṇī*, the *chāldivāri*." *Vāstuśāstra* Part I, Pg 289.

दुर्गे भूमिवशात्कार्या हट्टमार्गजलाशयाः।
सर्वत्र राज्ञ आदेशात्प्रासादभवनादिकम्॥ २०॥

कोष्ठे विद्याधरी बाह्या [५]द्विहस्तान्यधिकोदयौ।
गूढं युद्धासनं कोष्ठे तस्यां वा कारयेत्सुधीः॥ २१॥

गढमध्ये चतुर्दिक्षु मार्गं कुर्यात्प्रदक्षिणम्।
तत्र दुर्गे भवेद्रक्षा गजवाजिपदातिभिः॥ २२॥

तन्मार्गान्मध्यदेशे तु गृहाणि विनिवेशयेत्।
दृढानि पुरगोनृणां परेषां द्वेषिणामपि॥ २३॥

ब्राह्मणान्वासयेत्प्राच्यां क्षत्रं याम्योत्तरे विशः।
वापीकूपादिवारुण्यामुत्तरस्यां तु शूद्रकान्॥ २४॥

शिल्पिरङ्गकरानीशे वह्नौ तज्जीविनोऽन्त्यजान्।
नैर्ऋत्ये शौण्डिकान् वेश्यां वायव्ये लुब्धकादिकान्॥ २५॥

वराहः॥

कोणेषु वसतां दोषाः पुरग्रामगृहादिषु।
तेष्वेव वृद्धिमायाति अन्त्यजाः श्वपचादयः॥ २६॥

ईशकोणे न्यसेत्सूर्यं वह्निकोणे गणाधिपम्।
नैर्ऋत्ये च सहस्राक्षं वायव्यां तु जनार्दनम्॥ २७॥

पूर्वापरमुखादेवा कार्या न दक्षिणोत्तराः।
नगराभिमुखा श्रेष्ठा भङ्गदास्ते पराङ्मुखाः॥ २८॥

गणेशो भैरवश्चण्डी नकुलीशो ग्रहस्तथा।
मातरोमूर्त्तयो देव्याः शुभा दक्षिणदिङ्मुखाः॥ २९॥

हनुमान्वानरः श्रेष्ठो नैर्ऋत्यादिमुखो भवेत्।
गणेशो धनदो लक्ष्मीः पुरद्वारे सुखावहाः॥ ३०॥

५. हस्ताल्य - In A, हस्ताम्य - In D E

20. In a fort, according to the availability of land and with the permission of the king, market roads, water reservoirs, palaces, and houses, will be built.

21. The chamber of *Vidyādharīs* will be constructed outside and its height will be more than two hands. In that chamber, hidden seats for the warriors should be made by the expert architect.

22.Inside, circling the fort, there should be provision for streets on all four sides. In this way, the fort will be protected by elephants, horses, and warriors.

23. The houses are to be built in between two roads. Strong houses are to be built for cows and other people who are opposed to the enemies of the king.

24. Brahmins will reside in the Eastern (*Prācyām*) direction, *Kṣatriyas* in the South (*Yāmya*), *Vaiśyas* in the North. Water-tanks, wells, will be in the west and *Śūdras* will reside in the North.

25. Artists, actors will settle in the North-East (*Īśa*), those who survive based on such other professions and untouchables at the South-East (*Vahni*) corner, wine sellers and prostitutes towards the South-West (*Nairṛtya*) and the hunters (*Lubdhakas*) should be settled at the North-West (*Vāyu*) direction.

Varāha.

26. In a city village or house it is inauspicious if someone resides in a corner plot, but the same will be prosperous for untouchables and *Caṇḍālas.*

27. The Sun God will be placed in the *Īśa* corner, *Gaṇādhīpa* in the *Vahni* corner, *Sahasrākṣa* (*Indra*) in the *Naiṛtya* and *Janārdana* will be placed in the *Vāyu* corner.

28. The God should face either towards East or West, never towards South or North. It is best if they face towards the city other-wise the deities will break.

29. The temples of *Gaṇeśa, Bhairava, Caṇḍī, Nakula* as well as other planets, and mother goddess are regarded as auspicious if they face towards the South.

30. The apes (*Hanumān*), monkeys are best if their faces are towards the South-West (*Nairṛtya*) corner. *Gaṇeśa, Dhanada* (*Kubera*) and *Lakṣmī* bring hap-piness if placed on the palace gate.

वृत्तं वृत्तायताष्टास्त्रे अष्टपत्रं यवाकृतिः ।
स्वस्तिकं पुरुषाकारं दुर्गमित्यादौ सौख्यदम् ॥ ३१ ॥

एक द्वि शकटाकारं त्रिकोणं रसकोणकम् ।
वज्रत्रिशूलभुजगाकारं कर्णाधिकं त्यजेत् ॥ ३२ ॥

नगरं शोभितं कार्यं हट्टप्राकारगोपुरैः ।
प्रसादभवनोद्यानकीर्त्तिस्तम्भजलाशयैः ॥ ३३ ॥

पुरार्धेन भवेद्ग्रामो ग्रामार्धेन तु खेटकम् ।
खेटकार्धेन कूटं स्यात्कूटार्धेन तु कर्वटम् ।। ३४ ॥

पुरे ग्रामे क्रमान्मार्गाः खेटे कूटे च कर्वटे ।
कार्या सप्तदशाङ्केषु त्रिद्विसंख्या दिशं प्रति ॥ ३५ ॥

इति दुर्गनगरादिलक्षणम् ॥

दुर्गाणां रक्षणार्थाय यन्त्राः कार्या यथाविधिः ।
भवन्ति जयदा राज्ञां मद्य[६]मांसादिपूजिताः ॥ ३६ ॥

देवासुररणे दैत्यैः प्रबलैर्निर्जिताः सुराः ।
[७]ततो यन्त्रा गिरीशेन गदिता विश्वकर्मणे ॥ ३७ ॥

भिन्नास्ते यन्त्रपाषाणैः रक्तबिन्दुविवर्जिताः ।
उत्थानरहितादैत्या स्तदा देवैर्विनिर्जिताः ॥ ३८ ॥

चतुरशीतियन्त्रेषु नववायोर्जलस्य च ।
अग्नियन्त्रस्य षड्भेदाः षष्टिसंग्रामयन्त्रजाः ॥ ३९ ॥

अष्टहस्ता यस्य यष्टी स यन्त्रो भैरवो मतः ।
नवभिश्चन्द्रसम्पत्तिर्दशभिस्त्वादिभैरवः ॥ ४० ॥

६. मांश - In A
७. लक्षेयंगा - In C
After v35 Ms B writes सम्बत् १७९१ ।। पौष शुद्ध ४ बुधे ११ श्रीः

31. The fort brings happiness if its shape is circle, oval, eight cornered, eight sided, and shape of a barley, *Svastika* or *Puruṣa*.

32. One or two may be of the shape of a cart and a fort may have three or six corners in the shape of *Vajra*, trident or serpent; excess corners should be discarded.

33. The city should be decorated with markets, ramparts, *Gopuras*, palaces, houses, gardens, pillars of fame and water reservoirs.

34. A village will be half of a city, a *Kheṭaka* will be half of a village, a *Kūṭa* will be half of a *Kheṭaka*, and a *Karvaṭa* will be half of a *Kūṭa*.

35. In a city, village, *Kheṭaka*, *Kūṭa*, or *Karvaṭa* the roads should be serially constructed. Among the 17 number of roads there will be three or two roads in each direction.

These are the characteristics of a fort and a city-etc.

36. For the protection of a fort, machines should be manufactured in the prescribed method. The king will be victorious if he worships those with offerings of wine and meat.

37. While the war was going on between the Gods and demons, the powerful demons overpowered the Gods. At that time, Lord Śiva narrated the method of making weapons to *Viśvakarmā*.

38. Those weapons were of different types and made of stone, which were devoid of blood stains. (After their use) the demons were unable to get up and the Gods became winners .

39. Among eighty four types of machineries, nine are meant for using in the air, nine are for water. Firearms are of six types and war machines are of sixty varieties.

40. The weapon, which has an eight cubit long rod, is known as *Bhairava*, while *Candrasampatti* is known to have nine cubits and *Ādibhairava* is with ten cubit long rods.

यस्य रुद्रकरैर्यष्टी गजभीमः स उच्यते।
अर्कहस्तायता यस्य स यन्त्रो युग्मभैरवः॥ ४१॥

त्रयोदशकरैर्वह्निर्यमदण्डश्चतुर्दश।
तिथिहस्तो महारौद्र इत्यष्टौ भैरवा मताः॥ ४२॥

मर्कटी भैरवाख्यस्य त्रिकरा मध्यतः शुभाः।
द्वात्रिंशदङ्गुलां यष्टीं तस्या पृष्ठे तु कारयेत्॥ ४३॥

पिण्डे षडङ्गुला यष्टी पृष्ठे व्यासे कलाङ्गुलाः।
अग्रे वेदाङ्गुला [८]पृष्ठे कर्त्तव्या दृढकाष्टजाः॥ ४४॥

पृष्ठे छिद्रं तु यष्ट्याश्च मध्याद्वेदाङ्गुलं भवेत्।
मर्कटी सुदृढा पिण्डे कर्त्तव्याऽष्टाङ्गुला समा॥ ४५॥

लोहेन चर्मणा यष्टीं मर्कटीं कारयेद्दृढाम्।
अग्राङ्गुली [९]प्रकर्त्तव्येत्वष्टमात्रे सुलोहजे॥ ४६॥

गोः फणा वसुहस्ता च दैर्घ्ये सूत्रदुकूलजाः।
फणा कलाङ्गुला व्यासे दैर्घ्य तद्द्विगुणा मताः॥ ४७॥

नखाङ्गुला वा कर्त्तव्यो बाहुपाषाणवाहने।
पञ्जरं त्रिकरं दैर्घ्ये वेदाङ्गुलिसमन्वितम्॥ ४८॥

मर्कट्यङ्गे द्विहस्तं च पृथुत्वे(ऽ)ब्धिषडङ्गुलम्।
द्वौ स्तम्भौ पञ्जरस्यापि कुलिन्दाख्यौ प्रकीर्त्तितौ॥ ४९॥

मूर्ध्नि छिद्रे तयोर्यष्ट्याः पृष्ठछिद्रे इषु क्षिपेत्।
दृढां धातुमयीं कीलां पञ्जरस्यावलम्बने॥ ५०॥

पञ्जरं पूरयेद्धातुपाषाणैर्यन्त्रवाहने।
सुदृढं कीलकै पट्टी चर्मभिः कारयेदिदम्॥ ५१॥

८. पिंडे - In A
९. कर्तव्या अष्ट - In A

41. That rod which is eleven cubits long, is known as *Gajabhīma, (while) Yugmabhairava* has twelve cubits long rods.

42. *Vahni* is known to have thirteen cubit long rods and *Yamadaṇḍa* has fourteen cubits. *Mahāraudra* has 15 cubits long rods and these eight fall into the *Bhairava* category.

43. *Markaṭī* falls into the *Bhairava* category and it is auspicious if its middle part is three hands in length; at its back, a rod measuring 32 fingers in length is to be fixed.

44. A sixth *Aṅgula* rod should be fixed on the back side of the *Piṇḍa*(base) and the width of the rod will be two *Aṅgulas* (*Kalāṅgulas*). The front part of the base(*Piṇḍa*) will be four *Aṅgulas* and the back part should be made of strong wood.

45. The hole at the back of the rod will be measured at a distance of four *Aṅgulas, Markaṭī* should be firm at the base(*Piṅḍa*) and it should be equal to eight *Aṅgulas.*

46. Both the rod and the lever (*Markaṭī*) should be made strong with iron or leather belts. The front part should be made of iron and measure eight *Aṅgulas.*

47. A bandage used as a catapult (*Gophaṇā*) will be eight hands in length and the material will be made of silk thread. The cap will be two *Aṅgulas* in breadth and double the size in length.

48. The iron cage (*Pañjara*) will be three hands and four *Aṅgulas* in length (or fourfold), and it may be fitted with hands and claws for bringing stones.

49. The *Markaṭī* will be two hands in diameter and its breadth will be thirteen *Aṅgulas.* The two pillars of the *Pañjara* will be known as *Kulinda* .

50. There will be a hole on the top of those two rods/and on the back- side also, through which arrows are to be shot. Strong metal nails will support this *Pañjara* (cage).

51. The *Pañjara* should be filled up with stones, metals, and it should be made strong with the help of nails and leather covers.

स्तम्भास्तु षट्करा [१०]व्यासे दैर्घ्ये मूर्ध्नि त्रिहस्तकाः।
ऊर्ध्वे द्विभागौ त्र्यंशोऽधस्तत्रोत्पलनिवेशनम्॥ ५२॥

ऊर्ध्ववेल्लनिका तेन समापिण्डे युगाङ्गुलाः।
दशाङ्गुलान्तरे चान्या कर्त्तव्या चक्रवेल्लनी॥ ५३॥

चक्रवेल्लनिकामध्यादशीत्यङ्गुलनिर्गमा।
चक्रमानं द्विहस्ता तु पादोन त्रिकरावधिः॥ ५४॥

ऊर्ध्ववेल्लनिकाधस्तात्प्रान्ते लोहस्य कीलिका।
दक्षे कलाया रक्षार्थं ततो बन्धविमोक्षणम्॥ ५५॥

ज्योतिका रक्षकं मध्ये कारयेत्कीलकं पुनः।
पार्श्वयोर्वृद्धवेल्लन्यां तनिकाकर्षणाय च॥ ५६॥

विनाभ्यासेन सर्वेषां केवलं निष्फलः श्रमः।
तस्मादभ्यसतो लक्ष्यादखिलं प्राप्यते गुरोः॥ ५७॥

वाहयेत्प्रथमं शून्यं द्वितीये निक्षिपेद्बलिम्।
तृतीये माहिषं मुण्डं चतुर्थे गोलकं क्षिपेत्॥ ५८॥

तत्र भैरवभैरव्योः पूजा कार्या सदा नृपैः।
रक्तादिपुष्पैर्नैवेद्यैर्मद्यमांसै[११]र्जयार्थिभिः॥५९॥

[१२]दैर्घ्ये मन्वङ्गुलं प्रोक्तं व्यासायामे षडङ्गुलम्।
यन्त्रैर्हस्तमिते कैश्चित् कार्यं युक्त्या सुपञ्जरम्॥ ६०॥

स्तम्भाभ्रमणयन्त्रे तु कर्त्तव्या पञ्च पञ्च च।
हस्ततिथ्यङ्गुला दैर्घ्ये कर्त्तव्या तस्य वेल्लनी॥ ६१॥

प्रमाणं पूर्ववत्तस्य स्तम्भैर्भेदः प्रजायते।
लोके या ढिङ्कुली सोऽपि गौरीयन्त्रः प्रकीर्त्तितः॥ ६२॥

१०. कर्णो - In A
११. जयादि - In B, जपादि - In E
१२. दैर्ध्य - In B

52. The width of the pillars will be six hands and its length from the top part will be three hands in measurement. The upper part consists of two sections and the third section known as the lower part will contain sharp, flat, iron blades.

53. The upper disc will be equal in measurement to the third part and the base (*Piṇḍa*) will be four *Aṅgulas*. Another round disc should be fixed at the distance of ten *Aṅgulas*.

54. From the center of the round disc, the exit will be measured at a distance of eighty *Aṅgulas*. The measurement of the *Cakra* will be from two hands to $2\ ^{3}/_{4}$ th hands (minimized by one *Pada* up to three hands).

55. An iron nail will be fixed on the corner of the lower part of the upper disc. The right hand part is to be reserved for mechanical contrivance and its subsequent discharge.

56. One nail should be fixed for the fire-container inside and again for the pulling of the thread connecting the large side wheel.

57. Without practice, the effort of everybody will be fruitless. Therefore one should practise constantly under the instructor to attain success.

58. At first the target is in the air, in the second chance towards the *Bali*, in the third to the bulls-head and in the fourth the throw will be an iron ball.

59. So, a King will always worship *Bhairava* and *Bhairavī* with red coloured and other flowers, devotional gifts (*Naivedya*), wine, meat, prayers etc.

60. A well built *Pañjara* should be made after discussion; its length will be of fourteen *Aṅgulas*, breadth and diameter will be of six *Aṅgulas*; but, according to some, the arms will be measured with hands.

61-62. The columns should be made five in number in the revolving machine. The actual length of the disc will be fifteen *Aṅgulas*, if measured by *Hasta*. Its measurement will be as outlined before, the only difference being by columns. Among the people what is known as *Ḍhiṅkulī*, is the same as *Gourīyantra*.

एकस्तम्भेन मर्कट्या सर्वतोऽपि भ्रमत्ययम्।
यष्ट्यर्धे पक्षके तस्य दैर्घ्ये व्यासे त्रिभागतः ॥ ६३ ॥

पक्षयोश्च युगांशेन यष्ट्यासन्नात्र मर्कटी।
पाषाणं बन्धयेत्पृष्ठे भारः सर्वत्र कारणम् ॥ ६४ ॥

विधेयौ पक्षकौ स्तम्भे वेल्लन्या भ्रमणर्थकौ।
मर्कट्या यावती दैर्घ्ये ढिंकुली तावताधरः ॥ ६५ ॥

धरा दैर्घ्ये त्रिभागेन वेल्लनी पक्षकौ न्यसेत्।
उत्तमोऽनेकयन्त्रेषु गौरीयन्त्रः प्रकीर्तितः ॥ ६६ ॥

सर्वतो [१३]भ्रमणात्तेन सुखोपायेन सिद्धितः।
यन्त्रवाहाय सत्कृत्य दातव्यं नरनायकैः ॥ ६७ ॥

काञ्चनाभरणाक्षौमं ग्रामसद्वाहवाहनम् ॥ ६८ ॥

इति संग्रामयन्त्रलक्षणम् ॥

अग्नियन्त्रेषु नलेष्टाकाष्ठभल्लेश्ममोक्षणे।
सा तु रीतिमयी काष्ठादत्यायासेन साध्यते ॥ ६९ ॥

दृढा लोहमयी शस्ता सुबन्धैर्कटकैर्युता।
धत्तुरपुष्पवद्दैर्घ्ये त्रिगुणा षड्गुणावधिः ॥ ७० ॥

मुखे द्विगुणिता मूलात्सार्धा वाप्यधिका भवेत्।
केचिद्पृष्ठे प्रकुर्वन्ति शंखावर्त्तेन ढङ्कनम् ॥ ७१ ॥

केचित्सुमुद्रितां तत्र सूक्ष्मछिद्रेऽग्नियोजनम्।
औषधं प्रक्षिपेदस्यां मूले नालप्रमाणतः ॥ ७२ ॥

औषधाग्रे दृढं काष्ठं नालतुल्यमथायतम्।
नालमुखे क्षिपेद्गोलं काष्ठं वा लोहसंयुतम् ॥ ७३ ॥

---

१३. धूर्मवर्णं ते - In D

63. This machine moves all round by one pillar of the *Markaṭī*. (In a *Markaṭī* one column is moving it everywhere .) The wings will be on the half part of the rod and the length and breadth will be 1/3rd each.

64. The *Markaṭī* will be placed neither on the 1/4th part of the wings, nor near the rod. A boulder should be hung at the back for a uniform distribution of the pressure.

65-66. Two wings are to be set up on the pillar for moving the discs. The height of the *Markaṭī* will be similar to the scale of the *Ḍhiṅkulī*. The length of the scale will be divided into three segments. The disc and the two wings are to be placed therein. Among various arms of superior quality, *Gourīyantra* is one such.

67-68. It can easily move everywhere, and it is conducive to easily available comforts. The carriers of the machines are to be rewarded with gold ornaments, silks, villages and excellent vehicles for journeys, by the leader of the people.

Thus ends the definition of war machinery.

69. Among the fire arms (*Agniyantra*) the tubular weapon is used to throw bricks, wood, spears and stones. It is made of either brass or bell metal and there is a cardinal point by which one can easily aim at the target.

70. It should be strong, made of iron, close knitted and ornamented with a serpent belt (*Kaṭaka*). It will be like the *Dhattura* flower, but the length will be three to six times.

71. The front part will be twice the base, the base part is half or little more. Sometimes on the back a cover will be made like the whirls of a conch.

72. Some mark a small hole there for ignition. According to the size of the tube, medicament is to be inserted.

73. A piece of wood according to the size of the tube is to be placed in front of the medicament. Then, in the mouth of the tube, iron or wooden balls are to be put inside.

पृष्ठछिद्रेऽग्निसंयोगाद्गोलाद्यं याति दूरतः।
पुरप्राकारगेहादि ग्रामाराममविमर्दनम्॥ ७४॥

रिपूणां ते प्रकुर्वन्ति सैन्ये त्रासं च दारुणम्।
राज्ञा जयकरा एते वह्नियन्त्रा अनेकशः॥ ७५॥

विबुधैर्विहिताः पूज्याः पक्वान्नमदिरामिषैः।
हव्यवाहनलीवांशी चर्मनद्धाद्रिमुष्टिकाः॥ ७६॥

दैर्घ्यं कार्यार्धदैर्घ्यस्य चतुर्थांशेन विस्तरा।
ईषदार्द्रेण सूक्ष्मेण पूरयेदौषधेन ताम्॥ ७७॥

कुट्टयित्वा मुहुस्तस्यारिक्तमेकांगुलं मुखम्।
औषधार्धेन पृष्ठे स्याद्रन्ध्रं वह्नेर्यवप्रभम्॥ ७८॥

एकद्वित्र्यङ्गुलैकं बां [वांशं ?]सरलामत्र तोलयेत्।
सूर्योरुबुकसिंहास्य निर्वाणाङ्गारचूर्णकम्॥ ७९॥

अग्नियन्त्रौषधार्थं तु गृहीतव्यं यथोदितम्।
पञ्चषठ्सप्तचाष्टौ वा भागाश्चेति शिलाजतोः॥ ८०॥

गन्धस्यैकक्रमाच्चूर्णं सार्धं सार्धद्वियुग्मकम्।
तद्भेषजस्य मार्गोऽयं भेदा अन्येऽप्यनेकशः॥ ८१॥

वह्निसंयोगतस्तेषां दृश्यते बहुधा गतिः।
गैरेयं द्विगुणं गन्धात्कुर्यात्तोयेन गोलिकाम्॥ ८२॥

हव्यवाहा मुखे तारा वैरिणां पुरदाहकाः॥ ८३॥

इति अग्नियन्त्रलक्षणम्॥

74. With ignition at the back, the ball goes far and it destroys city gates houses, villages and pleasure gardens.

75. These fire arms create panic among the enemy's soldiers and these mostly bring victory for the Kings in many ways.

76-77. The weapon is to be worshipped with cooked rice, wine and meat. That part of the fire tube which is covered with skin, will measure eight *Aṅgulas* (*Dvimuṣṭikā*). The length will be for consideration of utility and the breadth will be 1/4th of the 1/2 of the height. That tube is to be filled up with slightly moistened minerals.

78. The minerals have to be repeatedly ground and the front part measuring one *Aṅgula* will be filled up and the residual ground minerals are to be poured into the small hole, measuring one *Yava*, at the back for ignition.

79. One should measure one, two, three *Aṅgulas* of the *Sūrya* (*Arka* (tree), the front part of the *Siṁha* (Olibanum tree), *Rubuka* (Castor oil) and burnt coal dust.

80. In addition to the minerals earlier prescribed for fire arms, five, six, seven or eight parts of bitumen are to be used.

81. One part of the sulphur (*Gandhaka*) is to be taken in proportion of half, half and a pair of two. This is the procedure of taking the minerals and there are innumerable other varieties.

82. After ignition, different directions of fire are marked. The balls are to be made with bitumen, with twice the amount of sulphur mixed with water.

83. From the mouth of the tube, the fire emits like stars and it will burn the city of the enemies.

Here ends the description of the fire arms.

अथ जलाशयाः ॥

युधिष्ठिरं प्रति श्रीकृष्णवाक्यम् ॥

वरं वर्षशतेनापि कृतैकाविहरी वने।
नासञ्चिता गृहे कोटीक्षणध्वंसि धनस्य हि ॥ ८४ ॥

सर्वस्वेनापि कौन्तेय भूमिस्थमुदकं कुरु।
कुलानि तारयेत्सप्त यत्र गौर्वितृषी भवेत् ॥ ८५ ॥

नन्दाभद्राजयावापी विजया च क्रमाद्युताः।
त्रिषठ्नवार्ककूटैः स्युरेकद्वित्रिचतुर्मुखैः ॥ ८६ ॥

कूपाः स्युर्वेदहस्तादि दशहस्तान्तविस्तराः।
श्रीमुखो विजयः प्रान्तो दुन्दुभिश्च [१४]मनोहरः ॥ ८७ ॥

चूडामणिश्च दिग्भद्रो जयो नन्दनशङ्करौः।
कुण्डं युगास्त्रं भद्रं स्यात्सुभद्रं भद्रसंयुतम् ॥ ८८ ॥

प्रतिभद्रैर्युतं नन्दं परिघं मध्यभिट्टवत्।
शतान्तमष्टहस्तादि चतुर्द्वाराणि कारयेत् ॥ ८९ ॥

मध्यभिट्टे च शालासु देवार्चास्तत्र विन्यसेत्।
सरोनामार्धचन्द्राभं वृत्ताकारं महासरः।

चतुरस्त्रं तु भद्रं स्यात्सुभद्रं भद्रसंयुतम् ।।९० ।।

अथ उद्यानम् ॥

आरामकारकोनाके वसेदिन्द्रायुतत्रयम् ॥ ९१ ॥

शूराणां पूजनं भोगः प्रीणनं प्राणिनां ततः।
पुरादिमध्ये बाह्ये वा कुर्यादुद्यानमुत्तमम् ॥ ९२ ॥

---

१४. नमोहरः - In D

Now the reservoirs:

It is *Śrīkṛṣṇa's* advice to *Yudhiṣṭhira* :-

84. It is better to roam around the forests for a hundred years than to reserve money in the house, for wealth may be destroyed within a moment.

85. So, O *Kaunteya*– even if you have to give all your money, dig one water reservoir in the land. If the cows are made free of thirst then your seventh generation will be relieved from worldly sufferings.

86. The water reservoirs named as *Nandā*[3], *Bhadrā, Jayā* and *Vijayā* will be serially connected with three, six, nine, and twelve projections with one, two, three, and four entrances.

87-89a. Dimensions of the *Kūpas*[4] will start from four hands up to ten hands. They are of manifold varieties known as - *Śrīmukha, Vijayā, Prānta, Dundubhi, Manohara. Cūḍāmaṇi, Digbhadra, Jaya, Nandana* and *Śaṅkara.* The *Kuṇḍas* will be square in shape and their varieties will be *Bhadra, Śubhadra* which is an addition to *Bhadrā, Nandā,* which is attached to *Pratibhadra* and *Parigha* which is similar to *Madhyabhiṭṭa.*

89b-90a. In breadth, a *Kuṇḍa* will be from eight hands to 100 hands and it will be accompanied by four entrances. In the *Madhyabhiṭṭa* as well as in *Śālā,* an image of God should be installed. *Sara* resembles the half crescent of the Moon while *Mahāsara* is round in shape. *Bhadra* is a square one, while *Subhadra* is joined together with *Bhadra.*

Now the garden:

90b-92. He, who lays out a pleasure garden, resides in the heaven for 420,000 years. There he does worship of the gods, has enjoyment and by pleasing the creating beings. The best type of garden is to be created either inside or outside the city.

---

3. Nandā - Ekavaktra and Trikūṭa
Bhadrā - Dvivaktra and Ṣatkūṭa
Jayā - Trivakra and Navakūta
Vijaya - Caturvaktra and Dvādaśakūta L.K. Shukla - P. 53

4. Here we find a Kūpa will be from 4 hands to 10 hands in dimension but in L.K. Shukla's book which mainly deals with Samārāṅgaṇa Sūtradhāra, reference of a Kūpa measuring 13 hands is also available.

गृहस्य वामे दक्षे वा एकद्वित्रिधनुःशतैः ।
नानाद्रुमलतोपेतं क्रीडास्थानशतैर्वृतम् ॥ ९३ ॥

तोयाशयः घटीयन्त्रधारागृहविराजितम् ॥ ९४ ॥

इति श्रीसूत्रधारमण्डनविरचिते वास्तुशास्त्रे पुरदुर्गजलाशयलक्षणाध्यायस्तृतीयः ।

93-94. It will be either on the right side or left side of the house, and its measurement will be one, two or three hundred *Dhanus*[5]. It is adorned with varieties of trees, creepers, hundreds of playgrounds, water-reservoirs, water-buckets, and bathrooms with showers.

Thus ends the third chapter of Vāstumaṇḍana, the book of architectures written by Śrī Sūtradhāra Maṇḍana. It describes the fort machineries and water reservoirs. There are 94 Ślokas.

5. F.N. चतुर्हस्तैर्धनुर्दण्डः: 4 hands = 1 Dhanu - 1 hand approximately 18 inches - 4 x 18 = 72 inches Dhanu 72 x 100 = 7200 inches = 60 ft.

चतुर्थोऽध्यायः

[गृहादिनिवेशः]

गृहं हि सर्वजन्तूनां लयस्थानं सुखास्पदम्।
त्रिवर्गसाधनं पुण्यमिष्टापूर्त्तप्रवर्त्तकम्॥ १॥

शीतवाताम्बुघर्मादि दुःखघ्नं मुनिभिर्मतम्।
वाटभित्तं पुरा कृत्वा तन्मध्ये कारयेद्गृहम्॥ २॥

चतुर्हस्तं गृहं व्यासे प्रोक्तं श्रीविश्वकर्मणा।
द्वात्रिंशत्करपर्यन्तं ततो दैर्घ्येऽपि तत्समम्॥ ३॥

साष्टमांशं सपादं वा सार्धं वा द्विगुणावधिः।
विस्तारादधिकं दैर्घ्ये श्रेष्ठं व्यासे भयावहम्॥ ४॥

द्वात्रिंशत्कर[१]विस्तीर्णं भवेद्ब्राह्मणमन्दिरम्।
प्रत्येकं क्षत्रियादीनां चतुर्हस्तैर्विहीनकम्॥ ५॥

दशाष्टत्रिचतुर्भागैरायामे क्रमतोऽधिकम्।
एतन्मूलगृहं प्रोक्तं तद्बाह्ये वाटभित्तिका॥ ६॥

प्राकारकोटभित्तीनां प्रमाणं तु यदृच्छया।
मध्यक्षेत्रे प्रकर्त्तव्यमायव्ययविशोधनम्॥ ७॥

सर्वक्षेत्रान्तरे शालालिन्दकोष्ठादिनिर्मितः।
कार्या पुत्रधनक्रीडाभोजनादिकं सन्ततेः॥ ८॥

---

१. विस्ताद्रं in B विस्तारं in CDE

Chapter IV

[Gṛhādiniveśaḥ]

Now the arrangement of the houses

1. For every living being, the house is the dwelling place and it is the place of enjoyment too. It also leads to the fulfilment of three goals in life and it encourages one towards the holy works, both material and heavenly.

2. According to the ancient sages it (house) protects us from the sufferings caused by cold, wind, water and summer heat. After constructing a road and enclosure, the house should be built inside.

3. According to *Srī Viśvakarmā*, the breadth of the house starts from four hands in measurement, and will extend up to 32 hands, and the length will be equal to that.

4. The length should be more than the breadth by 1/8th, 1/4th, 1/2 or double, but if breadth exceeds the length, it would be dangerous.

5. The house of a Brahmin should be 32 hands in extent. The house of *Kṣatriyas* and other castes should be 4 hands less, respectively.

6. Gradually the length will be more by 10, 8, 3, 4 parts than the breadth, it is said about the main building and on the outer side there will be an enclosure wall .

7. The dimension of the rampart, fort and enclosure wall can be done according to one's own requirement. Only in the central place, the *Āya, Vyaya* should be examined according to the rule. 7.

8. Within that enclosure *Śālā, Alinda, Koṣṭha* etc. should be made for the children, so that these can be used for preserving wealth, pleasure room, and dining place.

द्वात्रिंशत्करतो ग्रामभूमिभागं विशेषतः ।
गृहाणि भूपतीनां स्युर्यावदष्टोत्तरं शतम् ॥ ९ ॥

व्यासे हस्तैः समं राज्ञां गृहं दैर्घ्ये च पूर्ववत् ।
दृढं मनोहरं कुर्यादनेकाकारसंयुतम् ॥ १० ॥

महाराजगृहात् पुत्रमन्त्रिसामान्यभूभृताम् ।
हस्तैर्हीनान् गृहान्कुर्यात्तेषां युक्तिवशात्सुधीः ॥ ११ ॥

पुरस्य [२]षोडशांशेन मध्ये कोटं [३]सुनिश्चलम् ।
तन्मध्ये भवनं राज्ञः कलशध्वजभूषितम् ॥ १२ ॥

अष्टवर्गा अकाराद्याः पूर्वादिषु प्रदक्षिणे ।
स्थितास्तत्र गृहाणि स्युर्वर्गिणां नगरादिषु ॥ १३ ॥

गरुडस्त्वथ मार्जारः सिंहः श्वा सर्पमूषकौ ।
मृगो मेढश्च वर्गेशा वैरी यो यस्य सन्मुखः ॥ १४ ॥

दीपाम्नायः ॥

दीपाम्नाये अकाराद्यान्मध्याद्वर्गान् क्रमाल्लिखेत् ।
स्वरान्षोडशमध्ये तु क्षमीशानस्य कोष्ठके ॥ १५ ॥

स्ववर्गं मन्दिरे कुर्याद्दीपस्थानं तदेव हि ।
मन्त्रादिसाधनं तत्र सिद्धयेऽन्यत्र निष्फलम् ॥ १६ ॥

देशदीपे पुरं कुर्यात्पुरदीपे च मन्दिरम् ।
मन्दिरे शयनाद्यं च प्रोक्तमागमकोविदैः ॥ १७ ॥

वास्तुक्षेत्रं यथायोग्यं चतुरस्रं तथायतम् ।
षडस्रमष्टकोणं च वर्तुलं वर्तुलायतम् ॥ १८ ॥

---

२. षोडरगंशन in B

३. सुनिश्चयम् in DE

9. Especially in the village, the division of land starts from 32 hands, and the house of a land-lord will be up to 108 hands in length.

10. For a King, it is prescribed that both the breadth and length of the house will be same. (*i.e.* 108 hands) . It should be made strong, beautiful and in various shapes.

11. In comparison to the King's palace, the house of a prince, *Mantri* and ordinary landlords will be less by several hands. A learned man will do it according to his own judgment.

12. In the central 16th part of the city, a strong fort should be built. Therein, the King's palace should be built decorated with pitcher and flag.

13. Going round 8 *Vargas* from the east, starting from 'A', is the place, where the houses of *Vargis* should be built in all the cities.

14. *Garuḍa*, as well as the cat, lion, dog, snake, rat, deer, sheep are the lords of their own *Varga*. A *Varga* opposite to another *Varga* will be treated as each other's enemy.

Sacred tradition of the lamp

15 In the sacred tradition of the lamp, the *Vargas* should be drawn from inside, starting from 'A'. Among the 16th *Svaras*, 'Kṣa' should be placed on the house of *Īsāna* ..

16. In similar types of temples, the location of the lamp-stands will be similar . Then there will be accomplishment of the *Mantras*; in other place it will yield no result.

17. A city should be built in *Deśadīpa* and a temple should be erected in *Puradīpa* . There will be place for sleeping in a temple, say the people who are proficient in traditional doctrine.

18. Suitably, the plot of land will be either square or oblong in shape. It will be with six or eight corners, round and oval shaped.

राज्ञां द्विजानां [४]वेद्मस्तं न कार्यं क्षत्रियादिषु।
एकशालादितो गेहं दशशालावधि स्मृतम्॥ १९॥

वर्णानां वेदशालान्तं दिक्शालान्तं तु [५]भूभृताम्।
शाला व्यासे चतुर्हस्तात्तस्मान्नखकरावधिः॥ २०॥
साष्टमांशा सपादा वा सार्धा वाप्यायता मता॥ २१॥

अपराजिते॥

विस्तरे विंशतिर्हस्ता द्विरष्टाष्टादशापि वा।
चतुर्हस्तोदये शाला रङ्गभूफलकान्तरे॥ २२॥

[६]**मयमते॥**

चतुर्हस्तादितः शाला व्यासे जिनकरावधिः।
सार्धान्तमायता न णां सुराणामधिकापि सा॥ २३॥

इति।

शालां त्रिपञ्चसप्ताङ्कैर्विभागैः प्रविभाजयेत्।
एकद्वित्रियुगांशैस्तु समानोऽलिन्द इष्यते॥ २४॥

तथा च।

त्रिहस्तात् षट्करं यावल्लघोर्मानमुदाहृतम्।
श्रीविश्वकर्मणा तस्मात्प्रकर्त्तव्यं यथोचितम्॥ २५॥

प्रस्तारेण समुत्पन्नं तद्गृहं स्वामिनोरपि।
प्रीतिः परस्परं योज्या मण्डपाद्यं ततो बहिः॥ २६॥

४. वेदास्त्रं in BCDE
५. भूभुजाम् in B
६. यममते in B

19. It will be suitable for Kings and Brahmins, but it should not be done for *Kṣatriyas* and others. It is known that a house may have halls from one to ten.

20-21. For the four *Varṇas*, the house may have halls up to four, but for a King the house may have halls up to ten in number. The width of a *Śālā* may start from four hands and can go up to twenty hands (*Nakhakarā*), the length will be 11/8th, 11/4 th or 1 1/2; this is the opinion.

In the Aparājita

22. The extent may be twenty, sixteen or eighteen hands. In between the stage and the platform, the height of a *Śālā* will be of four hands.

According to Mayamata

23. Starting from four hands, the breadth of a *Śālā* may go up to 24 hands. The length of that *Śālā* may be half (of the breadth) for a King, but more for the Gods.

Thus it ends

24. *Śālā* should be divided into three, five seven and nine parts, *Alindas* should be added on the first, second, third and fourth parts.

As well as

25. The measurement of the *Laghu* is said to start from three hands and up to six hands by *Viśvakarmā*. So it should be done accordingly.

26. That house of the land-lord built according to the rules of *Prastāra* gives happiness to each other. *Maṇḍapas* and other things should be built outside.

शालायाः विस्तरात्सार्धा त्रिभागेनांशतोऽपि वा।
पट्टशाला भवेत् श्रेष्ठा व्यासे कैश्चित्समा मता॥ २७॥

पट्टशाला प्रकर्त्तव्या गूढजालकसंयुता।
प्रकाशा भद्रयुक्ता वाऽथवा पट्टत्रयानना॥ २८॥

गूढाग्रे मण्डपं कुर्यान्मध्यआच्छादनं विना।
पट्टशालाश्चतुर्दिक्षु आद्यालिन्दानुसारतः॥ २९॥

[७]वेदिकासनपट्टैश्च मत्तवारणतोरणैः।
भद्रजालक [८]उत्साद्यैः कर्त्तव्या द्विभूमिकाः॥ ३०॥

मण्डपाग्रे मुखद्वारं तस्योपरि सुशोभनम्।
द्वित्रिभूमं गृहं कुर्यान्माड[९]मुखा गवाक्षकैः॥ ३१॥

सर्वक्षेत्रे प्रकर्त्तव्या गवां गायादिकल्पना।
आय एव पृथक् मध्यक्षेत्रे भित्यन्तरे भवेत्॥ ३२॥

भाण्डागारोऽष्टषष्ट्यन्तं समः सार्धान्तमायतः।
महानसं तु लोकानां चतुर्हस्तं नवान्तकम्॥ ३३॥
धनधान्यालयं कुर्यात्तिथ्यन्तं पञ्चहस्ततः॥ ३४॥

मयः॥

अन्नालयं ह्यतिनतमत्युच्चं स्याद्धनालयम्।
तथैव दक्षिणागारमतिनीचं सुखालयम्॥ ३५॥

इति गृहनिवेशः॥

[१०]सृष्ट्या प्रवेश उत्सङ्गः प्रतिकायोऽपि सव्यतः।
वामावर्तो हीनबाहुः पूर्णबाहुस्तु सन्मुखः॥ ३६॥

---

७. वेक्षिका in B

८. सुधाद्यैः in A

९. मूषा in B

१०. Similar verbs are seen in A.P ch 83. V 11-12

27. If the extent of a *Paṭṭaśālā* is half, or one- third or one part of a *Śālā*, it is regarded as best, but their width may be same, this is the opinion of some people.

28. A *Paṭṭaśālā* should be made with concealed latticed windows. The appearance will be with a portico or with three *Paṭṭas*.

29-30. In front of the covered place, a *Maṇḍapa* should be built whose center will be without any cover. There will be *Paṭṭasālā* on four sides following the front *Alinda*. A two storeyed building is to be built with altar, seats, *Paṭṭa* (platform) *Mattavāraṇa* entrance, and latticed portico *(Bhadrajāla)*

31. The main door is to be erected in the front part of the *Maṇḍapa*. After that, a magnificent two three-storeyed *Māḍa* - shaped building with latticed windows should be built.

32. In all the cases one should have in mind the simile of a cow and a calf. *Āya* will be different in the central part and in between the walls.

33. The breadth of a storehouse will be from eight hands to sixty hands and the length will be either half or equal. A kitchen for the general public will be from four hands up to nine hands.

34. The room for the granary and treasury will be constructed from (minimum) five hands to (maximum) fifteen hands.

Maya.

35. The dining hall should be very low while the treasury will be very high. Likewise, the southern apartment and the house of pleasure will be very low.

Thus ends the arrangement of the house.

36. After construction, the main entrance named *Utsaṅga* and *Pratikāya* will be from the right side, *Hīnabāhu* from the left side, and *Pūrṇabāhu* from the front side.

गृहे मध्योन्नताभूमिर्निम्नाऽपीष्टा सुरालये।
गजस्कन्धा समोत्सेधा राजवेश्मादिभूमिका: ॥ ३७ ॥

ताम्रपात्रस्थितैर्धान्यं मृत्कन्दौषधिधातुभि:।
[११]सरत्नै: स्वस्वचिह्नाद्यैर्गर्भन्यासो गृहादिषु ॥ ३८ ॥

ब्राह्ममैत्रेंद्रवादित्यपुष्यस्वात्युत्तरे[१२]व च।
पित्रे पौष्णे श्रुतौ [१३]गर्भ: सद्युक्ते क्षे स्थिरोदये ॥ ३९ ॥

गर्भस्थानं गृहेष्विन्द्रे भल्लाटे वा गृहक्षते।
पुष्पदन्तेऽथवा द्वारदक्षिणस्तम्भकादध: ॥ ४० ॥

सगर्भं सर्वसम्पत्त्यै विगर्भं सर्वनाशनम्।
तस्मात् सर्वप्रयत्नेन गर्भं सम्यग्विनिक्षिपेत् ॥४१ ॥

इति गर्भन्यास: ॥

प्रतिहस्तं शिलाबद्धा भूमिर्युगयवानता।
इष्टका भित्तिविस्तारो गृहव्यास: कलांशत: ॥४२ ॥

पादोनो मध्यम: प्रोक्तो उत्तमार्धेन कन्यस:।
मन्वङ्गुलादे: केप्याऽहुस्त्रिंशन्मात्रावधिं तु तान् ॥४३ ॥

इति भिति: ॥

नागदन्तौ तु शालायां द्वौ द्वौ वामे च दक्षिणे।
एकशालार्कभागेन तस्मान्पदर्धेऽन्तरे पर: ॥४४ ॥

द्वारोर्ध्वाङ्गसमा शस्ता न गृहाभिमुखा: शुभा:।
दैवे दीपालयो वामे दक्षिणाङ्गे नृणां गृहे ॥४५ ॥

---

११. सरलै: in BCDE

१२. करे in A

१३. गर्त्त in BCDE

37. For a house the central part of the land is to be elevated, but for a temple low land is considered beneficial too. The site of the King's palace should be as high as the shoulder of an elephant.

38. The placing of the foundation deposit in a house and others should be performed with the grains kept in a copper plate, earth, roots, medicinal herbs and other ingredients with gems and the respective symbols.

39. By the moment Brahmā and *Maitra* belong to the Sun and the Moon, with the constellation of *Puṣyā, Svātī, Uttarā*, and by the moment of *Pitṛ* joins *Puṣya* star, the foundation deposit should be laid with these stars in the fixed position.

40.In a house, the foundation deposit is to be placed on *Indra, Bhallāṭa, Gṛhakṣata, Puṣpadanta* or under the pillar/column located on the right side of the door.

41. A correctly placed foundation deposit gives all kinds of wealth, whereas wrongly placed foundation deposit destroys everything. So, by all means one should lay out the foundation deposit properly.

Thus ends the laying out of the foundation of the deposit.

In the measurement of each hand, stones should be spread out and the ground will be lower by 4 1/8 th.

42-43. A brick wall will be 1/16th of the diameter of a house. It is medium if less by 14th part, *Uttama* if less by half, and *Kaniṣṭha* if less by 11/4th *Aṅgula*. Other people say it may be less by 30 *Aṅgulas* or 1/30th.

Thus ends the wall

44. In a *Śālā* two *Nāgadantas* are to be erected on the left and two on the right side. In a *Ekaśālā* house it may be kept on the 12th part or at intervals of 6th onwards.

45. It is auspicious if it is kept equal to the upper part of the door, but regarded as inauspicious if it faces the main house. In a temple, the lamp-stand is to be placed on the left side and it is on the right side in a dwelling of human beings.

अथ द्वारम् ॥

सप्ततिषष्टिपञ्चाशद्व्यासहस्तमिताङ्गुलैः ।
संयोज्य कार्यं गेहेषु त्रिविधं द्वारमुच्छ्रये ॥४६ ॥

गृहप्रासादयोर्द्वारं यानं [१४]शयनमासनम् ।
उदयार्धेन विस्तीर्णं षोडशांशाधिकं हि वा ॥४७ ॥

द्वारव्यासाद्विभागेन व्यासः शाखान्तरङ्गयोः ।
प्रतिशाखात्रिभागेन निर्गमे विस्तरे समा ॥ ४८ ॥

एलकापल्लवैर्युक्ता बकुलापुष्पकैरपि ।
उदुम्बरस्तूत्तराङ्गात्सार्धः कुम्भीसमोदयः ॥४९ ॥

द्वारविस्तारपादेन निर्गमो नागदन्तयोः ।
तदायव्ययधिष्ण्यांशा तारामैत्रीन्दुशोधितम् ॥५० ॥

[१५]वामभागाश्रितं वेश्म मूलद्वारं प्रकारयेत् ।
दक्षिणे चाश्वशालानां मध्ये द्वारं तु दन्तिनाम् ॥५१ ॥

तथा च-

गर्भे द्वारं न दातव्यं मध्यं नैव परित्यजेत् ।
द्वारव्यासजिनांशेन मध्यद्वारं निवेशयेत् ॥ ५२ ॥

मध्ये द्वारं तु देवानां द्विजानामवनीभृताम् ।
शेषानामपि सर्वेषां मध्यासन्नं विधीयते ॥ ५३ ॥

इति ॥

द्वारं गृहाणां सर्वेषां पट्टस्थाने प्रयोजयेत् ।
तुलाधस्तान्न दातव्यं केऽप्याहुर्नृपतेः शुभम् ॥५४ ॥

---

१४. शशनमासनम् in B

१५. Similar verse in AP ch 10 v18

Now the door:

46. For a house, the height of the door may be of three types measuring 70, 60, or 50 fingers of a hand.

47. The breadth of the door of a house, or palace, conveyance, bed, seat will be half of their length or may be more than 1/16th part.

48. The width of the inner part of the (door) frame will be equal to 1/7th part of the door width. Each frame, if divided by 3, will be equal to its projection and width.

49. The lintels will be decorated with the motifs of *Elakā* leaves as well as *Bakulā* flowers. The base will have the same height as half of the upper lintel.

50. *Nāgadanta* can be projected up to one *Pāda* (1/4th) of the breadth of the door . Then the *Āya, Vyaya,* and part of the edifice will be sanctified according to the position of the stars and the Moon.

51. In a house, the main door is to be erected on the left side, the door of the stable will be on the right side and the door of the elephants enclosure in the centre.

As well as:

52. A door should not be constructed in the inner chamber, but the middle part should not be discarded. The inner (*Madhya*) door should be placed on the 24th section of the total width of the gate.

53. The door of a mansion meant for Gods, Brahmins and Kings can be placed in the middle of a building, but for all other people the door is to be located near the middle of the room.

Thus ends this topic.

54. The doors of all types of houses are to be erected on the moulding of a base (*Paṭṭasthāna*); it should not be erected under the beam, but according to some, this is good for Kings.

अपराजितः

क्षेत्रेऽङ्कभक्ते [१६]तुर्यांशे द्वारं वामे दिशि न्यसेत्।
इन्द्रे गृहक्षते पुष्पदन्ते भल्लाटके क्रमात्॥५५॥

पृष्ठे द्वारे भवेद्रोगः कुक्षौ शोको महद्भयम्।
उपद्वारं न्यसेत्क्षेत्रे भक्ते नव नवांशकैः॥५६॥

जयन्ते इन्द्रे आदित्ये तथा सत्ये भृशेऽम्बरे।
पुष्णि वा [१७]वितथे गृहक्षते गन्धर्वभृङ्गयोः॥५७॥

मृगे पितृषु च द्वास्थे सुग्रीवपुष्पदन्तयोः।
वरुणो मुख्यभल्लाट सोमादिति दितिष्वपि॥५८॥

गवाक्षजालयोर्द्वारं शालाद्वाराधमुन्नतम्।
द्वारे त्रिभक्ते द्व्यंशं वा सर्वेषां सुसमं शिरः॥५९॥

द्वारोर्ध्वे द्वारमाद्येन समं सङ्कीर्णमेव वा।
गृहादीनां मुखात्पूर्वं भ्रमणं द्वारसंयुतम्॥६०॥

षोडशांश[१८]मधः शस्तमन्यथा तन्न चिन्तयेत्।
शालामानात्प्रतोली त्रिचतुःपञ्चगुणेन्तरे॥६१॥

तिथिहस्तसमुत्सेधा प्रतोली तूत्तमा मता।
त्रयोदशकरामध्या रुद्रहस्ता कनीयसी॥६२॥

विस्तारस्तु क्रमात्तासामष्टसप्तरसैः करैः।
त्रिद्व्येकभूमिका युक्ता अनेकरचनां चिताः॥६३॥

कपाटं दक्षिणे भागे गृहे वामे शुभार्गला।
कपाटयुग्मं पिण्डेन शाखापिण्डार्धसंमितम्॥६४॥

---

१६. कुर्यांशे in BC

१७. पितथे in B

१८. भवः in B

Aparājita

55. Dividing the measurement of the land by nine, the door is to be erected on the fourth part of the left side and in the sequence of *Indra, Gṛhakṣata, Puṣpadanta* and *Bhallāṭaka.*

If the door is erected on the back side, there may be fear of diseases and if erected in the middle there will be grief and a lot of fear.

56-58. The plot of land is to be divided into 9 x 9 and the secondary door *(Upadvāra)* may be erected on the position of *Jayanta, Indra, Āditya,* as well as *Satya, Bhṛṣa, Ambara, Puṣna, Vitatha, Gṛhakṣata, Gandharva, Bhṛṅga, Mṛga, Pitṛ, Dvāstha, Sugrīva, Puṣpadanta, Varuṇa, Mukhya, Bhallāṭa, Soma, Aditi* and *Diti*.

59. The door adorned with two latticed windows will be half of the *Śālā* door in height. Whether a door is divided into three or two parts, the crest is to be constructed uniformly.

60-61a. A door above the door will be equal or short in size than the former one. In front of the entrance of a house, a circumambulatory passage is to be constructed. Its position is appreciated if it is below the 116th below the level of the building, otherwise it should be discarded.

61b-62. The main entrance (*Pratolī*) will be thrice, four or five times more in measurement than the *Śālā*. The best type of the main entrance is 15 hands long in height, the medium one is 13 hands and the smaller one is eleven hands long.

63. By sequence their widths are 8, 7 and 6 hands respectively. They may be 3, 2 and 1storyed with plenty of decoration.

64. For a house, if the panel is on the right side and the door-bolt on the left, it is regarded as auspicious. Both the door panels are to be joined with the bodily frame, and the frames will be connected with half of the bodily frame.

कपाटस्य तु पिण्डेन सन्धिपालास्तु कारयेत्।
मध्ये यः सन्धिपालस्तु सार्धसंमितविस्तरः॥ ६५॥

सुद्रव्यं सुस्थितं कान्तं स्वदिग्भागे प्रयोजयेत्।
न विद्रुतं कृशं मध्ये नाध्मातं नातिपीडितम्॥ ६६॥

न कुब्जं न बहिर्यातं न ह्रस्वं न तथोच्चकैः।
वक्रं नान्तर्गतं श्रेष्ठं तद्द्वारं सर्ववास्तुषु॥ ६७॥

उपर्युपरि भूमीनां द्वारं कुर्यात्प्रदक्षिणम्।
नापसव्येन कुर्वीत द्वारमारोहणानि च॥ ६८॥

तन्मध्ये सद्मनो द्वारं कुर्याद्द्विपदस्य च।
न शूले न पदेनापि शिरापाते तदिष्यते॥ ६९॥

रथ्याचत्वरशृङ्गाटप्रासादप्रतिमाध्वजैः।
वापीकूपप्रणालादि सरःप्रस्रवणभ्रमैः॥ ७०॥

कुड्यकोणतरुस्तम्भद्वारपट्टतुलादिभिः।
दरोत्कटवल्मीकपङ्ककीलांत्यजालयैः॥ ७१॥
शिरामर्मादिभिर्विद्धं द्वारं स्याद्बहुदोषदम्॥ ७२॥

तथा च॥

द्वारद्रव्यैस्तुलास्तम्भनागदन्तगवाक्षकैः।
द्वारमध्येऽर्दिते रोगकुलपीडाधनक्षयाः॥ ७३॥

निरन्तरस्थितैर्द्रव्यैस्तिर्यक्क्रान्तैश्च मन्दिरे।
मर्मवेधो न दोषाय द्वारवेधोऽथवा क्वचित्॥ ७४॥

न प्राकारान्तरे वेधोऽथराजमार्गान्तरेऽपि।
न स्तम्भपट्टादिवेधस्तु न भित्यन्तरतो भवेत्॥ ७५॥

65. There will be a connector in between the panel and the bodily frame. The central connector will be half of the breadth of the door.

66. The doors should be made of good raw material, it should be strong, elegant and fixed in the proper direction. It should not be liquefied, lean, inflated in the middle or too twisted.

67. That type of door is best for all *Vāstu* which is not crooked, projected outside, too low or too high or curved inwards.

68. The doors made above the floors are auspicious. The landing and the door should be made on the right side.

69. In between the floors, the doors of the building as well as the abode (*Pada*) of the deities should be constructed. It is not desirable to make it on the corners *(Śūlas)* on the veins *(Śirā)* or in the important places.

70-72. A door faces multiple faults if it is obstructed by a main road or highway (*Rathyā*), courtyard, the place where four roads meet, palace, idol, flagstaff, tank, well, canal (*Praṇāla*), lake, spring, whirlpool, corner of a wall, tree, pillar, the panel of a door, lintels, cave, pile stack, mound of white ants, muddy place or the house of lower caste people. A door should not be erected in places which are the vital parts or veins of the construction.

As well as:

73. If any part of the door, beam of a balance, column, peg, or latticed windows comes in the centre of the door, then there will be disease, family distress and loss of wealth.

74. The constructions on the vital parts or the obstruction of the door is not to be considered faulty if it is obstructed by permanent objects, as well as a temple with slanting inclination, but occasionally there may be obstruction of the door.

75. There will be no obstruction at the interval of a wall, or the main street (*Rājamārga*) . If it is made by the broad rectangular fillet of a pillar or if it is from the inside of a wall, it is not regarded as obstruction.

उदयाद्द्विगुणां भूमिं त्यक्त्वद्म वेधो न जायते ॥ ७६ ॥

अथ गृहोदयः ॥

गृहव्यासकलांशस्तु युगैः सार्धं त्रिभिस्त्रिभिः ।
करैः समेत पट्टाध उदयस्त्रिविधो गृहे ॥ ७७ ॥

त्रिधा स पुनरेकैकस्तत्र ज्येष्ठोदयोऽङ्गुलाः ।
विंशत्यष्टादशकलाङ्गुलैः षण्णवतिर्युताः ॥ ७८ ॥

धिष्ण्यप्रकृतितिथ्यंशैर्युगाशीत्यङ्गुला युताः ।
मन्दिराणां यथायोग्यमुदयो मध्यतस्त्रिधा ॥ ७९ ॥
[१९]भैकविंशतितिथ्यंशैर्युता मात्रा द्विसप्ततिः ।
उदयः कन्यसे स्त्रेधा योजनीयो यथोचितम् ॥ ८० ॥

पञ्चभक्ते गृहोत्सेधे एकभागेन वेदिका ।
मत्तवारणमेकांशं तृतीयांशे न तं शुभम् ॥ ८१ ॥

गृहोदयेऽष्टभिर्भक्ते कुम्भिका भागमानतः ।
षडंशो भरणं शीर्षं चार्धार्धभागिकम् ॥ ८२ ॥

उर्ध्वे सतन्त्रिकः पट्टो भागोऽर्धा विस्तरे तुला ।
उच्चौ भागतृतीयांशे व्यासतुल्यं तुलान्तरम् ॥ ८३ ॥

राजगृहादौ

अष्टभक्ते गृहोत्सेधे भागेनैकेन कुम्भिका ।
सार्धवेदांशकः स्तम्भ उछालः (च्छायः ?) सार्धभागिकः ॥ ८४ ॥

---

१९. नैक-in A

76. If twice the height of a land is left then there will be no fault of obstruction.

Now the height of a house:

77. Three varieties of height of a house will be counted on the basis of these measurements, i.e. 1/16 th part of the width of the house is to be multiplied by 4,2, 3 respectively and the calculation should start from the base of the floor.

78. Again, each of them is to be divided into three types, beginning with *Jyeṣṭha* whose height is to be measured by 20, 18, 16 *Aṅgulas* added by 96.

79. For temples, the height of the each variety of the building can be any one of 27, 21, 15 *Kara* added by 84 *Aṅgulas* as per requirements.

80. Similarly for the smaller type of the three varieties of measurement, the height will be 27, 21, 15 added by 72 *Aṅgulas* respectively.

81. The height of the house is to be divided into five parts and one part will form the altar. One part will be the *Mattavāraṇa* and it is not auspicious on the third part.

82. If the height of the house is divided by eight, the base of the column, (*Kumbhikā)* will form one part, the supporting part (*Bharaṇa*) will include six parts and the top part will constitute (half and half) portion.

83. On the upper part of the building, the fillet will be added with cord. On the middle of building height, there has to be lintel. On the third part of the height, another linted is to be erected of length, equal to the width.

In the Royal Palace.

84. The height of a house, if divided into eight parts, the *Kumbhikā* will take one part, the pillar will occupy four and half parts, while the remaining would constitue *Ucchāla*.

[२०]हीरग्रहणमंशेन शुण्डिकादिविराजितम्।
सतन्त्रिकः सपादांशः [२१]पट्टः सा त्र्यंशनिर्गताः ॥८५॥

भागार्धेन जयन्ती स्यात्क्रम एव तले तले।
उदुम्बर समाकुम्भी स्तम्भाद् द्विगुणविस्तरा ॥८६॥

स्तम्भतुल्याकृतिः कार्या भरणं चापि तादृशम्।
गृहव्यासकरमितैरङ्गुलैः स्तम्भविस्तराः ॥८७॥

स्तम्भपट्ट तुलाश्रेण्यां स्थानं मानं न लङ्घयेत्।
शालयोरन्तरे भित्तिस्तत्पार्श्वं स्तम्भकाबली ॥८८॥

अग्रालिन्दे न कर्त्तव्ये नायं सार्वत्रको विधिः।
भित्तेरुपरि भित्तिस्यात्स्तम्भं स्तम्भोपरि न्यसेत् ॥८९॥

भित्तेरुपरि वा स्तम्भं स्तम्भोर्ध्वे नैव [२२]भित्तिका।
भरणं द्विगुणं स्तम्भाद्व्यासे स्तम्भसमं शिरः ॥ ९० ॥

दैर्घ्यं सप्तगुणं यावत् शीर्षात् पट्टः सपादकः।
सुरूपं वा विरूपं वा सर्वमङ्गं [२३]प्रयोजयेत् ॥९१॥

भितिविस्तारपादोना वरंडी विषमस्तरा।
भित्तिव्यास[२४]समोत्सेधा विधेया गजपृष्ठवत् ॥९२॥

अन्तमूलं प्रणालं स्यात्तुला दैर्घ्यार्धमायतम् ॥९३॥

---

२०. हारगृह-in C, द्वीरग्रह-in D and, हीरगृहा-in E
२१. पदः in A
२२. भिभिका in B
२३. प्रजोजयेत् in A
२४. सप्तोत्सेधा in B

85. On one part there will be *Hīra* and others are to be decorated with *śuṇḍikā. Paṭṭa* (horizontal band) with cord will be one fourth in measurement and will be raised from the balance part.

86. *Jayantī* will be erected occupying the half part serially one after another. *Udumbara* (threshold bottom sill) and *Kumbhī* (one of the moulding of a basement) are of same size and these are double in width than the pillar.

87. Pillars will be similar in shape and size and *bharaṇī* will be likewise. The width of the pillar in a house will be determined by the width of a house. Each arms length of the width of the house is equal to one finger length of the width of the pillar (For example 20 arms width of the house will have 20 finger width of the pillar).

88. The band on the pillar and rows of lintels- their prescribed position and measurement should not be disturbed and deviated. In between the halls there will be walls and on that side there will be rows of small pillars.

89. Portico in the front part may not be erected universally. Wall will be built over the wall and column is over the column.

90. Neither there will be pillar on the wall nor there will be wall on the pillar *Bharaṇa* will be double of the column in width, and the top part will be equal to the pillar.

The top of the horizontal band with prop will be up to seven times of the length. Whether pleasant or non pleasant each part has to be included. 91.

92. The width of *Varaṇḍī* (veranda?) will be less by one fourth of the width of the wall, and it will be placed in an uneven level. Its height will be equal to the width of the wall resembling the back of an elephant.

93. The origin of the chute for draining waste water will be from inside the house and its width will be up to half of its length.

अथ भूलम्भः

गृहं व्यासेऽष्टहस्तान्तमेकभूमं प्रकारयेत्।
ततो दश दशर्ध्यन्तं क्रमवृद्धया[२५]तलं न्यसेत्॥९४॥

एकभूमं द्विभूमं वा क्षुद्राणां भवनं नृणाम्।
शूद्राणां त्रितलं कुर्याद्वैश्यानां तु चतुस्तलम्॥९५॥

क्षत्रियादेः [२६]पञ्चभूमं द्विजानां रागभूमिकम्।
सप्ताढ्यं मण्डलीकानां भूभुजां नवभूमिकम्॥९६॥

एकादशतलं गेहं विदध्याच्चक्रवर्त्तिनाम्।
उदयेऽर्कार्कभागेन हीना ऊर्ध्वोर्ध्वभूमिकाः॥९७॥

अधस्तलक्रिया युक्तिं कुर्यादूर्ध्वतलेष्वपि।
कुट्टिमार्थं सुधाचूर्णं शर्करा कर्करेष्टकाः॥९८॥

कदली पुरमाषाद्यैर्युक्ताः योज्या गृहादिषु॥९९॥

अथ वृक्षाहरणम्

धनिष्ठापञ्चकं त्यक्त्वा सुनिमित्ते शुभे दिने।
वनं गत्वा बलिं दत्वा कर्मयोग्यं वरेद्द्रुमम्॥१००॥

मन्त्रः

ॐ [२७]अपक्रामन्तु भूतानि देवराक्षसगुह्यकाः।
युष्मभ्यं तु बलिर्भूयाच्छं मे दिशत पादपाः॥१०१॥

२५. ललं in B
२६. पंचतलं in B
२७. Similar verse in Maymatam ch 15 v 89,90

Now the number of storeys (and their dimension)

94. The one - storeyed house will be up to 8 hands in breadth. Then it can gradually be increased up to 10 or 10 1/2 according to the requirement of the storeys.

95. One or two storeyed buildings can be built for the lowest category people. Three storeyed buildings are to be built for *Śūdras* and four storeyed for *Vaiṣyas.*

96. Five storeyed (buildings) for *Kṣatriyas,* six for Brahmins, seven for *Maṇḍalikas* (lord of a province), and nine storeyed will be for Kings.

97. Eleven storeyed buildings should be built for the *Cakravartti* (King). When the number of storeys increases, the height of each upper floor will be less by 1/12th part.

98. The nature of work should be same for the bottom as well as for the top floor. Lime powder, limestone, gravel, brick powder should be used for plastering.

99. A house should contain bananas, paddy, lentils and others.

Now the collection of woods :-

100. Barring *Dhaniṣṭhā* etc. the 5 stars-(*Dhaniṣṭhā, Śatabhiṣā, Pūrvabhādra-padā, Uttarabhādrapadā* and *Revatī*), one should go to the forest on an auspicious day and for a good cause give offerings to the woods which are suitable for construction.

Mantra :-

101. *Om,* disperse the *Bhūtas,* Gods, Demons and *Rākṣas.* Offerings have been made to you, be patient and show me the woods.

शिवमस्तु महीपुत्रा देवताश्च सगुह्यकाः ।
कर्मैतत्साधयिष्यामि क्रियतां [२८]देवपर्ययः ॥१०२ ॥

एवमुक्त्वा द्रुमं नत्वा कुठारमभिमन्त्रयेत् ॥१०३ ॥

मन्त्रः

ॐ नमो रुद्राय देवाय [२९]पिङ्गलाय महात्मने ।
विश्वदेवाय विश्वरूपाय [३०]विश्वकर्मणे नमो नमः[३०] ॥१०४ ॥

मूलं हस्तं विहायोर्ध्वं छित्वा तत्राभिलक्षयेत् ॥१०५ ॥

वारिश्रावः शुभो नेष्टः क्षीराज्यास्त्र मधुश्रवः ।
पूर्वे सौम्येऽथवेशाने पतितः शुभदो द्रुमः ॥१०६ ॥

गृहाद्यर्थं त्यजेद्वृक्षं चैत्यप्रासादपार्श्वगम् ।
भूतावासं श्मशानस्थं सकीट[३१]व्रणकोटरम् ॥१०७ ॥

सवल्मीकं स्वयं शुष्कं सनीडं चान्त्यजैः श्रितम् ।
दवालीढं बहुशिरं सरित्सङ्गम[३२]सम्भवम् ॥१०८ ॥

सक्षीरकण्टकं भग्नं पथि सर्वजनैः श्रितम् ।
[३३]संसेवितं खगमृगैर्वातेन तडिदाहतम् ॥१०९ ॥

वापीकूपतडागादि वास्तुजातं रुजायुतम् ।
आम्रं बिभीतकं चिञ्चां नीपं श्लेष्मातकं धवम् ॥११० ॥

२८. वो विपर्ययःin BCDE
२९. Ms A omits v104 from पिङ्गलाय to विश्वदेवाय
३०. नमस्ते विश्वकर्मणे in D
३१. घृण-in
३२. संभिवं in B
३३. संसेविकं in B

102. Let it be propitious for you, O son of Earth, Gods and good Demons, I shall perform the act, please change your residence.

103. Saying so, lowering the trees one should consecrate the axe.

Mantra :-

Om, salute to the God *Rudra, Piṅgala* the *Mahātman, Viśvadeva,*

104. *Viśvarūpa, Viśvakarmā*, salute to them again and again.

105. Leaving the main branches, one should cut the upper part and examine that.

106. Water shedding trees are beneficial, but milky trees or the trees which shed honey are not suitable. If the trees are felled towards the East, North or North-East, it gives good results.

107. For the construction of a house, those types of trees are to be discarded which grow beside a temple and holy ground (*Caitya*), nested by spirits, trees which are grown on cremation grounds or infected with insects.

108. Trees covered with white ants, those which have dried up by themselves, trees with nests, those which are used as a shelter by *Śūdras*. Trees with sinews, those which grow on the confluence of the river.

109. Milky and thorny trees, broken on its own, trees which are resting places for all passersby, which are the abode of birds and of animals, which are broken by wind and lightning.

110a. Trees which grow near a tank, well, pond or such place, and diseased trees should be discarded.

अरिष्ट[३४]पञ्चकं तद्वत्कोविदारमुदुम्बरम्।
शुभाः पुण्यवनाद्रिस्था दृढाः साराः समाद्रुमाः ॥१११ ॥

शाकः शिरीषः श्रीपर्णी शिंशपा सरलः शमी।
सुरद्रुमः सप्तपर्णः शाल्मली सर्जकोऽशनः ॥११२ ॥

तमालतालहिन्तालशालकालाः सकट्फलाः।
नालिकेरः (नारिकेलः) सखर्जुरश्चीरः कदरखदिरौ ॥११३ ॥

विम्बो निम्बः कदम्बश्च जम्बुः स्तम्बो मधुद्रुमः।
पिशितः पनसः पिण्डी पूगपत्तङ्गपद्मकाः ॥११४ ॥

राजादनो धन्वनश्च चन्दनो रक्तचन्दनः।
तिनिसस्तिमिर[३५]श्रोणिं तिन्दुकस्तिलकस्तरुः ॥११५ ॥

अजकर्णोऽर्जुनो भूर्जोऽशोको वंशोविकङ्कतः।
क्षीरिणी रोहिणी रोध्री होमो हारिद्रकोऽञ्जनः ॥११६ ॥

पुरुषो लंकुचः सिंहो गवाक्षी च शुभा मयमते गृहे।
कालस्कन्धः कोविदारः करवीरः कलिद्रुमः ॥ ११७ ॥

[३६]कालागरुः कर्णिकारः कपित्थश्चापि किंशुकः।
कण्टः करञ्जः कर्चूरस्तिन्दुकश्च महाद्रुमाः ॥११८ ॥

बदर्युदुम्बरो बाणो विल्वश्च बकुलो वटः।
पुत्रजीवः पारिजातः पिण्डी पालाशपिप्पलौ ॥११९ ॥

पाटला पद्मकः पीलुः प्लक्षः पथ्यापिक प्रियः।
श्लेष्मातकः सप्तपर्णः शिरीषः सरलः शिवाः ॥१२० ॥

३४. चंपकं in A
३५. स्त्रौणि/स्त्रीणि in BDE
३६. Ms A omits v 118

110b-111. *Āmra, Bibhītaka, Ciñcā, Nīpa, Śleṣmātaka, Dhava, Ariṣṭa pañcaka* as well as *Kovidāra,* and *Udumbara,* are beneficial if they are grown in an auspicious forest. They are hard, vigorous, and straight types of trees.

112-116. *Śāka, Śirīṣa, Śrīparṇī, Śimśapā, Sarala, Śamī, Suradruma, Saptaparṇa, Śālmalī, Sarjaka, Aśana, Tamāla, Tāla, Hintāla, Śālakāla, Sakaṭphala, Nālikera, Kharjura, Cīra, Kadara, Khadira, Vimba, Nimba, Kadamba, Jambu, Stamba, Madhudruma, Piśita, Panasa, Piṇḍī, Pūga, Pattaṅga, Padmaka, Rājādana, Dhanvana, Candana, Raktacandana, Tinisa, Timira, Śroṇi, Tinduka, Tilaka, Ajakarṇa, Arjuna, Bhūrja, Aśoka, Vaṁśa, Vikaṅkata, Kṣīriṇī, Rohiṇī, Rodhrī, Homa, Hāridraka, Añjana, Puruṣa, Laṁkuca, Siṁha, Gavākṣī*– are regarded as auspicious for a house.

according to Maya:-

117-118. *Kālaskandha, Kovidāra, Karavīra, Kalidruma, Kālāgaru, Karṇikāra, Kapittha, Kiṁśuka, Kaṇṭaka, Karañja, Karcūra, Tinduka* – these are the big trees *(Mahādruma).*

119. *Badarī, Udumbara, Bāṇa, Vilva, Bakula, Vaṭa, Putrajīva, Pārijāta, Piṇḍī, Palāśa, Pippalī* .

120-121. *Pāṭala, Padmaka, Pīlu, Plakṣa, Pathya, Pika, Priya, Śleṣmātaka,*

शिलीन्ध्रः शाल्मली सर्पमार शम्याकशाबराः ।
देवयोग्या इमे वृक्षा मानुषेभ्यस्तनर्थदाः ॥ १२१ ॥

तस्मात्सर्वप्रयत्नेन न गृह्णीयान्नरालये ।
न वृक्षानयनं कार्यं धनिष्ठादिपञ्चके ॥१२२ ॥

यदेकद्वित्रिजातीयैः भूरुहैः भवनं कृतम् ।
तत्तनोति श्रियं नित्यं बहुभिर्बहुभीतिदम् ॥१२३ ॥

मतान्तरे ॥

एकैव शस्ता श्रीपर्णी शिंशपा सरलोऽर्जुनः ।
हारिद्रकस्तिन्दुकश्च पद्मकः पनसस्तथा ॥१२४ ॥

चन्दनः सुरदारुश्च योज्या नैतेऽन्यसंयुताः ॥१२५ ॥

अथ सन्धिविधिः-

[37]मूले मूलं न युञ्जियादग्रेणाग्रं च दारुणः ।
न पुराणैः नवमथो मूलं याम्येऽपरे शुभम् ॥१२६ ॥

ऊर्ध्वद्रव्येष्वधोमूलं पार्श्वद्रव्येषु मध्यतः ।
शायिते स्यादधोमूलमग्रमूर्ध्वे प्रयोजयेत् ॥१२७ ॥

चतुष्ट्यां नैर्ऋते मूले कुर्यादग्रद्वयं शिवे ।
न सन्धिः स्तम्भयोर्मध्ये ब्रह्मस्थानेऽपि तं त्यजेत् ॥१२८ ॥

एकस्मिन् पंक्तिसन्धाने सन्धिरेकाकृतिर्भवेत् ।
उपर्युपरि चैवं स्याद्विपरीते विपत्करम् ॥१२९ ॥

37. Similar verses are found in the Mayamata Part I ch. 17 v. 9 onward.

Saptaparṇa, Śirīṣa, Sarala, Śiva, Śilīndhra, Śālmalī, Sarpamāra, Śamī, Ākaśābarā– These trees are most suitable for Gods but disastrous for men.

So, with all efforts, these trees should not be brought for human dwellings.

122. On the constellation of *Dhaniṣṭhā*[1] and other five stars, collection of the wood should not be done.

123. If the house is built with one, two or three types of wood, it is beneficial for ever, if the construction is done with various types of trees, it is dangerous.

According to another opinion:

124. *Śrīparṇī, Śiṁśapā, Sarala, Arjuna, Hāridraka, Tinduka, Padmaka,* as well as *Panasa* are best for construction if they are not joined with each other.

125. *Candana* and *Suradāru* can be joined with one another but not with other types of wood.

Now the rules for assemblage:-

126 The bottom part of a tree should not be joined with the bottom (of another tree), as also the upper part should not be joined with another upper part. The old part should not be assembled with a new one, and it is auspicious if the root part is assembled with the right and other parts of a tree. .

127. One should assemble the upper part with the lower part (of a tree), the side branches with the middle part, the bottom part should be arranged below, and the top above.

128. Of all the four directions, the root part should be joined in the South-West direction *(Śiva)* and the upper two parts in the North East direction. No joints should be done in a pillar and it should also be discarded in the centre (*Brahmasthāna)* .

129. In a single row the joints should be of the same type, from top to bottom. Any deviation will lead to failure.

1. Dhaniṣṭhā, Śatabhiṣā, Pūrvā Uttarabhādrapadā and Revatī.

अन्तरग्रं बहिर्मूलं स्वामिनस्तु विनाशनम्।
द्रव्यविस्तारमध्यस्थं रन्ध्रं शीघ्रविनाशकृत् ॥१३०॥

इति श्री वास्तुमण्डने वास्तुशास्त्रे गृहनिवेशद्वारभूलम्भवृक्षाहरणं सन्ध्यादिलक्षणाध्यायश्चतुर्थः। श्लोकाः ॥१३०॥

(While making the combination)

130. If the top portion is placed at the bottom, and the bottom outside, it causes death of the owner and if there is any hole in the middle of the breadth of the wood, it gets destroyed very soon.

Thus ends the fourth chapter of the Vāstumaṇḍana which comprises housing, door, height of a house, collection of woods and joinery, etc. There are Ślokas 130.

पञ्चमोऽध्यायः

[गृहविन्यासः लक्षणसमुच्चयः]

यस्यां दिशि पुरो द्वारं तां प्राची परिकल्पयेत्।
न्यास ईशादितः कार्यो भोजने शयनेऽन्यथा ॥१ ॥

विवेकविलासेऽपि।

पूर्वादिदिग्विनिर्देशो गृहे द्वार[१]व्यपेक्षया।
भास्करोदयदिक्पूर्वा न विज्ञेया यथा श्रुते ॥२ ॥

पूर्वे द्वारं गृहे कुर्यादास्थानं पृथु चाङ्गनम्।
अग्नौ महानसं धेनुं महिषी व्यञ्जनालयम् ॥३ ॥

याम्ये जलगृहं नृत्यशालां भोजनमन्दिरम्।
नैर्ऋत्ये स्नानसूतानां देहचिन्तापदं बहिः ॥४ ॥

पश्चिमे दीर्घिकास्थानं वायौ स्नेहान्नयोगृहम्।
सौम्ये धनाङ्गनोद्यानस्थानमीशे सुरालयम् ॥५ ॥

मध्ये मुख्यगृहं स्वामि[२]वाञ्छया शयनास्पदम्।
पश्चिमास्या गृहे देवा स्थाप्या दक्षिणतोमुखः ॥६ ॥

याम्योत्तरास्या गावः स्युर्न प्राक् पश्चिमतोमुखाः ॥७ ॥

---

१. अपेक्षया in DE

२. वांछना in A

Chapter V

[Gṛhvinyāsaḥ Lakṣaṇasamuccayaḥ]

Now the planning of a house and its peculiarities will be described.

1. The planning (of a house) should be done in such a way that the door should be placed in the Eastern direction. Planning will start from the North-East corner excepting that the bedroom and dining room should not be placed therein.

   This is also quoted in Vivekavilāsa.

2. According to necessity, the door should be planned in the Eastern side of a house, but the Eastern direction will not to be determined by the phenomena of sunrise as it is known.

3. In a house the door should be built facing the East, and there will be a broad courtyard. In the South-East corner (*Agni*) there will be a kitchen, cowshed, and the kitchen for the chief queen.

4. In the South (*Yāmya*) there will be a water reservoir, dancing court, dining hall and in the South-West (*Nairṛtya*)[1] there will be bathroom for children and the place for the care of the body.

5. The site for ponds will be in the West and in the North-East (*Vāyu*) corner the storage for rice and oil will be constructed. In the North (*Saumya*) there will be the treasury and garden; the temple should be in the North-East (*Īśa*) corner.

6. The main room will be in the centre position and it can be used as the master's bedroom, if one wishes so. In a West-facing house, the God should be kept facing towards South.

7. The cow-shed will face either towards South or North, never towards East or West.

1. Nairṛtya is the direction of Nirṛti (South-West).

वीक्षः ।

वामाङ्गे वस्त्रशस्यार्थं देवार्चाभेषजालयम् ।
दक्षिणे दीप[३]नयानतोयोच्छिष्टपदं न्यसेत् ॥८ ॥

अथ राजगृहविन्यासः ॥

पुरादौ त्रिचतुर्थांशे कारयेत् राजमन्दिरम् ।
पश्चिमे सौम्यतो वाऽपि तत्तु दुर्गेषु भूवशात् ॥९ ॥

अपराजिते ॥

एकद्वित्रिसहस्रैस्तु हस्तैः राजगृहं त्रिधा ।
तुङ्गराजगृहं रम्यं मन्दिरोद्यानदीर्घिकाः ॥१० ॥

त्रिप्राकारं सपरिखं स्याच्चतुर्गोपुरं वरम् ।
पूर्वास्यं दक्षिणास्यं वा नोदक् प्रत्यग्दिशामुखम् ॥११ ॥

एकाशीति पदे क्षेत्रे मध्ये ब्रह्मपदेऽकंणम् ।
मण्डपं वा न्यसेद्द्रव्य[४]माये द्वारं गृहं सभा ॥१२ ॥

विवस्वत्यभिषेकार्हं मित्रे मुख्यगृहं न्यसेत् ।
पृथ्वीधरे सभामापे भाण्डागारं प्रकारयेत् ॥१३ ॥

आपवत्सेऽम्बरागारं सावित्रे भोजनास्यादम् ।
कुर्यात्सवितरि श्रेष्ठं सव्यं जनमहानसम् ॥१४ ॥

इन्द्रे राजाम्बिकागेहमिन्द्रराज [५]उपस्करम् ।
रुद्र[६]व्यये [७]महिष्याश्च राजस्त्रीणां गृहा अपि ॥१५ ॥

३. मंयान – in A
४. Here आय denotes the place for Aryamâ
५. पुरस्करम् in BCDE
६. द्वये in A
७. महिषश्व in A

After Examination *(Vīkṣya)*

8. On the left side of a house there will be the dressing room, granary, temple and medicinal room. On the right side the room for lighting and other accessories should be made.

Now the planning of a King's palace

9. The royal palace should be erected in the front part of the city occupying three-fourths of the area. In a fort, according to the nature of the soil, one should construct a palace either in the West or in the North

In the Aparājitapṛcchā

10. According to the measurement of 1, 2 and 3 thousand hands, the King's palace may be of three types. The royal palace will be elevated, consisting of the temple, garden and lakes.

11. The best palace will be adorned with three ramparts, a moat and four *Gopuras* (main gates). It will face either the East or South, but never the West or North.

12. If the land is divided into 81 *Pādas,* the central part should be drawn as *Brahmapada.* In the approach (*Āya*) there shall be gateways and pavilions.

13. The coronation hall will be on the *Vivasvata* (South) and the main rooms on the *Mitrasthāna* (Western side). The halls should be on the *Pṛthvīdhara* and the treasury (*Bhāṇḍāgāra*) on the site of *Āpa.*

14. *Ambarāgāra* - the sky gazing room [2] - is on the *āpavatsa* (North East side) and the dining hall is on the *Sāvitra* (South). The best one on the East (*Savitari*) and the community kitchen should be placed on the left (*Savya*).

15. On the *Indra* (East) and *Indrarāja* (South-West), the houses of the King as well as the Queen Mother will be built, and on the *Rudra* (North-West) the house of the Queen and other women of the royal palace, related to the King, will be made.

---

2 At that period, there seems to be a particular room which was used to gaze the sky and *Rana Kumbha* was specially interested in that and a hanging room was found in the palace of *Kumbhalgarh.*

ईशे सुरालयं याम्याननं वा पश्चिमामुखम्।
पराङ्मुखं तु पर्जन्ये राज्याधिकरणं न्यसेत्॥१६॥

जये श्रीकरणानेकाभ्यासमण्डपदीर्घिका।
शक्रकणं शास्त्रगृहं सूर्ये व्ययगृहाङ्गणे ॥१७॥

सत्ये पराङ्मुखा धर्माधिकाराध्ययनालये।
भृशेऽन्नगेहं व्यापारं व्योम्नि मुख्यं महानसम्॥१८॥

वह्नौ पक्वान्नं गोस्थानं पुष्णि सभ्यासनालयम्।
वितथे वर्मबल्ल[बल्य?]रायुधानां भोजनस्य च॥१९॥

गृहक्षतेऽकंणं कुर्याद्रक्षकाणां च संश्रयम्।
यमे सेनेक्षणावसं गन्धर्वे रतिनृत्ययोः॥२०॥

भृङ्गे [८]रध्वानथ मृगे देहचिन्ता पदं बहिः।
पित्र्ये स्नानालयं द्यूतं द्वास्थे सलिलकेलयः॥२१॥

यद्वा युद्धालोकनार्थं [९]मिदं गजसमोच्छ्रयम्।
नानायुद्धगृहं तत्र प्रकुर्वीत पराङ्मुखम्॥२२॥

सुग्रीवे मल्लयुद्धार्हं पुष्पदन्ते खलूरिणाम्[काम्]।
वरुणे युवराजस्याऽसुरे [१०]धान्यञ्जनालयाः॥२३॥

शोषे [११]शस्त्रविषस्त्रीणां रोगेऽन्तर्वशिकौषधम्।
वायौ खरोष्ट्रान्नागे तु धात्री सैरन्ध्रिदीर्घिकाः॥२४॥

---

८. रथ- in E

९. मिहं in A

१०. धान्येन्द्रजालयोः in A

११. शास्त्र- in B

16. The temple should be built on the *Īśa* (North-East) and it will face either South or West. In the place of *Parjanya* the royal court should be built, which will face West, having its face on the back.

17. In the *Jaya,* the place for the clerical community, hall for practice, pavilion, water tanks, in the *Śakra,* the painting gallery and the room for teaching and in the *Sūrya* the place for disbursement on the courtyard of the palace should be built.

18. In the *Satya,* schools and the legal court will be built facing back to back. On the *Bhṛśa,* the storage room for business affairs and on the *Vyoma* the main kitchen will be placed.

19. On the *Vahni* - the room for cooked food and cowshed, on the *Puṣṇī* the meeting room, on the *Vitatha* - the room for preserving armour, spears and other weapons as well as the dining room will be constructed.

20. The painting room as well as the place for guards or sentinels should be built on the *Gṛhakṣata.* On the *Yama,* the watch tower for observation of the troops and the pleasure room for dancers on the *Gandharva* should be constructed.

21. In the *Bhṛṅga* there will be a road, and following it there will be a room for diseased persons (*Dehacintāpada*) outside *Mṛga.* There will be a bathing room and the place for playing dice in the *Pitṛsthāna,* and the place for water sports in *Dvāstha* (*Dauvārika*).

22. Otherwise this palace should be built as high as an elephant to watch the battlefield or behind this, one room for the rehearsal of the battle can be built.

23. The wrestling place will be on the *Sugrīva* and on *Puṣpadanta* there will be the parade place for military exercise. For the *Varuṇa* prince's house, in the *Asura* granary and dressing room for women should be placed.

24. Weapons and poison for emergency use of the seraglio in the *Śoṣa,* rooms for the keeper of the seraglio in the *Roga,* the stable for donkeys and camels in the *Vāyu* and the pond for *Dhātrī* and *Sairandhrī* in the *Nāga* should be erected.

मुख्ये कन्यागृहं कुर्याद्भल्लाटे श्वेतभेषजम्।
सोमे संवाहिकां शैले मलस्थानं रजस्वला: ॥२५॥

अदितौ स्नानसूतानां दित्यामुष्णाम्बुमर्दने।
पूर्वेऽकणं सभास्थानं पार्श्वयुग्मे बलालयम् ॥२६॥

राज्ञां विशेषत: शक्रे प्रयुक्तं द्वारमुत्तमम्।
त्रिपञ्चभूमिकं मुख्ये योजयेद्वा गृहक्षते ॥२७॥

पुष्पदन्ते च भल्लाटे द्वारं नीचतलान्वितम्।
नृपचित्तवशाद्धवारं विमानानि निवारणम् ॥२८॥

स्त्रीणां निवासं शयनं कुड्यमन्यञ्च कारयेत्।
अश्वशाला तु वामाङ्गे सौम्या स्याद्द्विवगुणान्तरे ॥२९॥

हस्तै: शतेनाशीत्या वा षष्ट्या वाप्यायता त्रिधा।
तिथि विश्वशिवव्यासा क्रमादुच्चारसान्तकम् ॥३०॥

याम्योत्तरास्या अश्वा: स्यु: स्थानं हस्तद्वयोदयम्।
गजशाला दक्षिणें(ऽ)गे शुभा चतुर्गुणेन्तरे ॥३१॥

सप्ताष्टनवहस्तोच्चा: शालास्तम्भा गतत्वच:।
गजानां प्राङमुखी श्रेणी स्थाप्या वा दक्षिणानना ॥३२॥

श्री। इति श्रीसूत्रधारमण्डनविरचिते वास्तुशास्त्रे वास्तुमण्डने गृहविन्यासाध्याय: पंचम: ॥ ५ ॥ श्री।

25. The chamber of the girls in the *Mukhya* and the white medicinal herbs in the *Bhallāṭa* should be kept. In the *Soma,* the room for shampooing and in the *Śaila* toilets and confinement room for women are to be built.

26. In the *Aditi* there will be bathing place for children and in the *Diti* there will be place for massage and hot water. In the East there will be the drawing room, place for meeting and on both the sides there will be room for wrestling.

27. For a King's house the best type of door is to be erected, especially in the direction of *Śakra.* Three or five storied buildings are to be built either in *Mukhya* or *Gṛhakṣata.*

28. On the *Puṣpadanta* or *Bhallāṭa,* the door should be erected on the lower storey. According to the desire of the King the door and the edifices are not to be erected.

29. Residential places of women, bedrooms, walls, are to be constructed. Stable for horses is to be erected on the left side and it is auspicious if placed in double intermediate space (*Dviguṇāntara*).

30. These will be of three types, 100, 80 or 60 hands in length. The width will serially be 15, 13, 11 and may end in 9 hands.

31. The horses will stay facing towards the south or north and that place will be raised by two hands. The hall for elephants will be placed on the southern part and it is auspicious if placed at four times distance.

32. The hall will be 7, 8 or 9 hands high and the pillars of the hall will have coating on them. The row of elephants will face either the East or South.

Thus ends the 5th chapter of Vāstumaṇḍana in Vāstuśāstra comprising the arrangement of the house written by Śrī Sūtradhāra Maṇḍana.

षष्ठोऽध्यायः

[शालादि गृहलक्षणम्]

ध्रुवादीनि प्रवक्ष्यामि वासाय पुरवासिनाम्।
शस्तानि निन्दितान्येषां भवन्ति भवनानि च ॥१॥

अलिन्दा द्वित्रिवेदान्तशाले गेहे ध्रुवादिवत्।
मुखे द्वि [१]अधिका कार्या मण्डपस्य च वृद्धये ॥२॥

शालामध्ये द्विषट्दारु [२]एकं कुर्याद्विनापि तम्।
मध्येऽपवरकं [३]वापि फलकैर्दृढकाष्ठजैः ॥३॥

छन्दास्तु षड्जात्युत्पन्ना भेदैर्भिन्ना द्विरष्टभिः।
तैरुक्तं क्रमरूपाद्यै गृहसंख्या ह्यनेकधा ॥ ४ ॥

खण्डपाण्डुवाजिमयतृणपर्णसुपट्टकैः।
उदितः षड्विधः छन्दः प्रयोज्यो गृहकर्मणि ॥ ५ ॥

पट्टछन्दे यथा भेदाः शालालिन्दादिका मताः।
विपरीता तृणछन्दे षोडशैव प्रकीर्त्तिताः ॥ ६ ॥

हीनोदयाः पाण्डुसंज्ञा वाजिनस्तूच्छ्रयेऽधिकाः।
फलकान्ते चतुर्हस्तः शेषछन्देषु [४]चोच्छ्रयः ॥ ७ ॥

१. त्र्यधिका – in B
२. एवं – in A
३. चापि – in A
४. वोच्छ्रयः – in D.E

Chapter VI

[Śālādi Gṛhlakṣaṇaam]

Description of Ekaśālā and other houses

1. Now I shall relate about the apartment, beginning with *Dhruva* and others for the dwelling of citizens, and whether auspicious or inauspicious.

2. It is universally accepted that 2, 3 and 4 porticos (*Alinda*) will be built in the *Śālā* or a house. Two more porticos are to be added at the entrance, for the extension of the pavilion.

3. In the center of the *Śālā* house, two *ṣaḍdārukas*[1] are to be erected, failing which at least one should be given, and outside it, the central lying- in-chamber should be made with strong wooden planks.

4. The shapes (patterns) or *Chanda* are of six types having sixteen varieties. They have been described according to the serial order, the number of houses being innumerable.

5. *Khaṇḍa, Pāṇḍu, Vāji, Tṛṇa, Parṇa, Paṭṭa*[2] - these six types of designs are to be used in the construction of the houses.

6. The division of *Paṭṭa Chanda* is done according to the *Śālās* and *Alindas*. *Tṛṇacchcnda* is of opposite type and they have sixteen varieties.

7. *Pāṇḍu* type of construction is less in height whereas *Vājicchanda* has greater height. For the remaining varieties of designs, the height will be similar to 4 hands at the extremity of the wooden plank.

---

1. *Ṣaḍdāru*- a kind of wooden structure made of six logs of wood.
2. *Khaṇḍacchanda*- Of the component parts of a human dwelling, which are mainly in the middle of the house.
   Pāṇḍu – Belonging to the storied mansions built in stone.
   Vājicchanda - Stone architecture.
   Tṛṇacchanda - *Śālās* with thatched roof.
   Parṇa - Śālās with roof made of leaves.
   Paṭṭacchanda- *Chādana* type, *Śālās* with *Pāṭana* roof.
   A. P. ch 68. Verse 11 writes pūrṇa for *parṇa.*

अथ प्रस्तारः

यदृच्छया लिख्य गुरून्सर्वस्याधो लघुं लिखेत्।
यथोपरि तथा शेषं भूयः कुर्यादमुविधिम्॥ ८॥
ऊने दद्याद्गुरून्सर्वं लघ्वन्तं प्रस्तारेदिति॥ ९॥

प्रस्तारः।

नष्टे रूपे बुधैः पृष्ठे गुरुरूने समे लघुः।
विषमे चैकमाधाय दलयेत्पुनरेव हि॥ १०॥

नष्टम्।

उद्दिष्टे स्थापयेदङ्कान् क्रमाद् द्विगुणितानधः।
लघुस्थानोद्ध्वैरङ्कैः संख्या स्यादेकमिश्रितैः॥ ११॥

उद्दिष्टम्।

प्रस्तारवर्णैस्तु समानैकाद्यानेक भू लिखेत्।
ततः संकलनं कुर्यादुपात्यस्य निवर्त्तनात्॥ १२॥

एकादिलघुविज्ञानं द्वितीयस्थानतो भवेत्।
मेरुश्च खण्डमेरुश्च सूची तद्वल्लघुक्रिया॥ १३॥

द्वौ भागौ विलिखेत्तिर्यगेककाङ्केन संयुतौ।
अंशवृद्ध्य क्रमेणाधो मेरौ वा खण्डमेरुके॥ १४॥

एकैकाङ्कं लिखेत् पंक्त्यमादावन्ते च सर्वतः।
ऊर्ध्वसङ्कलनेनाधः पंक्तौ पंक्तौ च मध्यतः॥ १५॥

आदौ सर्वगुरौ रूपं प्रान्ते सर्वलघुर्भवेत्।
शेषेष्वेकाद्यलिन्दानां संख्या प्राज्ञैरुदाहृता॥ १६॥

इति मेरुखण्डे मेरुसूचीछन्दः॥

Now Prastāra

8. At one's convenience (free choice) the *Guru*[3] should be drawn and under all *Guru, Laghu* can be arranged. The layout should be the same in the beginning as well as in the end and that order can be repeated.

9. In the layout, the arrangement of the *Guru* will be less and *Laghu* will be at the end.

Prastāra

10. According to the scholars in the form, *Naṣṭa Guru* will be placed at the back and *Laghu* will be less in number and is to be placed at the even place. In case of uneven number, one should count again taking one of them.

Naṣṭa

11. In the form *Uddiṣṭa*, the numbers are to be placed serially and the lower part will be multiplied twice. The numerals coming from *Laghu* will make a number with the addition of one.

Uddiṣṭa

12. Those which are equal to the letters (*Guru, Laghu*) of *Prastāra* should be written in one place. Then the whole thing should be summarized for the completion of the penultimate.

13. The first *Laghu* is known to be placed in the second place. Likewise in the *Meru, Khaṇḍameru* and *Sūcī Laghu* will be placed in the same manner.

14. Two sections are to be drawn slantingly so that they can be joined together. In the *Meru* and *Khaṇḍameru* the section will gradually increase downwards.

Each row will start with one letter and it will end with the same. By arranging the upper line, lower line and the middle line, *Guru* will be placed in the beginning of each line and *Laghu* at the end.

15-16. According to the wise people, at the end the number of the porticos starting from one will emerge in this manner.

This is Merusūcīchanda in Merukhaṇḍa.

3. According to A.P. *Guru* means wall and *Laghu Alinda*. *Prastāra* means permutation combination of *Guru*

इष्टरूपे लघून्पूर्वमन्ते तु विलिखेद्गुरून्।
पूर्ववत्प्रस्तारे तावद्यावद्रूपविपर्ययम्॥ १७॥

लघोः पृष्ठे गुरून्दद्याच्छेषांस्तस्माल्लघून्यसेत्।
पूर्वरूपे तु यावन्तोलास्तावन्तोऽपरेष्वपि॥ १८॥

खण्डप्रस्तार इत्येषपताकाछन्सूचकः।
लघुक्रियाङ्कसंघात पृथगुपायदर्शितः॥ १९॥

इति खण्डप्रस्तारः।

लघुस्थाने गृहमुखादलिन्दं सृष्टितो न्यसेत्।
तत्पर्यायाः क्षणे मुखाःपदेऽलिन्दे लघुस्तथा॥ २०॥

चतुर्गुरूणां प्रस्तारे एकशालानि षोडश।
ध्रुवादीनि गृहाणि स्युस्तेभ्यो वेदोत्तरं शतम्॥ २१॥

प्रस्तारो रूपभेदो स्याद्गृहाणि षोडशैव हि।
तेषु मन्वङ्कदिग्विश्वपञ्चमं तु परित्यजेत्॥ २२॥

तेभ्यः षोडशतश्चैकशालानि सयुगांशतम्।
एकैकस्य सहस्रं तु पुनरष्टौ तथैकतः॥ २३॥

द्वापञ्चाशद्द्विवशालानामेकैकस्य क्रमेण च।
[५]द्विसहस्रमिता वृद्धिः पुनरष्टौ तथैकतः॥ २४॥

द्वासप्ततिस्त्रिशालानि त्रीणि त्रीणि क्रमात्ततः।
सहस्राणि भवन्त्येवं तथैवाष्टाष्ट चैकतः॥ २५॥

५. Comp A.P ch 93.V 22-23

17. In the desired form, *Laghu* is to be drawn first and *Guru* will be drawn at the end. When change is desired, the previous method will be applied in the *Prastāra*.

18. *Guru* will come after *Laghu* but *Laghu* will come at the end. In the previous form, as many as *Laghu* forms desired will be placed, and in others the same will follow.

19. *Khaṇḍaprastāra* is indicative of *Patākā Chanda*. The multitude of placing of *Laghu* (short) numerals has been shown in a different manner.

Thus ends the Khaṇḍaprastāra.

20. From the beginning of the construction of the house, *Alinda* should be placed in the place of *Laghu*; alternatively the same procedure will be followed in the centre, and the same placement will be followed by placing *Laghu* for *Alinda*.

21. There are sixteen types of *Ekaśālā* houses in the *Prastāra* of four Gurus. *Dhruva* and other houses will have hundred and four varieties.

22. These houses will be sixteen in number according to the form of *Prastāra*. Among them fourteenth (*Manu*), ninth (*Aṅka*), tenth (*Dik*), thirteenth (*Viśva*) and fifth houses should be discarded.

23. From those 16 types of *Ekaśālā* houses, one hundred and four varieties will come up. Each of them will have one thousand varieties again from each one of them, eight varieties will come up.

24. Of the 52 varieties of *Dviśālā* constructions, gradually each one of them will have 2000 varieties and again there will be eight varieties from each one.

25. 72 varieties of *Triśālās* are to be increased serially by three. In this way, the varieties will be increased up to 1000, likewise each one of them will have eight varieties.

चतु:शाल[६]गृहाणि हि षट्पञ्चाशं शतद्वयम्।
वृद्धिर्वेदसहस्राणां पूर्ववत्पु[७]नरष्ट च॥ २६॥

कोट्येका तिथिलक्षाणि सहस्राणि युगाष्टं च।
तेषां गृहाणां संख्या तु प्रोक्ता श्रीविश्वकर्मणा॥ २७॥

एकदित्रिचतु:शालं गृहं प्रस्तारतो भवेत्।
पञ्चादिदशशालान्तं तेषां संयोगतो मिथ:॥ २८॥

गृहाणां पञ्चशालानां षड्विधा योजना मता।
यथा।
पञ्चशालं भवेद्योगाच्चतु:शालैकशालयो:॥ २९॥

त्रिशालयुग्मशालाभ्यां द्व्येकशालत्रिशालत:।
द्विद्विशालैकशालेन द्व्येकशालाद्विशालत:॥ ३०॥

योगात्पञ्चैकशालानां तत्षोढैवं पराण्यपि।
नवधा रसशालानां सप्तशाले शिवोन्मिता॥ ३१॥

अष्टशाले तिथिमिता नवशालेऽष्टभूमिता(का:)।
योजना दशशालानां त्रयोविंशतिधा मता॥३२॥

यन्नाम जन्मभादन्यत्तद्वद्धै[८]ईष्टत: कृतम्।
नृपालोके गृहे ग्रामे तेन चिन्त्यं शुभाशुभम्॥ ३३॥

गढदुर्गपुरग्रामनामानि विविधान्यपि।
कृतानि विबुधैर्बुद्ध्या तथा भवतु वेश्मनि॥ ३४॥

---

६. गृहाणां in ACDE
७. पुनरेव च in D, E
८. हर्षत: in B

26. *Catuḥśālā* type of houses will have 256 varieties. The variety may increase up to 1000, and like the previous one, each of them may have eight varieties again.

27. According to *Viśvakarmā* the number of *Śālā* houses will be one *Crore*, fifteen *lakh* and forty eight thousand.

28. One, two, three, four *Śālā* houses can be constructed through the *Prastāra* principle. The principle of combination (of one to four *Śālā* houses) will apply for houses from the fifth to tenth. *Śālā* houses or the mutual combination of these *Śālā* houses will give rise to the fifth to tenth *Śālā* houses.

Such as

29. By the addition of *Catuḥśālā* and *Ekaśālā* one form of *Pañcaśālā* house will be formed.

Pañcaśālā type of houses will have six ways of formation. Other combination[4] will be of *Triśālā* and *Dviśālā,* two *Ekaśālās* and one *Triśālā,* two *Dviśālās* and one *Ekaśālā,* three *Ekaśālās* and one *Dviśālā* or five *Ekaśālās.*

30-31. Likewise there will be combinations for six *Śālā* houses and others. There will be nine ways of combinations for six *Śālā* houses and eleven ways for *Saptaśālā.*

32. *Aṣṭaśālā* houses will have 15 types of combination and *Navaśālā* houses will have 8 combinations. Twenty three varieties of combination are given for the application of *Daśaśālā.*

33. The name which is other than the birth name acquired by the birth star is kept for welfare. The auspicious and inauspicious characters should be determined by this method for the King's palace, house and village.

34. As the names of the moat, fort, city, village etc have been named differently by the wise men after consideration, similarly the names of the dwelling places will be named.

---

4. 1. 4 *Śālā + 1 Ekaśālā* 2. 3 *Śālā+ 1 Dviśālā*
3. 3 *Śālā + 2 Ekaśālās* 4. 2 *Dviśālā + 1 Ekaśālā*
5. *1 Dviśālā+ 3 Ekaśālā* 6. 5 *Ekaśālās*

लोकशास्त्रविरुद्धानि [९]नामानि परिवर्जयेत्।
दशरुद्रार्कसूर्यैश्च [१०]गुरुभिर्लघुकल्पना॥ ३५॥
एकद्वित्रिचतु:शाले क्रमेणोक्ता स्वयम्भुवा।
अधिकान्याद्यरूपाणि प्रस्तारस्य परित्यजेत्॥ ३६॥
यद्विश्वकर्मणो वाक्यं भेदैर्भिन्नास्तु षोडश।
प्रस्तारस्य त्रयो भेदा: सूचिता विश्वकर्मणा॥ ३७॥
गृहाग्रेऽलिन्दबाहुल्यात् पूर्वरूपाण्यतस्त्यजेत्।
एको भेदो गृहोत्पत्ते: सहस्रादि द्वितीयक:॥ ३८॥
एकैकस्य तथैवाष्टाविति भेदास्त्रयो मता:।
धान्याद्यष्टौ समा[११]न्यग्रे पुन[११]र्लघुयुतानि च॥ ३९॥
तेषामलिन्दसंयोगादेकैकस्याष्टकं भवेत्॥ ४०॥

अथ एक शालानि॥

ध्रुवं धान्यं जयं नन्दं खरं कान्तं [१२]मनोहरम्।
सुमुखं दुर्मुखं क्रूरं [१३]सुपक्षं धनदं क्षयम्॥ ४१॥
आक्रन्दं विपुलं चैव विजयं नामवत्फलम्।
खरं च दुर्मुखं क्रूरं क्षयमाक्रन्दकं त्यजेत्॥ ४२॥
इति ध्रुवादीनि॥
धान्याद्येकैकान्तरेऽष्टमुखालिन्दयुतानि चेत्।
तदा रम्यं श्रीधरं च मुदितं वर्धमानकम्॥ ४३॥
करालं च सुनाभं च ध्वाक्षं समृद्धिमित्यपि।
इति रम्यादीनि॥

---

९. नानापि in B. C, D, E
१०. प्रस्तृतैलिदकल्पना in A
११. न्य ग्रै तु न° in A
१२. मनोरमम् in A
१३. विपक्षं, in A

35. Those names which are against popular usages and the scriptures should be discarded. In place of 10, 11 (*Rudra*) and 12 (*Sūrya*)[5], which are *Guru*, the *Laghu* can be inserted therein.

36. It has been said by Svayaṁbhuva that in the place of one, two, three and four *Śālā* coming serially, the excess of the first form in a *Prastāra* should be given up.

37. Though according to the sayings of Visvakarmā there are sixteen different types of divisions, three divisions of *Prastāra* are indicated by Viśvakarmā.

38. Previous forms should be discarded if there are extra *Alindas* in front of the house. The construction of the house starts from single form but from the second there may be 1000 forms.

39. For each of the three divisions there will be eight varieties. The front part of the eight varieties of *Dhānya* and others will be equal; again they will be joined with *Laghu*.

40. With the addition of *Alindas,* each will have eight varieties again.

Now the varieties of Ekaśālā

41-42. *Dhruva, Dhānya, Jaya, Nanda, Khara, Kānta, Manohara, Sumukha, Durmukha, Krūra, Supakṣa, Dhanada, Kṣaya, Ākranda, Vipula, Vijaya-* give results true to the meaning of their names, so one should discard *Khara, Durmukha, Krūra, Kṣaya,* and *Ākranda.*

Thus ends Dhruvā etc.

If *Dhānya* and other varieties are endowed with *Alindas* in eight directions at intervals, then these will be termed as *Ramya, Śrīdhara, Mudita, Vardhamānaka, Karāla, Sunābha, Dhvāṁkṣa* and *Samṛddhi.*

Thus ends Ramya etc.

5. Here *Arka* and *Sūrya* indicate number 12.

ध्रुवादिमध्ये षड्दारु सुन्दरादीनि षोडश॥ ४४॥

सुन्दरं वरदं भद्रं प्रमोदं विमुखं शिवम्।
सर्वलाभं विशालं च विलक्षमशुभं ध्वजम्॥ ४५॥
उद्योतं भीषणं शून्यमजितं कुलनन्दनम्॥ ४६॥

इति सुन्दरादीनि॥

पूर्वालिन्द [१४] युतोऽष्टेषु पुनः षड्दारुके सति।
हंसं सुलक्षणं सौम्यं हयं भावुकमुत्तमम्॥ ४७॥

रुचिरं सन्ततं क्षेममाक्षेपमुच्छ्रितं वृषम्।
उच्छन्नं व्ययमानन्दं सुनन्दं चेति षोडश॥ ४८॥

इति हंसादीनि॥

ध्रुवादिमध्येऽपवर्कोऽलङ्कृतादीनि षोडश।
अलङ्कृतमलङ्कारं रमणं [१५]पूर्वमीश्वरम्॥ ४९॥

पुण्यं सगर्भं कलशं दुर्गतं [१६]रक्तमीप्सितम्।
भद्रकं वञ्चितं दीनं विभवं कामदं तथा।। ५०॥

इत्यलङ्कृतादीनि।

एतेषु चापवर्कस्य मध्ये षड्दारुके सति।
प्रभवं भावितं रुक्मं तिलकं क्रीडनं मुखम्॥ ५१॥

यशोदं कुमुदं कालं भासुरं भूषणं तथा।
वसुन्धरं धान्यहरं कुपितं चित्तवृद्धिदम्॥
कुलोदयं च विज्ञेयं गुणाभिधानं शाश्वतम्॥५२॥

१४. युतष्ब्वेषु in A

१५. पूर्णम् in A

१६. रिक्षम् in A

43-46. Placing a wooden structure known as *Ṣaḍdāruka*, in the *Dhruva* and other *Ekaṣālā* houses, *Sundara* etc. sixteen varieties of houses can be formed. They are *Sundara, Varada, Bhadra, Pramoda, Vimukha, Śiva, Sarvalābha, Viśāla, Vilakṣam, Aśubha, Dhvaja, Uddyota, Bhīṣaṇa, Śūnya, Ajita,* and *Kulanandana.*

Thus ends Sundara etc.

47-48. If eight *Śālās* with *Alindas* in front again have *Ṣaḍdāruka* structure, then another sixteen varieties will be formed. They are *Haṁsa, Sulakṣaṇa, Saumya, Haya, Bhāvuka, Uttama, Rucira, Santata, Kṣema, Ākṣepa, Ucchrita, Vṛṣa, Ucchanna, Vyaya, Ānanda, Sunanda.*

Thus ends Haṁsa etc.

49-50. If *Apavarka* is added to the *Dhruva* type of *Śālā*, sixteen varieties will be formed. They are *Alaṁkṛta, Alaṅkāra, Ramaṇa, Pūrva, Īśvara, Puṇya, Sagarbha, Kalaśa, Durgata, Rakta, Īpsita, Bhadraka, Vancita,* ~*Dīna, Vibhava* as well as *Kāmada.*

Thus ends Alaṅkṛta etc.

If *Ṣaḍdāruka* construction is added to the *Apavarka*, then the following similar varieties will come up. They are *Prabhava, Bhāvita, Rukma, Tilaka, Krīḍana, Mukha, Yaśoda, Kumuda, Kāla, Bhāsura, Bhūṣaṇa, Vasundhara, Dhānyahara, Kupita, Cittavṛddhida, Kulodaya–*

51-52. These are eternal according to their quality.

इति प्रभवादीनि।

अपवर्को द्विषड्दारु मुखेऽलिन्दो यदा भवेत्।
चूडामणि प्रभद्रं च क्षेमे शेखरमुच्छ्रितम्॥ ५३॥

विशालं भूतिदं हृष्टं विरोधं कालपाशतः।
निरामयं सुशालं च रौद्रं मेघं मनोरमम्॥ ५४॥
सुभद्रं चैकशालानामिति वेदोत्तरं शतम्॥५५॥

इति चूडामण्यादीनि॥

अपवर्कस्तु फलकैः कृतं शालान्तरे गृहम्।
दक्षिणे तद्गृहे शस्यं वामपार्श्वे तु योषिताम्॥ ५६॥

[१७]प्रस्तारे लघुसंस्थाने भवनस्य नवांशतः।
शाला स्यादग्निकोणादौ तदा पञ्चादशालयाः॥ ५७॥

ईश्वरं वृषभं चन्द्रं रोगं पापं भयप्रदम्।
नन्दनं खादकं ध्वाक्षं विवृतं विलयं क्षयम्॥ ५८॥
[१८]याम्यं हि विपरीतं च सुभद्रं तिथिसन्मितम्॥ ५९॥

इति एकशालानि॥

१७. प्रस्थाने in B,C,D,E

१८. याम्याहं in A

Thus ends Prabhava etc.

53-55. If the corridors are built in front and the apartments *(apavarka)* are made of two ṣa*ḍdārukas,* then the following sixteen varieties will be formed. They are- *Cūḍāmaṇi, Prabhadra, Kṣema, Śekhara, Ucchrita, Viśāla, Bhūtida, Hṛṣṭa, Virodha, Kālapāśa, Nirāmaya, Suśāla, Raudra, Megha, Manorama, Subhadra.* With these the total of *Ekaśālā* houses will be hundred and four in number.

Thus ends the Cūḍāmaṇi etc.

56. In different apartments, if the inner apartment is to be made of wooden planks (*Phalaka*), the right section of that house is regarded as auspicious and the left part will be suited for women.

57. If the combination with *Laghu* starts from the ninth place of the house, then there will be fifteen apartments starting from the South-East corner (*Agni*) to others.

These fifteen apartments are *Īśvara, Vṛṣabha, Candra, Roga, Pāpa, Bhayaprada, Nandana, Khādaka, Dhvāṁkṣa, Vivṛta, Vilaya, Kṣaya, Yāmya,*

58-59. *Viparīta, Subhadra*– these are according to the order of the lunar days.

Thus ends Ekaśālās

अथ द्विशालानि।

[१९]हस्तिनी महिषी गावी छागली च यथाक्रमम्।
युग्मानि हंस विमलं संज्ञयाष्टाष्ट निर्दिशेत्॥ ६०॥

द्विहंसं च द्वि [२०]चक्राह्वं द्विसारसमथापि वा।
द्वि कोकिलमिति प्रोक्तं हस्तिन्यादि क्रमेण तु॥ ६१॥

चतुरस्त्रं समं कृत्वा त्रिपुटे नवकोष्ठकम्।
मध्यकोष्ठपदं त्यक्तवा शालायुग्मानि चिन्तयेत्॥ ६२॥

दक्षिणस्यां [२१]तदाग्रेय्यां हस्तिन्युत्तरदिङ्मुखाम्।
पितृवारुणसंयोगान्महिषी पूर्वतो मुखा॥ ६३॥

दक्षिणाभिमुखा गावी सोमे रोगे च संस्थिता।
वरुणाभिमुखा शस्ता ऐन्द्रे [२२]रोगे च छागली॥ ६४॥

श्रीधरं च मुखालिन्दे याम्याग्रस्थे जयावहम्।
श्रीजयं प्रदक्षिणास्थे मुखयुग्मे तु कामदम्॥ ६५॥

याम्याग्रमुखतोऽलिन्दे जयन्तं नाम शोभनम्।
प्रदक्षिणेऽलिन्दयुग्मे [२३]विशालमिति निर्दिशेत्॥ ६६॥

अग्रे तृतीयालिन्दे तु जायते सोमसम्भवम्।

---

१९. We find similar verses in A.P ch 93,94

२०. चक्रं च, in D

२१. तथा-in A

२२. रुद्रे च लांगली in B,C,D,E

२३. विलास in A

Now the variety of Dviśālā

60-61. Serially they are *Hastinī*, *Mahiṣī*, *Gāvī* and *Chāgalī*. The pair of white swans etc. should have eight designations. They are two swans (*Haṁsa*), two drakes (*Cakras*) and two cranes (*Sārasa*) and two cuckoos (*Kokilas*). It is known that serially they are for *Hastinī* and others.

62. Equalizing four corners and keeping nine inner *Pādas* (*Koṣṭha*) within a three-fold set up, and a triangle (nine *Pādas*), one should think of a twin apartment, leaving the central chambers.

63. Constructed on the Southern and South East (*Āgneya*) corner of the plot, the *Hastinī* type of house will face the Northern side. The *Mahiṣī* type of house will be constructed on the Western as well as the South-East corner of the plot and it will face the Eastern side.

64. The *Gāvī* type of house will be built on the North and North-West corner and it will face the Southern direction. The *Chāgalī* type of the house will be constructed on the East and North-West corner and it will face the Western side.

65. *Śrīdhara* will have *Alindas* in the front part. *Jayāvaha* will have *Alindas* on the fore part of the South. *Śrījaya* should be placed at the place of circumambulation and *Kāmada* is to be placed on the main pairs.

66. *Jayanta* and *Śobhana Śālās* have *Alindas* on the front part of the South. *Viśāla* type of *Śālā* will have two *Alindas* at the place of circumambulation.

हस्तिनी क्रमगे द्वारे इदं युग्मगृहाष्टकम्॥ ६७॥

एतान्येवान्यसंज्ञाभिर्दिग्भेदान्नामपर्यये।
गजं भीमं पराक्रमं जयन्तं भासुरं तथा॥ ६८॥

[२४]वशिष्ठं च समुद्रं महिषीपृष्ठसम्भवात्।
सुनाभं वर्त्तकं सौम्यं चन्द्रं तेजश्च दीपकम्॥ ६९॥

कुलोद्योतं सुनेत्रं च गावीपृष्ठोद्भवानि हि।
पाशुपतं महाकालं सुतेजस्तेजवर्द्धनम्॥ ७०॥

[२५]वाशवं दशभूतानां रुद्रतेजः समुद्भवम्।
छागलीपृष्ठजातानि गृहान्येतानि निर्दिशेत्॥ ७१॥

इति युग्मगृहद्वात्रिंशद्भेदलक्षणम्।

द्विपञ्चाशद्द्विशालानां लक्षणं वक्ष्यते क्रमात्।
सिद्ध्यर्थं यमसूर्यं च दण्डाख्यं वातसंज्ञकम्॥ ७२॥

चुल्लिकाचप्रमुखादि द्विशालानि प्रचक्षते।
अनेकभेदभिन्नानि [२६]लघुप्रस्तारयोगतः॥ ७३॥

मुषाभेदं क्रमैस्तानि भिन्नाभिन्नक्रमेण च।
तथा निलयकरणं मुषालिन्द सुमार्गतः॥ ७४॥

प्राग्ग्रीवादिविधानेन द्विशालानि [२७]च पर्ययात्।
यथासम्भवमेतानि कथयामि समासतः॥ ७५॥

निर्वाहस्तत्र मुषानामनिर्वाहश्च नामतः।
छन्दतो गुणतो रूपादशुभानि शुभानि च॥ ७६॥

---

२४. बसिष्टं in A
२५. वासनं in B,C,D,E
२६. अलिन्द प्रस्तार in D,E.
२७. विपर्ययात् in A.P

67. *Somasambhava* type of *Śālā* will have a third *Alinda* in the front. According to this order of the door, *Hastinī* will have eight pair of houses.

68-71. According to the difference in directions, they may be known serially by different names. They are *Gaja, Bhīma, Para, Ākrama, Jayanta* as well as *Bhāsura, Vaśiṣṭha, Samudra.* These we get from the back part of *Mahiṣī.* Starting from the back of the *Gāvī* type, we get *Sunābha Varttaka, Saumya, Candra, Teja, Dīpaka, Kulodyota* and *Sunetra* and *Pāśupata, Mahākāla, Sutejaḥ, Tejavardhana, Vāśava* – all these are born out of the prowess of *Rudra* from the elements. These houses are to be shown as coming out of the back of *Chāgalī.* [7]

Thus ends the variety of 32 types of pairs of houses.

Now[8] the characteristics of 52 types of *Dviśālās* are being described serially. *Siddhārtha, Yamasūrya, Daṇḍa, Vāta, Cullī* and *Kāca*- they are the varieties of *Dviśālā* houses.

72-73.L They may be of multiple varieties resulting from the arrangement of *aghuprastāra.*

74 . Gradually the different number of ventilators of different or uniform sizes are to be described, so the house could be built with ventilators, corridors on good roads.

75. As far as possible I shall briefly describe *Dviśālā* according to the position of the *Prāggrīva*[9] etc deviating from customary obsarvance.

76. The alteration of these auspicious and inauspicious character depends on the rhythmical disposition and the designation of the arrangement of Guru. Accomplishment and non-accomplishment of the ventilators are known by their names.

---

7. Aparājitapṛcchā writes : *Hastinī Haṁsasaṁbhūtā Gāvī Sārasasaṁbhavā*
Chāgalī Kokilodbhūtā Mahiṣī Cakrabākajā ch. v
8. Similar Ślokas A.P. ch-94 Pg- 239.
9. *Prāggrīva*- the eastern recess between the cupola and the entablature
Note : See Bṛhatsaṁhitā of Varāhamihira for variety of Dviśālā.

हितार्थाय नरेन्द्रणां [२८]वर्णिनां लिङ्गिनामपि।
हस्तिनी महिषी चापि द्विशाला यत्र वेश्मनि॥ ७७॥

तत्सिद्धार्थमिति ज्ञेयं [२९]वित्तसम्पत्तिकारकम्।
भवेद्गोमहिषीभ्यां तु यम[३०]सूर्यमृतिप्रदम्॥७८॥

दण्डाख्यं छागली गावी शालाभ्यां दण्डभीतिदम्।
वाताख्यं छागली युक्ता महिष्युद्वेग [३१]कारकम्॥७९॥

महिष्यजाभ्यामुद्वेगकरी चुल्लीति नामतः।
काचं करेणुगावीभ्यां सुहृत्प्रीतिविनाशनम्॥८०॥

एकमुषाममुषं च न द्विशालेषु कारयेत्।
अस्याकारं तु चुल्लीं च सर्वभित्तिस्त्रिभिस्तथा॥८१॥

चत्वार्याद्यानि [३२]भिद्यन्ते लघुप्रस्तारयोगतः।
प्रत्येकमेकादशधा मन्दिराण्यभिधानतः॥८२॥

अन्ये चतुर्धा भिद्यन्ते प्रत्येकं द्वे तथान्तिमे।
एकमुषादिको भेदस्तद्बाह्याबाह्यहेतुकः॥८३॥

वसुधारं भवेत्तेषामाद्यं सिद्धार्थकं ततः।
कल्याणकं शाश्वतं च शिवं कामप्रदं तथा॥८४॥

श्रीदशान्तं निष्कलंकं [३३]नीवीसंज्ञं च [३४]पूरकम्॥
सिद्धार्थमनुयायीनि गृहाण्येकादशक्रमात्॥ ८५॥

---

२८. वर्गाणां C वर्णाणां in D,E
२९. चित्त in C,D,E
३०. सूर्प्प in A
३१. कारिका in B, C, D, E
३२. भेद्यन्ते in A
३३. निवि in D, E
३४. पुरुषां in A

For the welfare of the Kings, people of the four castes and of religious sects, *Hastinī* and *Mahiṣī* type of *Dviśālā* should be done in a building. This is known as *Siddhārtha* which bestows wealth and prosperity.

77-78. *Yamasūrya* causes death to the owner of the Go (*Gāvī*),*Mahiṣī* type of houses (*Sālā*).

79. *Daṇḍa* causes fear of punishment to the owner of *Chāgalī* and *Gāvī* type of *Śālā*. *Vāta,* if associated with *Chāgalī* and *Mahiṣī,* causes anxiety.

80. *Cullī* associated with *Mahiṣī* and *Ajā* is the cause of anxiety. The *Kāca* variety associated with female elephant *(Kareṇu)* and *Gāvī* causes loss of friendship.

81. *Dviśālā* type of *Śālā* should not be constructed with one ventilation or without any ventilation. Its shape will be like *Cullī* which will be adorned with three walls.

82. The earlier four types vary according to the arrangement of *Laghu Prastāra*. These are again sub-divided into 11 varieties and they come within the category of temple.

83. Others divide them into four types and each of them into two groups at the end. The variety begins from one ventilation according to their external and internal positions.

84-85. The first of that variety is known as *Vasudhāra*, then *Siddhārtha, Kalyāṇaka, Śāsvata, Śiva, Kāmaprada, Śrīda, Śānta, Niṣkalaṅka, Nīvīsaṁjña, Pūraka*–these eleven types of houses fall under the *Siddhārtha* group.

संहारं यमसूर्यं च कालं [३५]वैवस्वतं यमम्।
करालं विकरालं च कबन्धं मृतकं शवम्॥८६॥

यमसूर्यस्य भेदेन कथितं महिषं तथा।
प्रचण्डचण्डे दण्डाख्यमुद्दण्डं काण्डकोटरे॥८७॥

विग्रहं निग्रहं धूमं निर्धूमं दन्तिदारुणम्।
इत्येकादशभेदास्तु दण्डे दण्डभयप्रदाः॥८८॥

मरुत्पवनवाताख्यमनिलं सप्रभञ्जनम्।
धनाख्यं मोदविध्वंसि प्रलयं कलहं कलिः॥८९॥

कलिशूलञ्च वातस्य भेदा उद्वेगदायकाः।
रोगं चुल्ल्यनलं भस्म चुल्लीभेदचतुष्टयम्॥९०॥

काचस्यानुच्छलङ्काचं कुलघ्नं च विरोधकम्।
द्विपञ्चाश[३६] द्विशालानि नामभेदेन निर्दिशेत्॥९१॥

प्राग्दक्षिणगतेऽलिन्दे वसुधारं धनप्रदम्।
प्राक् पश्चिमे तु सिद्धार्थं सर्वोपद्रववर्जितम्॥९२॥

याम्यापरस्थे कल्याणं शाश्वतं पूर्वसौम्यगे।
शिवं याम्योत्तरेऽलिन्दे [३७]कामदं पश्चिमोत्तरे॥९३॥

मुखे द्वौ पश्चिमे चैकः श्रीपदं सम्प्रदे प्रभोः।
पूर्वयाम्योत्तरेऽलिन्दः शान्तं शान्तिप्रदायकम्॥९४॥

प्राक् पश्चिमोत्तरेऽलिन्दे निष्कलङ्कं समृद्धिकृत्।
याम्यापरोत्तरेऽलिन्दे धनेशं धनवर्धनम्॥९५॥

---

३५. विवस्वतं in A

३६. शालानां नमभेदानि in A

३७. B, C, D, E, omit from v 93d to 95a

Saṁhāra, Yamasūrya, Kāla, Vaivasvata, Yama, Karāla, Vikarāla, Kabandha,

Mṛtaka, Śava, Mahiṣa–these are said to be the divisions of *Yamasūrya* as well as the *Mahiṣī* type. *Pracaṇḍa, Caṇḍa, Daṇḍākhya, Uddaṇḍa, Kāṇḍakoṭara, Vigraha, Nigraha, Dhūma, Nirdhūma, Danti, Dāruṇa* - these are the eleven types of *Daṇḍa* and there is fear of punishment in these types of houses.86-88.

Marut, Pavana, Vātākhya, Anila, Prabhañjana, Dhanākhya, Modavidhvaṁsi, Pralaya, Kalaha, Kali, Kaliśūla– these are the divisions of *Vāta*, which are causes of anxiety.

89-91. The four divisions of *Cullī* are– *Roga, Cullī, Anala,* and *Bhasma,* and the divisions of *Kāca* are *Ucchala, Kāca, Kulaghna* and *Virodha.* In this way 52 types of *Dviśālās* are mentioned here.

92. If there are *Alindas* towards the Eastern and Southern directions, it is called *Vasudhāra* and it bestows wealth. *Siddhārtha,* with *Alindas* to the East and West, is devoid of any trouble.

Kalyāṇa is known to have *Alindas* towards the Southern and Western directions and *Śāśvata* has *Alindas* towards the East and North.

93. *Śiva* has *Alindas* towards the Southern and Northern directions and *Kāmada* has *Alindas* to the West as well as to the North.

94. *Śrīpada* with two *Alindas* in front and one to the West is auspicious for its owner. *Śānta* brings peace in the house with *Alindas* to the East, South and North.

95. *Niṣkalaṅka* brings prosperity, with *Alindas* towards the East, West, and North. *Dhaneśa,* with *Alindas* to the South, West and North brings in more wealth.

मुखे द्वौ सौम्यतश्चैकः कुवेरं वित्तवृद्धिकृत्।
संहारादीनि दिग्भेदादे [३८]भिरेव क्षणैर्विदुः ॥९६॥

रोगं प्राग्याम्यगेऽलिन्दे चुल्ली याम्यापरस्थिते।
अनलं पश्चिमे सौम्ये [३९]भस्माख्यं पूर्वसौम्यगे ॥९७॥

उदङ्मुखाभ्यां मूषाभ्यां काचभेदे [४०]छलं गृहम्।
प्राग्याम्योत्तरगे काचं कुलघ्नं दक्षिणे द्वये ॥९८॥

दक्षिणापरसौम्यस्थे विरोधं स्याद्गृहं क्षणे।
उक्ता [४१]न्येवं द्विपञ्चाशद्द्विशालानि समासतः ॥ ९९ ॥

तथा च॥

द्विशालं शोभनं वेश्मपूर्वोत्तरमुखं सदा।
पूर्वोत्तरास्यं सिद्धार्थं लाङ्गलं सौख्यदायकम् ॥१००॥

मत्स्यपुराणेऽपि।

सिद्धार्थं वर्ज्यं वर्ज्यानि द्विशालानि सदा बुधैः ॥१०१॥

इति द्विशालानि॥

अथ त्रिशालानि

चतुर्गुरूणां प्रस्तारे त्रिशालानि ध्रुवादिवत्।
गृहे सप्तदशे कार्यं चतुर्दिक्षु लघुद्वयम्॥ १०२॥

अष्टादशे त्रिशाले तु मध्ये षट्दारुकं न्यसेत्।
पूर्वादिद्वारभेदेन त्रिशालानि द्विसप्ततिः॥ १०३॥

---

३८. भिरैव in A, B
३९. तस्याक्षं in B, E
४०. बलं in A
४१. न्येकं in A, C, D, E

96. *Kuvera* with two *Alindas* in front and another towards the North increases one's property. *Saṁhāra* and other types are known by designation in accordance with place and direction.

97. *Roga* has *Alindas* to the East and South, *Cullī* has *Alindas* to the South and West. *Anala* has *Alindas* to the West and North and *Bhasma* has *Alindas* to the East and North.

98. (A *Dviśālā* house named) *Chala* of *Kāca* variety has two ventilators on the North. If the ventilators are on the Eastern, Southern and Northern sides, it is known as *Kāca*, and if two ventilators are on the South, it is known as *Kulaghna*.

99. *Virodha* type of house is designated to have *Alindas* towards the Southern and Northern direction In this way, 52 types of *Dviśālā* houses are precisely described.

Then again

100. The *Dviśālā* house is always pleasant if it faces towards the East and North. *Siddhārtha* as well as *Lāṅgala* bring happiness if they face East and North.

It has been also said in the Matsyapurāṇa

101. Of the *Siddhārtha* variety of *Dviśālā* which are not appreciable, (they) are to be discarded by the learned persons.

Thus ends the variety of Dviśālā

Now[10] *Triśālās*

102. Like *Dhruva* and others, *Triśālā* is always built on the *Prastāra* of four *Gurus*. In the seventeenth type of house, two *Laghus* will be made in four directions.

On the central part of the eighteenth type of *Triśālā ṣaḍdāru* should be inserted.

103. According to the placing of the doors starting from the East, the *Triśālā* may be of seventy-two types.

---

10. A. P. ch 97 mentions 79 *triśālā* houses.

कालदण्डं तु पूर्वास्यं सुनाभं दक्षिणामुखम्।
जयन्तमाद्यं वारुण्यां सौभाग्यं रिपुमर्दनम् ॥१०४॥

[४२]कालदण्डं प्रचण्डं च श्रीजयं च धनावहम्।
मायासद्मं महाकान्तं मनोहररमाप्रिये ॥१०५॥

[४३]विमुख्यं क्रोधनाख्यं च स्वामिभक्तं धनेश्वरम्।
कालाख्यं विकरालं जनप्रियं सिद्धिकामदम् ॥१०६॥

प्रीतिमुखा सर्वलाभमुद्भवं रसदारुणम्।
सुनाभं च शुभं शान्तं जयं च विभवोद्भवम् ॥१०७॥

कुवेरं यक्षपक्षाख्यं विवक्त्रं कलिसौम्यके।
सुवक्त्रं क्षयं कालाख्यं विपुलं राज्यवर्धनम् ॥१०८॥

आत्मकं दारुणाख्यं च सुनाभादीन्यष्टादश।
जयन्तं भासुरं भीमं श्रीजयं [४४]च विशालकम् ॥१०९॥

शस्तं च शाश्वतं सारं दुर्दयं क्रोधनं तथा।
सौख्यं पुष्टं च जानीयादभयं घोरमीश्वरम् ॥११०॥

आनन्दं शुभपत्रं चोत्तुंगमष्टादशं मतम्।
रिपुमर्दनं सुनेत्रं बलं चाति[४५]बलं तथा ॥१११॥

अशुभं च शिवं सर्वात्मकं [४६]विशालमित्यपि।
शिवं सर्वालवैशाद्वं क्रूरं च श्रीकरं प्रभम् ॥११२॥

---

४२. Similar verses in A.P ch93 8–9

४३. B, C, D, E विमुखं

४४. A वा

४५. B, C, D, E बलाशुभम्

४६. B, C, D, E वैशालम्

104. *Kāladaṇḍa* is facing the East, *Sunābha* faces the South, *Jayanta* faces the West and *Ripumardana* faces the North.

105-107a. *Kāladaṇḍa, Pracaṇḍa, Śrījaya, Dhanāvaha, Māyāsadma, Mahākānta, Manohara, Ramāpriya, Vimukhya, Krodhanākhya, Svāmibhakta, Dhaneśvara, Kāla, Vikarāla, Janapriya, Siddhikāmada, Prītimukha* bestow benefits and *Udbhava* is full of awful potentialities.

107b-109a. Eighteen types of *Sunābhas* are *Sunābha, Śubha, Śānta, Jaya, Vibhava, Udbhava, Kuvera, Yakṣa, Pakṣa, Vivaktra, Kalisaumya, Suvaktra, Kṣaya, Kālākhya, Vipula, Rājyavardhana, Ātmaka, Dāruṅa.*

109b-111a. Eighteen varieties of *Jayanta* are *Jayanta, Bhāsura, Bhīma, Śrījaya, Viśālaka, Śasta, Śāśvata, Sāra, Durdaya, Krodhana, Saukhya, Puṣṭa, A bhaya, Ghora, Īśvara, Ānanda, Śubhapatra, Uttunga.*

111b-112. Eighteen varieties of *Ripumardanas* are *Ripumardana, Sunetra, Bala, Atibala, Aśubha, Śiva, Sarvātmaka, Viśāla, Śiva, Sarvālavai, Krūra, Śrīkara, Prabhu.*

कालनेत्रं विनेत्रं लक्ष्मीधरं श्रियः पतिः।
महाजयं जयाख्यं चाष्टादशं नामवत्फलम् ॥११३॥

यथा युग्मोद्भवा भेदाः स्युर्द्विशालत्रिशालयोः।
तथा युक्त्या विधातव्याश्चतुःशालगृहेष्वपि ॥११४॥

मत्स्यपुराणे

सौम्यशालाविहीनं यत्त्रिशालं धन्यं हि तत्।
क्षेमवृद्धिकरं नृणां सर्वव्याधिभयापहम् ॥११५॥

शालया पूर्वया हीनं [४७]सुक्षेत्रमिति विश्रुतम्।
धन्यं यशस्यमायुष्यं शोकमोहविनाशनम् ॥११६॥

चुल्ली तु याम्यया हीनं त्रिशालं चैव [क] शालया।
कुलक्षयकरं नृणां सर्वव्याधिभयावहम् ॥११७॥

हीनं पश्चिमया यच्च पक्षघ्नं नाम विश्रुतम्।
मित्रबन्धुसुतान् हन्ति तथा सर्वभयङ्करम् ॥११८॥

इति त्रिशालानि।

अथ चतुःशालानि॥

प्रस्तारेऽष्टगुरूद्भूते सुनाभादीनि नामतः।
चतुःशालगृहाणि स्युः षट्पञ्चाशं शतद्वयम् ॥११९॥

इति श्रीसूत्रधारमण्डनविरचिते [४८]वास्तुशास्त्रे वास्तुमण्डन शालादिगृहलक्षणोऽध्यायः षष्ठः॥ श्लोकाः॥११९॥

---

४७ B, C, D, E omit V 116 bed, and v II7a

४८ वास्तु मण्डने वास्तुशास्त्र in BCDE

113. *Kālanetra, Vinetra, Lakṣmīdhara* – the husband of *Śrī, Mahājaya, Jaya* –they give results according to their names.

114. As the twin varieties of *Dviśālā* and *Triśālā* has been found, likewise for the *Catuśśālā* house also, the same principle should be followed.

In the Matsyapurāṇa

115. *Triśālā* without a hall in the Northern direction is known as *Dhanyaka*. It increases the prosperity of the King and removes all sorts of sorrows and misery.

116. (*Triśālā*) without a hall in the Eastern side, is known as *Sukṣetra*. It gives prosperity, fame and long life and removes all sorts of sorrows and misery.

117. *Cullī* type of *Triśālā* is devoid of one *Śālā* to the South. It destroys the family of the King by bringing all sorts of dangerous diseases.

118 *Triśālā* without a hall in the West is known as *Pakṣaghna*. It destroys progenies and friends and brings all sorts of evils.

Thus ends the variety of Triśālā.

Now the varieties of *Catuśśālā* :

119. *Sunābha* and other *Catuśśālā* houses have been built from the *Prastāra* of eight *Gurus*. They are two hundred and fifty six in number.

Thus ends the sixth chapter of Vāstumaṇḍana written by Maṇḍana Sūtradhāra. It describes Ekaśālā and other houses.

सप्तमोऽध्यायः

[दूषणभूषणानि]

गृहारम्भे गेहकर्तुर्विनाशः शिल्पिसम्भ्रमे।
स्तम्भस्कन्धाच्च्युते कुम्भे शिरोरोगं विनिर्दिशेत् ॥१॥

कुम्भापहारे सर्वस्य कुलस्यापि क्षयो भवेत्।
मृत्युः स्थानाच्च्युते कुम्भे स्तम्भे भग्ने तथा विदुः ॥२॥

करसंख्याविनाशे तु नाशं गृहपतेर्विदुः।
बीजौषधिविहीने तु भूतेभ्यो भयमादिशेत् ॥३॥

स्तम्भाः भयरङ्कराः पूर्वं योजिता अप्रदक्षिणाः।
हीनाधिकां गतौ वास्तौ सर्वथा तु विवर्जयेत् ॥४॥

प्रासादो देवराज्ञो वै त्यजे[१]त्प्रासादजं गृहम्।
सिंहकर्णकपोताली सिंहसम्बरणध्वजान् ॥५॥

कपिशीर्षाणि कलशं दण्डमामलसारकम्।
स्तम्भं सभद्रं वाष्टास्रं वृत्तं सरूप[२]पल्लवम् ॥६॥

कुम्भी सभद्राभरणं पल्लवाद्यं च किन्नरान्।
पत्रशीर्षं कुमाराढ्यं रूपं लेपविनिर्मितम् ॥

प्राग्भू कुम्भी विना शैलं न कुर्याद्वर्णवेश्मसु ॥७॥

---

१. देव राज्ञोस्या त्यजेत् in A
देव राजोस्तु त्यजेत् in C

Chapter VII

[Duṣṇabhūṣaṇāni]

Now the defects and decorations of a construction are to be described

1. At the time of the building construction, any confusion amongst architects may lead to the death of the owner. If a pitcher falls from the top of the column, then it leads to affliction of the head.

2. In the case of theft of a pitcher, the entire family may be ruined. In the case of dislocation of the pitcher as well as breach of the column, there should be fear from death.

3. It is said that mistakes in measurement by finger/hand may lead to the death of the house owner. Without spreading seeds and medicinal plants there will be fear from spirits.

4. If a column is erected prior to circumambulation, it is dangerous. If there is diminution or excess of the measurement of the *Vāstu*, it should be totally discarded.

5-7. Even if it is the palace of Gods or of Kings, a house inside the palace should avoid *Siṁhakarṇa*[1], *Kapotālī*[2] *Siṁha,* rolled up flag-staff, battlements, pitcher, pillarette, post, crowning part, pillars with eight-sided or round-projected moulding or without a sprout(*Pallava*). The base of a column with projected moulding with a twig and *Kinnaras,* leaves on the top, plastered form of *Kumāra* (*Kārtikeya*), in front of the land, the base of a column without any stone in front of the site should not be constructed in the dwelling abode of the four *Varṇas.*

---

1. It is a moulding in shape of *Nāgarī Thakāra* according to P. K. Acharya.
2. Roll cornices or overhanging cornice .

मयः ॥

गृहे स्तम्भः शुभो वृत्तः षडष्टास्र कलास्रकः ।
शिला देवालये ग्राह्या द्विजावनिपयोरपि ॥८ ॥

पाषण्डिनां च कर्त्तव्या न कार्या वैश्यशूद्रयोः ।
क्रियते यदि मोहेन धर्मकामार्थनाशकृत् ॥९ ॥

तथा च ॥

इतिहासपुराणोक्तं वृत्तान्तं प्रतिरूपकम् ।
निन्दितं च गृहे नेष्टं शस्तं देवकुले च यत् ।१० ॥

करालं भीषणं रौद्रमशस्तं दुष्टमेव च ।
गृध्रकङ्ककपोतादि कपिसंग्रामभीषणम् ॥११ ॥

वर्जयेद्गृहचित्रेषु श्रेयस्तत्र न विद्यते ॥१२ ॥

भोजः ॥

यानीन्द्रजालतुल्यानि यानि मिथ्याकृतानि च ।
भीषणानि च यानि स्युर्न [३]कुर्यात्तानि ॥१३ ॥

नग्नं तपस्वीलीलां च मायादीनि न योजयेत् ।
प्रेताः पिशाचाः रक्षांसि क्रव्यादा मृगपक्षिणः ॥१४ ॥

मृगर्क्ष व्याघ्रमार्जारवराहद्वीपिजम्बुकाः ।
तरक्षुखरकंकोष्ट्रप्रमुखा वा निशाचराः ॥१५ ॥

गृहे न कार्या [४]वाद्यादौ व्याधिबन्धक्षयावहाः ।
नागदन्ततुलास्तम्भभित्तिमुखा गवाक्षकाः ॥१६ ॥

---

२. वल्लवम् in B

३. वेश्मनि in B, C, D, E,

४. वाटादौ । वायादौ in B, D, E

Maya

8. For a house a column, round-shaped, six, eight or sixteen sided is regarded as auspicious, stone pillars are accepted in a temple and for the houses of Brahmins and Kings.

9. (The stone pillar can be built for) heretics (*Pāṣaṇḍī*) also but not for *Vaiśya* and *Śūdra*. If it is done out of infatuation then it will be against the principles of virtue, desire and money.

As well as

10. Historical and *Purāṇic* events and their corresponding images are forbidden in a house and it is not considered desirable and auspicious and which is cursed even among the Gods.

11-12. Frightful, terrible, violent, inauspicious, corrupted pictures, (scenes of) dreadful fights among vultures, purple herons, pigeons, monkeys etc. should be discarded in the household pictures. There is no welfare in it.

Bhoja

13. Those (acts) which are like magical tricks, contradictory deeds and which are dreadful should not be performed in the house.

14-16a. The naked sports of ascetics, witchcraft and likewise, ghosts, goblins, demons, carnivorous birds and animals, deer, bear, tiger, cat, boar, leopard, jackal, hyena, ass, purple heron, camel etc. or nocturnal animals should not be kept in a house or in the garden, as they bring disease, confinements, and loss.

क्षणमध्ये न दातव्या [५]न चैते विषमाः शुभाः ।
[६]प्राग्भूमेरूर्ध्वभूमिं च विस्तारे वोदयेऽधिकाम् ॥१७॥

[७]संलग्नान्यासनं कुम्भी स्तम्भो भरणाशीर्षके।
पट्टश्च तन्त्रिके मानिन [८]कुर्यात्सर्ववेश्मसु ॥१८॥

अल्पलेपं बहुलेपं समसन्धिः शिरोगुरूः ।
सशल्यं पादहीनं च वास्तु शीघ्रं विनश्यति ॥१९॥

अन्यवास्तुचितं द्रव्यं न युञ्जादन्यवास्तुनि।
प्रासादे न भवेत्पूजा गेहे क्रीडन्ति राक्षसाः ॥२०॥

मयः ॥

विनष्टवास्तुसंजातं द्रव्यं सर्वविपत्करम् ॥
तस्मात्सर्वप्रयत्नेन शुद्धद्रव्यं [९]प्रगृह्यताम् ॥२१॥

अन्यपृष्ठे यदा चान्यत्प्रासादं मन्दिरं पुरम्।
खादकं नाम तद्वास्तु परस्परविरोधकृत् ॥२२॥

कुक्षिद्वारं गृहे वापि यत्र स्यात्सुरसद्मनि।
विभ्रमं नाम तद्वास्तु भ्रामयेत्तत्पतिं गृहात् ॥२३॥

कुक्षिभागे गृहं चान्यत्कुक्षिदन्त विरोधकृत्।
अग्रोन्नतं न तन्मध्ये [१०]उद्धतं हन्ति सन्ततिम् ॥२४॥

अधिकं विस्तरे कर्णे पञ्चहस्ताधिकोच्छ्रयम्।
यद्बहुद्रव्यकाष्ठाढ्यं न भवेच्छाश्वतं गृहम् ॥२५॥

---

५. न वैते in B, D, E,

६. प्राग्भूमंमेरूभूमिं in B

७. संलग्नाभ्यासनं in A, B, D, E

८. कुर्याद्वर्णवेश्मसु in A

९. विधीयताम् in B

१०. उद्धतं हते in A उद्धृतं in D उद्द्धतं in E

16b-17. A peg, balancing beam, and latticed windows towards the foundation wall should not be placed directing towards the centre, they are not regarded auspicious if uneven. The upper part of the floor should not be greater in length and breadth than the lower part.

18. It should not be attached with the base of a column and pillar which is ornamented on the top. A broad rectangular fillet (*Paṭṭa*) should be measured with a chord in all types of houses.

19. The *Vāstu* will collapse soon if it is less plastered or plastered heavily, if the joints are one over the other in one line, if the upper portion of the construction is heavy, and if the ground has nails in it and if it is without any columns.

20. Materials meant for one *Vāstu* should not be applied to another. Then there will be no ceremony in the palace and the demons will overpower the house.

Maya

21. Materials[3] for *Vāstu* may be dangerous, if they are collected from a demolished house. So, one should procure pure materials with the utmost care.

22. If a palace, temple, or city is constructed otherwise than on the surface prescribed, it is known as *Khādaka*, and that *Vāstu* stands in contradiction with each other.

23. If a door is erected in the center of a house or temple, that type of *Vāstu* is known as *Vibhrama* and it will cause the owner to leave the house.

24. If a house is constructed in the central part, which contradicts another house in the centre, the front should not be raised high between the two houses, as in such a case it kills the progeny.

25. If the corner part is projected more (than the prescribed measurement) and its height is more than five hands and if the wood is used in excess for construction, then that house does not stand for long.

3. Similar *Ślokas* in S.S. chapter 48

भोजः ॥

द्रव्यं द्रव्याधिकं हन्ति कुलमायामतोऽधिकम्।
उच्छ्याभ्यधिकं पूजां सन्ततिं विस्तराधिकम् ॥२६ ॥

कर्णशाला यदा लग्ना आग्नेयां दिशिमाश्रिताम्।
अग्निदं नाम तद्वास्तु कुरुतेऽग्निभयं फलम् ॥२७ ॥

नैऋत्ये बाह्यतो लग्ना नैऋत्तं व्याधिमृत्युकृत्।
[११]वायव्ये शालिका लग्ना वायव्यं वायुभीतिदम् ॥२८ ॥

ईशाने बाह्यतो लग्ना दैविकं देवदोषकृत्त्।
दिशायां विदिशायां वा वास्तुवेधविशोधनम् ॥२९ ॥

जीर्णे नीचानां नीचमेवेष्टं श्रेष्ठानां श्रेष्ठमिष्यते।
नवतरे वापि वेधदोषं विवर्जयेत्।
श्रेष्ठमानं निकृष्टानां सर्वथा न प्रयोजयेत् ॥३० ।।

अधोभूमिक्रियायुक्तिः स्यादूर्ध्वोर्ध्वतलं प्रति ।३१ ॥
विपरीते विपत्तिः स्यादिति शास्त्रार्थनिश्चयः ॥
कुर्याद्ब्रह्मपदं न्यस्तो भार [१२]पट्टः कुलक्षयम् ॥३२ ॥

ब्रह्मस्थलोर्ध्वगद्रव्यसन्धानं विपदां पदम्।
ब्रह्मस्थानस्थितः स्तम्भः स्वामिनस्तु विनाशनम् ॥३३ ॥

तुलादीन्युपरि [१३]द्रव्याण्यत्र दोषो न विद्यते।
गर्भाधानञ्च क्रमणं स्वभित्तिं मुखवासके ॥३४ ॥

[१४]शिलास्तम्भतलं कुंड्यं नृणां वासे न कारयेत्।
अन्योन्यद्रव्यविद्धं च हीनमित्युत्तमाङ्गकम् ॥३५ ॥

---

११. व्यायव्ये A, B, D

१२. प्रद in A

१३. द्रव्याणामत्र in D द्रव्याणां यत्र E

१४. Similar veres are found in Mayamatam ch 27 v 95

Bhoja

26. Excess of materials will cause loss of the same and excess of length will cause the destruction of the family, excess of height will be inauspicious and excess of breadth will cause harm to the progeny.

27. If the corner hall is directed towards the South-East corner of the land, that *Vāstu* is termed *Agnida* and it will cause fear from fire.

28. If a *Śālā* is attached to the South-West corner externally, it is termed *Nairṛtam*, which causes illness and death. If the hall is attached to the North-West corner of the plot, it is termed *Vāyavya* which causes fear from wind.

29. (If a *Śālā*) is attached to the North-East corner externally, it is termed *Daivika* and causes providential disturbance (*Devadoṣa*). Whether in the right direction or in the wrong direction the obstruction of *Vāstu* should be corrected.

30. In an old house or in a new one, the fault of obstruction should be discarded. The inferior one is best suited for the inferior, while the superior one is best for the superior.

31. By no means should the best measurement be applied for the worst one. Construction of the base (plinth) is advisable according to the type of upper storied construction, and the reverse will cause negative results – this is the essence of the teaching of the *Śāstras*.

32-33. If the weight of the broad rectangular fillet is put on the *Brahmapada,* it destroys one's family. Assembling of materials above the *Brahmasthala* brings in danger and if a pillar is erected on the *Brahmasthāna,* it is disastrous for the owner.

34. Materials kept over the beam will not produce any ill effect. The foundation deposit's location, verandah and the median partition wall are in the principal building.

35. Neither the pillars, nor the base, nor the walls of houses meant for common men should be made of stone. At the time of construction, other materials should not be mixed up and if the foundation is weak and the upper structure is strong, this is not recommended.

त्यक्त श्रेण्यूर्ध्वमूलस्थस्तम्भं स्तम्भविवर्जितम्।
गृहं हीनाधिकं स्तम्भं विषमस्थं तुलातलम् ॥३६ ॥

आदि[१५]पदानुसारेण [१६]न्युनाधिकायुतं बहिः।
भिन्नं प्राग्भुविमुखाभिद्वारै रविकरानिलैः ॥३७ ॥

मुखे नतं हीनमध्यं [१७]पट्टानुगजलप्लवम्।
भिन्नशालं मानहीनं दुष्पदं प्रविभाजितम् ॥३८ ॥

विकृतं च गृहं भर्त्तुरनिष्टफलदायकम्।
मूलगृहात्समीपस्थं कुर्यान्नोच्चं [१८]न चाधिकम् ॥३९ ॥

यत्स्यान्मुखविनिष्क्रान्तं चलितं तत्प्रकीर्त्तितम्।
वलितं पृष्ठनिष्क्रान्तं दिङ्मूढं भ्रान्तमुच्यते।।४०।।
विसूत्रं कर्णहीनं स्यात्फलमेषां प्रचक्षते।
चलिते चलति स्थानं बलिते विग्रहो भवेत् ॥४१ ॥

भ्रान्तं योषिद्विनाशाय विसूत्रं भूरिशत्रुकृत्।
भर्तुस्तुल्याभिधानं च गृहं दूरात्परित्यजेत् ॥४२ ॥

सर्वदोषकरी ज्ञेया गर्भे चन्द्रावलोकनी।
मुखाद्वित्तविनाशाय कामोच्छित्यै गवाक्षकः ॥४३ ॥

द्वौ स्तम्भौ क्षणमध्ये वा दद्याद्गर्भं न पीडयेत्।
एकोऽलिन्दो न कर्त्तव्यो वामतः पृष्ठतस्तथा ॥४४ ॥

---

१५. पट्टा in A
१६. न्यूनाधिक्य in B, D, E
१७. पदा in B, C, D, E
१८. नवा in B , C, D, E

36. One should discard the pillar standing in the foremost part (*Śreṇī*) of the wall, a house without pillars, with excess of pillars or shortage of pillars, and having uneven lintels.

37. Following the measurement of the first part, the outer surface will be made small or large. The door facing other than the Eastern side or in the wrong direction will be devoid of sunshine and wind.

38. If the front part is low and middle part is less, then the slab is considered to be flooded with water. If *Śālās* are different from the prescribed measurement, they are considered short of the standard.

39. The *Vikṛta* type of house brings evil fortune to the owner of the house. If it is to be constructed near the main house, it should be neither high nor broad.

40 That house, the forefront of which juts out is called Calita, and the house whose back part juts out is known as the *Valita Bhranta* type of house is bewildered of right direction.

41. The *Visūtra* type of house is without any corners and the results of these varieties are described herein. In the *Calita* type of house the place changes. There will be disturbances in the *Valita* type of house.

42. The *Bhrānta* type of house causes death of women folk and *Visūtra* brings lots of enmity. The house which has been named after the owner should be avoided from a distance.

43. That construction is to be considered defective in all respects if the *Candrāvalokanī* is built in the centre. If the window is placed in an unplanned manner, then it causes loss of wealth and proper ventilation.

44. Two pillars can be erected towards the centre, but the plinth area should not be disturbed. The single portico should not be erected from the left or from the back side.

भोजः ॥

यद्द्विशालं त्रिशालं वा चतुःशालमथापि वा।
अलिन्दरहितं वेश्म तदनिष्टफलप्रदम् ॥४५ ॥

ग्रन्थान्तरे ॥

पुरतः पृष्ठतः पार्श्वे यदि वाऽलिन्दवर्जिता।
न शस्यते शाला देवागारे तु शस्यते ॥४६ ॥

न देवधूर्त्तसचिवःचत्वाराणां समीपतः ।
कारयेद्भवनं प्राज्ञो दुःखशोक[१९]भयं ततः ॥४७ ॥

तथा च।

सुरवैरिनृपामात्यचौरपाषण्डपापिनाम्।
चत्वारां त्यज धूर्त्तानां समीपे दुःखदं गृहम् ॥४८ ॥

न कुर्यादर्हतः पृष्ठे अग्रतः शिवसूर्ययोः ।
पार्श्वयो र्ब्रह्मविष्णोश्च गृहं चण्डयाः समन्ततः ॥४९ ॥

शिवसूर्यजिनादीनामन्तरे न शुभं गृहम्।
मार्गश्चैको यदा गच्छेदुभयोर्गृह[२०] पार्श्वयोः ॥५० ॥

मार्गवेधस्तदा स स्याच्छोकसन्तापकारकः ।
गृहपृष्ठं समालोक्य प्रवेशो न शुभङ्करः ॥५१ ॥
मार्गान्तरे त्वादिभूमिः समभित्त्या न दूषणम् ॥ ५२ ॥

मत्स्यमते।

स्तम्भं वा भवनं वापि द्वारं वासगृहं तथा।
दिङ्मूढे कुलनाशः स्यान्न च सम्बर्द्धयेद्गृहम् ॥५३ ॥

---

१९. फलं in A

२०. पृष्टयो in B

Bhoja

45. Whether it is *Dviśālā, Triśālā* or *Catuśśālā* a building without any portico yields bad results.

According to another work

46. A *Śālā* house without any portico in the front, back or side is inauspicious, but it is praiseworthy for a temple.

47. A wise man should not build a house near a temple or near a wicked person's house or a councilor's residence or near the sacrificial ground as these cause fear or grief and sorrow.

Also

48. A house gives painful results if built near a temple, or the house of a warrior, enemy, King, councilor, thief, heretic, sinful men. One should avoid building near a courtyard or a cunning person's house.

49. One should not build one's house in the rear of a Buddhist temple or in the front of a *Śiva* and *Sūrya* temple, nor on the side of a *Brahma* and *Visṇu* temple, nor around a *Caṇḍī* temple.

50. A house, if built in between the temple of *Śiva*, *Sūrya* or *Jina* and if the road runs by both sides of a house, it is not regarded as auspicious.

51. Then it is known as obstruction of road and it causes grief and sorrow. The entrance facing the exit is not auspicious.

52. But if the main plot of land is on the other side of the road and it is equal to the wall there is no fault.

So says the Matsyapurāṇa

53. If the correct orientation is not done for a pillar, house, door, as well as a dwelling place, then there will be destruction of one's family, and one should not extend his house in such a manner.

यदि सम्बर्द्धयेद्गृहं सर्वमेव विवर्द्धयेत्।
प्राग्वर्धिते मित्रवैरं याम्ये शत्रुभयं गृहे ॥५४॥

पश्चिमेऽर्थविनाशस्यान्मनस्तापस्तथोत्तरे।
आग्नेयेऽग्निभयं विन्द्याद्राक्षसे तु शिशुक्षयम्॥५५॥

[२१]वायव्येऽनिल [२२]रुक्कोपं ईशाने शस्यसंक्षयम्॥५६॥

मयः॥

वृद्धिं गृहादिवास्तूनामिच्छेद्यदि समृद्धितः।
प्रागुत्तरे सर्वतो वा वर्धयेन्नान्यतो गृहम्॥५७॥

ग्रन्थान्तरे।

संवर्धनं च वास्तूनां वास्तुसम्बरणानि च।
द्वाराणां परिवृत्तिश्च मृत्यवे स्यान्न संशयः॥ ५८॥

मयः।

इष्टव्यासायामं प्रागेवालं विचिन्त्य कर्त्तव्यम्।
तस्माद्धीनं यत्तत्सततं विपदांपदं भवति॥५९॥

भोजः।

स्थापितद्वार[२३] संरोधे गृहिणो जायतेऽश्मरी।
कृतानि यत्र चीयन्ते गवाक्षालोकनानि च॥६०॥

तत्र प्रसूतिर्न भवेन्निष्पन्नापि विनश्यति।
कुड्यं भित्वा न कर्त्तव्यं द्वारं तत्र सुखेप्सुभिः॥६१॥

---

२१. व्ययब्ये. in A
२२. सष्कोपं. in A
२३. मम्बोध. in DE

54. If there is any occasion of extension of the house, one should extend it in all directions. If any extension is done in the East there may be quarrel with friends, if in the South there is a fear from enemies.

If extended in the West there is loss of wealth, and if in the North there will be mental agony.

55-56. If in the South-East, there will be fear from fire. In the South-West, there will be loss of child, and if in the North-West there will be fear from the wind and there will be loss of grains if in the North-East.

Maya

57. If one wants to extend his house or *Vāstu* with prosperity, he should extend it towards the East, North or on all sides, not on other sides of the house.

In other works

58. While carrying out extension or diminution of a house, the alteration of a door will cause death, and there is no doubt about this.

Maya

59. Desired length and breadth should be ascertained properly, (before starting a construction). If less than the prescribed measurement, it always brings danger.

60. If there is any obstruction to the constructed door and if the windows already set up and other sources of light are diminished or cut down, the inmates of the house will turn into gravel.

61. Then there will be no birth, and those conceived will be lost. So, one who wants to attain happiness should not build a door by breaking the wall.

द्वारे च जलनिःश्रावं नैव कुर्याद्विचक्षणः।
निम्नोन्नतं करालं च सम्मुखं पृष्ठदेशगम् ॥६२ ॥

वामावर्त्तं च न शुभं द्वारमग्रतरं गृहे।
स्तम्भं द्वारं च भित्तिं च विपरीतं न कारयेत् ॥६३ ॥

कटुकण्टकि दुर्गन्धिः गुह्यकाद्याश्रयान्द्रुमान्।
न धारयेत् समीपस्थान्पुरप्रासादवेश्मनाम् ॥६४ ॥

[२४]शालासु भिन्नशालासु सन्धिकर्म न कारयेत्।
देवतास्थापनं पिण्डशालासु न विधीयते ॥६५ ॥

अन्योन्यसन्धिबिद्धं च शिखा कीलस्य वेधनम्।
धर्मार्थकामसौख्यानां विनाशं नित्यमादिशेत् ॥६६ ॥

अज्ञैः सन्तापवद्भिर्वा परद्रव्यैश्च निर्मितम्।
त्वरितं [२५]पूर्णतां नीतं स्थपतिद्वयकारितम् ॥६७ ॥

विनष्टवास्तुसञ्जातद्रव्यैरपि विनिर्मितम्।
अतृप्तवास्तुदेवं यद्गर्भविन्यासवर्जितम् ॥६८ ॥

अक्रमेण कृतं वापि वास्तु तद्याति शून्यताम्।
अनुवंश न भुञ्जीत न शयीत कदाचन ॥६९ ॥

भुञ्जानस्यार्थनाशस्याच्छयानस्य न निवृत्तिः।
यत्र भुक्तं यथास्थानं पात्रधान्याम्बरादिकम् ॥७० ॥

भग्नभाण्डगतं चान्नं मुखवातोपसाधितम्।
रजस्वला श्वा न दृष्टं सन्ध्ययोर्वा विदिङ्मुखम् ॥७१ ॥

---

२४. Similar verse in Mayamatam ch 27 v 73 cd 74 ab

२५. पूर्णतानान्तं in A

62-63. A wise person should never make a water-outlet through the door. The front and back part of the door should not be too high or low or frightening. A door should not to be made in such a way as to turn to the left from the front of the house. The pillar, door and wall should not stand in opposition to each other.

64. Thorny, pungent, foul smelling trees, and others inhabited by ghosts should not be planted near a city, palace, or residential building.

65. One should not attach one type of *Śālā* with another type. One should not consecrate a deity in the *Piṇḍaśālā* (disjoined house).

66. If the joinings clings to one another and the tenor obstructs the nail (peg), it always indicates the destruction of *Dharma, Artha, Kāma,* and *Soukhya* (friendship).

67-68. If a house is built by an ignorant or distressed person with other than the prescribed material or if it is completed quickly by two architects or if a house is built with the material collected from waste, and if the plinth is devoid of a ground plan, the *Vāstudeva* is dissatisfied.

69. If a house is built without any order, it becomes useless. One must not sleep or take food on supporting floorboards (or genealogical table).

70. A man eating food there suffers monetary loss, and one sleeping there suffers prolonged drowsiness. It is not proper to leave utensils, rice and clothing in an open place (then it brings no good).

71. And in the same place if the food is kept in a broken utensil, the food is cooled by the mouth-wind, the place is covered with dust, it is not visible in the evening or is in the wrong direction, then it brings no good.

भग्नासनगतैर्यद्वा [२६]आसन्दीस्थैश्च भुज्यते।
यत्रोपघातवत्किञ्चिद्भक्ष्यं पेयमथापि वा ॥७२ ॥
पंक्तिभेदो वृथापाकः पाकभेदः सदाकलिः ॥७३ ॥

आभ्युक्षणं च संध्यायां यत्र कण्टकिनो द्रुमाः।
भार्या पुनर्भूवल्मीकं यत्र निष्पातवल्लरी ॥७४ ॥

मुसलोलूखले स्त्रीणामास्या (?) तद्वदुदुम्बरे।
[२७]मन्त्रस्यावस्करे शस्त्रः पक्वा पक्वान्नलङ्घनम् ॥७५ ॥

स्थालीपिधाने वा दर्व्यास्तलेनाग्निसमर्पणम्।
उच्चैर्वदन्ति वा रात्रौ नीचैर्ज्वलति वानलः ॥७६ ॥

पितॄनभिवन्दत्येवं पुत्रभार्यास्तथा पतीन्।
यत्र धान्यं विप्रकीर्णं काकमूषिकभोजनम् ॥७७ ॥

अपावृतं पयस्त्विष्टे उच्छिष्टैः स्पृश्यते घृतम्।
बालानां प्रेक्षमाणानां वृद्धा भक्ष्यं च भुञ्जते ॥ ७८ ॥

पाचयन्त्यात्मनोऽर्थेऽन्नं वृथैवं मांसभक्षिणः।
उत्सूरशायिनो यत्र पुरुषाश्च प्रागे निशाः ॥७९ ॥

आश्रमस्थान्विधर्मस्थाः प्रद्विषन्ति परस्परम्।
परस्वा [२८]दानुरुचयो विपण्यभ्यवहारिणः ॥८० ॥

अशुश्रूषुर्गुरोः शिष्यो यत्र शिष्यसखागुरुः।
शास्तिप्रेष्यांश्च भर्तारं गुरूणां परतो वधुः ॥८१ ॥

कृतघ्ना नास्तिकाः पापा निर्मर्यादा हतः त्विषः।
अभक्ष्यभक्षिणो यस्मिन्नाचाररहिता नराः ॥८२ ॥

---

२६. आदिस्यैश्च तु in B, C, D, E

२७. मन्त्रश्चाव in B, C, D, E

२८. दान्नरू in A

72. (If in the same place) one sits on a broken seat, or eats food sitting on a small couch, where small amount of food as well as drinks are treated like an oblation (it brings no good).

73. If one deviates from the proper method of cooking (*Paṅktibheda*), then the cooking becomes waste and wrongly cooked food is always the cause of difference of opinions (it brings no good).

74. In the evening the wife should sprinkle water where the thorny trees grow, in ant hills where the creepers are without leaves.

75. A pestle, wooden mortar and the seats for ladies will be made out of the fig tree. The pollution of chanting of the *Śastras* is same as the spoiling of cooked rice.

76. It is harmful if one puts fire under the lid of a utensil, or under the ladle, or if one speaks out loudly at night and the fire burns at a very low flame.

77. (It is equally harmful) if one endears one's son, wife or husband in the same way as showing obeisance to one's father and where the grains are scattered to feed the cows or rats.

78- 79. Also, if the milk which is desired for sacrifice is kept uncovered, and the clarified butter is touched by impure hands, and if in front of the children, who are watching eagerly, the elder persons eat edibles (it is despisable). Like the male persons who sleep in the evening before nightfall, those meat eaters who cook rice for their own interest are also despisable.

80, 81. Residents of *Āśramas* and those who belong to different faiths are jealous of each other. They are greedy of the wealth of others and consume articles from the shop. When a disciple is disobedient to his *Guru*, and when the disciple is like a friend to his *Guru*, and when the wife wants punishment for her husband in front of his *Guru* (this situation is not acceptable).

82. Ungrateful (persons), heretics, sinners, those who transgress the law, wretchedly drunk, those who eat inedible foods and where the people do not follow any custom (the situation is not desirable).

भर्त्तादीपश्च भवने यत्र पश्यति मार्जनीम्।
अमार्जितानि भाण्डानि तत्रालक्ष्मीभयं सदा ॥८३ ॥

वेदशास्त्रविहीनं यन्नास्तिका क्रान्तमद्द्विजम्।
ऊर्णनाभादिलालाभिः कीर्णं संस्कारवर्जितम् ॥८४ ॥

स्त्रीजितं स्वामिहीनं च लिङ्गिभिः परिवारितम्।
श्लेष्मवातोच्छिष्टमलैः प्रलिप्तं गोरसादिभिः ॥८५ ॥

केशभस्मतुषाङ्गारप्रेतवृक्षैर्युतं गृहम्।
कपालास्थिसमाकीर्णं श्वापदैः परिपूरितम् ॥८६ ॥

मार्जारनकुलादीनां संघुष्टं कलहारवैः।
द्रव्याश्मकाष्ठैर्देवानां पूर्णं तद्विलयं व्रजेत् ॥८७ ॥
तस्माद्दोषान्परित्यज्य शुभं ग्राह्यं गृहादिषु ॥ ८८ ॥

अथ शुभानि-

सुमङ्गलकथोपेतं सुश्रद्धाह्यष्टरूपकम्।
वृषाजविषमध्वाज्य वीणाभरणचन्दनैः ॥८९ ॥

ताम्रपात्रहयादर्शस्वर्णैर्नित्यं समन्वितम्।
सदानुलिप्तं सन्ध्यासु गृहमम्बुसमुक्षितम् ॥९० ॥

कृतपुष्पबलिं नित्यं सूर्यावेक्षितदीपकम्।
नित्याग्निसलिलं सूर्योद्दिष्टं [२९]श्रेयं श्रियःप्रदम् ॥९१ ॥

यत्र देवपितृब्रह्माऽतिथिर्गुर्वर्चनं सदा।
मिथो मैत्रीबालवृद्धं बन्धुं स्वजनयोषिताम् ॥९२ ॥

२९. Omitted in BD

83. If the master of a house looks at the lamp as well as the brooms, and the utensils are unwashed, there is always fear of loss of property and affluence.

84. And (the house which is) without the chanting of the Vedas, which is infested by heretics, and devoid of Brahmins, full of cobwebs and devoid of any rituals (is not praiseworthy).

85. A house which is controlled by the womenfolk and without a master, full of persons belonging to other religious faiths, full of mucous, rheum, and full of impure things and besmeared with the urine of cows (is not praiseworthy).

86. A house with hairs, ashes, smouldering fires, trees resided by ghosts, full of skull and bones and full of wild beasts (is not praiseworthy).

The house which resounds with cries of the quarrels of cats and mongooses and where the substances, stones and wood forming the idols are scattered, that house will shortly be destroyed.

87-88. So, one should discard the vices and include auspicious items in the house.

Now the auspicious elements :

89-90. The house is to be full of holy discussions, which are of great veneration and of pleasing character. It will be always adorned with bulls, goats, water, honey, ghee, *Vīṇā* (flute), ornaments, sandal wood, copper vessels, gold. The house will be always decorated and sprinkled with water in the evening.

91. There should always be offering of flowers and the lamps will face the Sun. Daily offering of fire and water dedicated to the Sun is desirable and beneficial.

92. Where there will be daily worship of gods, manes (*Pitṛ*), *Brahmā*, guests and preceptors and where there are good relations among children and old people friends, relations and women.

सुशीला योषितो योग्यं वयसः शयनासनम्।
तिष्ठत्सु गुरुवृद्धेषु कनीयांसो न चासते ॥९३॥

यत्र पद्मो महापद्मौ सुरभिर्मोदकाशिनी।
वृषभैरावतौ [३०]तद्वल्कल्यं ते धान्य[३१]सञ्चयः ॥९४॥

अशस्त्रा देवता यत्र सशस्त्राश्चहवं विना।
आश्वासनं विषण्णार्त्तदीनानां त्रस्तरोगिणाम् ॥९५॥

यत्र भूतदयादानं तपः शौचं तथोद्यमः।
बहुद्वाराणि न यत्र गृहे तत्र सुखं श्रियः ॥९६॥

इति श्री सूत्रधारमण्डनविरचिते [३२]वास्तुशास्त्रे वास्तुमण्डने दूषणभूषणाध्यायः सप्तमः श्लोकाः९६॥

---

३०. omitted in B, D

३१. सेचयः in B

३२ वास्तुमण्डने वास्तुशास्त्रे in B, C, D, E,

93. Where the ladies are obedient, and where the seats and beds are worthy of age. Where the juniors will not take their seats in the presence of the preceptor and aged people.

94. Where lilies and lotuses are fragrant and pleasing, and where there are bulls and elephants with proportionate storing of paddy.

95. Where there are Gods without weapons, and if decorated with weapons it will be without battle. Where there is consolation for the depressed, the distressed and the frightened having diseases.

96. Where there is compassion and charity for living beings and penance, purity and enterprise. Where there is not a multiplicity of doors, in that house happiness and prosperity stay forever.

Here ends the 7th chapter titled Defects and Decorations, in Vāstumaṇḍana, the Vāstuśāstra written by Maṇḍana Sūtradhāra.

अष्टमोऽध्यायः

[प्रकीर्णकाध्यायः]

गृहप्रकाराः

शाला तु शुद्धा सम्बद्धा संयुता च परिभ्रमाः ॥
छन्दभिन्ना प्रतिभिन्ना सम्पुटा च प्रतिक्रमाः ॥१ ॥

अलिन्दरहिता शाला शुद्धोक्ता केवला बुधैः ।
अग्रालिन्देन सहिता सम्बद्धा स्याद्दशान्तकम् ॥२ ॥

अलिन्दवेष्टिता बाह्ये शालाश्रेणिस्तु संयुताः ।
पृथगैकैकशालाया अलिन्दश्चान्तरे यदा ॥३ ॥

परिभ्रमा तदा ज्ञेया सर्वशान्तिकरी नृणाम् ।
छन्दभिन्नापवरके फलकेभित्तिकान्तरे ॥४ ॥

शालामध्ये तु षड्दारौ प्रतिभिन्ना सदोत्तमा ।
भित्तिमध्ये यदालिन्दास्तथा बाह्ये च सम्पुटा ॥५ ॥

पृथक्शालाग्र कपिलाद्यलिन्दाग्रे प्रतिक्रमा ।
गृहमाला गृहनाभिः गृहसंघट्ट एव च ॥६ ॥

गृहाणकश्च विज्ञेयं गृहभेदचतुष्टयम् ।
गृहमाला गृहैः कुक्षौ पृष्ठेऽग्रे पंक्तितः स्थितेः ॥७ ॥

दिग्विदिक्ष्वग्रतः पृष्ठे कुक्षौ संघट्ट ईरितः ।
नानाकारापवरकैः सालिन्दैर्गृहनाभिका ॥८ ॥

Chapter VIII
[Prakīrṇakādhyāyaḥ]

Now the varieties of the houses.

Śālā houses may be of eight types, they are *Śuddhā, Sambaddhā,*

1. *Saṁyutā, Paribhramā, Chandabhinnā, Pratibhinnā, Sampuṭā* and *Pratikramā.*

2. A *Śālā* house without any corridor is known as *Śuddhā* by the learned people. *Sambaddhā* type of *Śālā* is connected with the front corridor.

3-4. When rows of *Śālā* houses are surrounded by corridors from outside - they are known as *Saṁyutā.* In each of the separate *Śālā* houses, if there are corridors in between they are known as *Paribhramā.* It bestows all sorts of peace to the human being. When the inner chamber is endowed with a slab in between the partition wall, it is known as *Chandabhinnā.*

5. When a contrivance made of six logs of wood, is placed inside the *Śālā* (which is) beneficial at all times, it is known as *Pratibhinnā.* When the corridors are inside the wall, as well as outside, it is known as *Sampuṭā.*

6-7a. In front of each separate *Śālā,* if there is a corridor designated as *Kapilā* and others then the *Śālā* is named as *Pratikramā.* There are four varieties of houses known as *Gṛhamālā, Gṛhanābhi, Gṛhasaṁghaṭṭa* and *Gṛhāṇaka.*

7b. In the *Gṛhamālā* type of houses, there will be rows of rooms in the front, centre, as well as in the back.

8. The *Saṁghaṭṭā* variety of houses will have rooms on all sides, in the front, back and in the centre. *Gṛhanābhi* is known to have different sizes of inner apartments and corridors.

[१]अधौ भूविस्तृता ऊर्ध्वोर्ध्वभूम्य: स गृहाणक: ।
[२]एकद्वारं भवेद्वेश्म निलयं पूर्वपश्चिमे ॥९ ॥

त्रिद्वारं करणं प्रोक्तं चतुर्भिश्चतुरं विदु: ।
माडमौण्ड [३]शुद्धशेखरस्तुङ्गार:सिंहावलोकना: ॥१० ॥

राजवेश्मसु षट्छन्दा विश्वकर्मादिभि: स्मृता: ।
[४]माडमर्धोदयं छाद्यं घण्टाकूटादिभिर्युतम् ॥११ ॥

मौडं तु भद्रे माडाढ्यं मध्येशृङ्गयुतं तले ।
सर्वभूम्यो वरं शुद्धं क्रान्तं चतुष्किकम् ॥१२ ॥

सुरसद्मादिशिखराकारं [४]छन्दं तु शेखरम् ।
भद्रे भद्रे तवंगाढ्यं तुङ्गारं द्विघ्ननिर्गतम् ।
सिंहावलोकनं कुर्यात्सिंहकर्णैर्विभूषितम् ॥१३ ॥

मय: शाला तु केवला जाति र्विमानं शिखरान्वितम् ।
बद्धाकारशिरोहर्म्यं नानाकाराङ्गसंयुतम् ॥१४ ॥

अनेकभूमा मालाविबद्धा स्यात्सा तु मालिका ।
प्रागुदक् प्रागवाक् प्रत्य[५]गुदग्द्वेतु लाङ्गले ॥१५ ॥

स्वामिनो [६]मरणं स्याद्धि श्रियै याम्ये प्रतीच्यपि[७] ।
अवाक् प्रत्यगुदक् सम्पत् प्रागवागपरो जय: ॥१६ ॥

---

१. अधोतु विस्तृता in B D E
२. Similar verse in *Aparājitāpṛchhā* ch 69 v 13
३. शेषस्तुंगार: सिंहावलोकना: in DE
४. omitted in BDE, तत् शुद्धां दिखरम in C
५. गुदग्जे in BCD
६. रमणं in BCDE
७. Similar verse in Mayamatam ch 26 v 18

9-11. When construction of the ground level is wider than the upper levels, then it is known as *Gṛhāṇaka.* A house with one door is known as *Veśma,* (a house) with doors in the East and West is known as *Nilaya.* (A house) with three doors is known as *Karaṇa* and with four doors is known as *Catura.* *Viśvakarmā* and others prescribe varieties of designs in the royal mansions - they are *Māḍa, Mauṇḍa, Śuddha, Śekhara, Tuṅgāra, Siṁhāvalokana.* The eves board of the *Māḍa* palace will be constructed at half of the height and it will be adorned with bells and summits (*Kūṭa*) or a square aedicule.

12. The central offset of the *Mauḍa* palace is like *Māḍa* and the middle and lower parts will be adorned with peaks. Of all the sites, this one is favourable, it should be unmixed and extended with four pillared pavilions *(Catuṣki).*

13. Temples of the gods and others will be shaped like peaks and the *Chanda* will be *Śekhara.* The *Tuṅgāra,* another *Chanda* of royal mansion, will be projected on the central offset on its body, which will be multiplied by two. *Siṁhāvlokana* should be adorned with *Siṁhakaraṇa.*

14. Maya Śālā houses are of the *Vimāna* type (7-storied) with *Śikharas* (crests). Rooms on the top part will be close knit and these (*Harmya*) will be of different shapes and sizes.

15-16. *Mālikā* is multi-storied and looks like a garland. If the two main buildings of a *Lāṅgala* house are to the East and South or to the East and North or to the West and North, this will bring about the owner's death; if good fortune is desired, they have to be placed to the South and the West. Building to the North, West, and South brings fortune, and building to the East, South, and West brings victory.

दक्षिणे पश्चिमे हीनशालं सूर्प्पं तु दोषदम्।
लाङ्गलं गणिकादीनां सूर्प्पमुग्रोपजीविनाम्॥१७॥

लाङ्गले चैव सूर्प्पे च पृथक्शालासु सर्वदा।
शालाविरहितस्थाने कुड्यद्वारं प्रयोजयेत्॥१८॥

[८]द्वारशोभा द्वारशाला द्वारप्रासादहर्म्यके।
द्वारगोपुरमित्येवं पञ्चभेदं हि गोपुरम्॥१९॥

[९]अथ श्रीधरादिप्रासादाः॥

एकभागश्चतुःस्तम्भश्चतुर्द्वारः सजालकः।
छाद्यघण्टायुतो माडशोभितःश्रीधरो मतः॥२०॥

पञ्चयुग्मकरे क्षेत्रे सार्धत्रिंशद्विभाजिते।
मध्ये नवपदं कार्यं भागार्धं भित्तिकाद्वयम्॥२१॥

मध्यं तु षोडशस्तम्भं स माडं पञ्चभूमिकम्।
भद्रं सार्धं द्विभूमं स्याच्चतुःस्तम्भं च भागिकम्॥२२॥

चतुर्दिक्षुश्चतुर्द्वारः प्रतापवर्धनः शुभः।
तत्र त्र्यंशायतं भद्रं मुखभद्रं च भागतः॥२३॥

प्रतिभद्रं दशस्तम्भाः षट्शरा मध्यबाह्यगाः।
भद्रे माडं द्विभूम्योर्ध्वे गृहे पञ्चतलोर्ध्वतः॥२४॥

---

८. Similar verse in Mayamatam ch 24 v.11

९. Mss DE write following verses :-

श्रीधरश्चैव प्रासादः प्रतापवर्द्धनः परः।
लक्ष्मीविलाससंज्ञश्च श्रीनिवासश्चतुर्थकः॥
क्षीणिभूषणनामानो पृथ्वीजयश्च षष्टमः।
षट्ष्वेतेषु च प्रासादे श्रेष्ठः स्यादुत्तरोत्तरः॥

17. The *Sūrppa* type of houses without *Śālā* (main building or hall) to the South and West, cause misfortune. The *Lāṅgala* type of houses are suitable for courtesans and people of that ilk. *Sūrppa* houses are for cruel avocations (*Ugropojīvinām*),

18. In *Lāṅgala* and *sūrppa* type of houses and in all those with only one main building, a wall with a door must be disposed so as to border them where there is no main buildings.

19. *Dvāraśobhā, Dvāraśālā, Dvāraprāsāda, Harmya,* and *Dvāragopura*– these are five respective divisions of gateways (*Gopuras*).

Now the Śrīdhara and other palaces

20. The *Śrīdhara* type of palace is known with one section having four pillars and four latticed doors and it is adorned with bells hanging from the roof. It belongs to the *Māḍa* variety.

21. In a land measuring 25 hands (lengthwise) and 15 hands (in breadth), 9 *Padas* should be kept reserved in the centre and two walls will be erected on the half segment.

22. That *Māḍa* type of palace will be five-storeyed and the central part consists of sixteen pillars. The *Bhadra* will be constructed on the second half storey and in a part there will be four pillars.

23. *Pratāpavardhana* is auspicious with four doors in the four directions. There the portico will be 1/3rd in breadth and the central offset will be from another part.

24 *Pratibhadra*[1] consists of ten pillars and there will be 6 pillars at the centre and 5 in the outer part. In the *Bhadra* (central offset in the plan) *Māḍa* will be constructed above the second storey and in the (other type of) house it will be above the fifth storey.

1. *Pratibhadra* :– Sub-division in plan 8 elevation, adjoining the *Bhadra*

लक्ष्मीविलासः प्रासादो नृपाणां तनुते श्रियम्।
क्षेत्रेंशैः पञ्चविंशत्या स्तम्भैः षट्त्रिंशतायुते ॥२५॥

दशमांशसमा भित्तिः चतुर्द्वारं प्रकारयेत्।
भद्रं नवांशमेकांशः मुखभद्रत्रयान्वितम् ॥२६॥

सार्धं त्रिभूमिकं सर्वे स्तम्भाजिनयुतं शतम्।
माडो त्रिपञ्चभूम्यर्धे श्रीनिवासः श्रियःप्रदम् ॥२७॥

अष्टाष्टभक्ते क्षेत्रे तु गर्भः स्यात् सप्तभागिकः।
भित्तिरर्धांशकामध्ये चतुःषष्ठिधरान्वितः ॥२८॥

चतुर्द्वारोऽत्र भद्रं तु पञ्चविंशतिभागिकम्।
भद्रे त्र्यैकांशकं तत्र प्रतिभद्रत्रयं न्यसेत् ॥२९॥

भद्रे स्तम्भाश्चतुः पञ्च सर्वेऽशीत्या शतद्वयम्।
भद्रे माडं त्रिभूम्योर्ध्वे गृहे षड्भूमिकोपरि ॥३०॥

[१०]क्षीणोभूषणसंज्ञोपमा वासो भोगसौख्यदः।
क्षेत्रे तु दशभिर्भक्ते द्वे भित्ती भागमानतः ॥३१॥

शतस्तम्भं युतं मध्यं सार्धसप्ततलान्वितम्।
सप्तपञ्चत्र्येकभागे भद्रेऽष्टाविंशतिर्धराः ॥३२॥

सार्धं त्रिभूमे सर्वत्र स्तम्भाः [११]सार्धशतद्वयम्।
पृथ्वीजयोऽयं प्रासादो राज्ञो सुखजयप्रदम् ॥३३॥

पञ्चविंशतिहस्तादेरष्टोत्तरशतावधिः।
प्रतापवर्द्धनादीस्तु यथायोग्यं प्रकारयेत् ॥३४॥

---

१०. क्षीणी in B

११. सार्कं in B

25. The *Lakṣmīvilāsa* type of palace is conducive to the prosperity of a King. Here, 25 parts of the land will have 36 pillars.

26. The wall will be equal to the $1/10^{th}$ part and four doors are to be erected. The *Bhadra* will have nine parts out of which one part will contain three *Mukhabhadras.*

27. The *Śrī-nivāsa* brings prosperity if it is three and half storeyed with 124 pillars. There *Māḍa* will be constructed on the 3rd and 5th storeys.

29. If the land is divided into 64 parts (8x8), the foundation will be on the 7th segment. The wall/partition will come within the half of the sixty four scale. There will be four doors and the *Bhadra* will be on the 25th part. The *Bhadra* (central offset) will be divided into three units and in one unit three *Pratibhadras* will be raised. 28-

30. In a *Bhadra* (central offset) the number of the pillars can be 4, 5, and in total from 80 to 200. In a *Bhadra*, the *Māḍa* will be above the third storey and in a house it will be above the sixth storey.

31-33. The *Kṣīṇobhūṣaṇa* type of residence is conducive to enjoyment and prosperity. If the total area of the land is divided by 10 (10x10)[2], two walls are to be measured accordingly. The middle portion will contain 100 pillars and it will be $7\frac{1}{2}$ storeyed. In the 7th, 5th, 3rd, and in the 1st part of the *Bhadra*, there will be 28 scales. In all cases of $3\frac{1}{2}$ storeyed buildings, there will be 52 pillars. So, the *Pṛthvījaya* type of palace will augur victory for the King.

34. According to the prescribed manner *Pratāpavardhana* and others are to be constructed from 25 hands up to 108 hands.

2. It will be 100 square *Padavinyāsa* which is found in *Rājavallabhamaṇḍana* also.

एतांस्तु राजप्रासादान् गवाक्षछाद्यजालकैः ।
सिंहघण्टासंवरणैः सदण्डकलसध्वजैः ॥३५ ॥
सिंहकर्णकपोतालीकपिशीर्षैर्विभूषयेत् ॥३६ ॥

अथ सभा ।

क्षेत्रे षोडशभक्ते तु मध्यं स्याच्चतुरंशकम् ।
बाह्य एकांशकोऽलिन्दः सभा नन्देति सा मता ॥३७ ॥

भद्रा द्विभागभद्राढ्या चतुर्भद्रैर्युता जया ।
द्विद्व्यलिन्दा चतुर्दिक्षु पूर्णा भद्रैर्युता मता ॥३८ ॥

क्षेत्रे नवांशे तु कलास्तम्भैर्दिव्या सभा मता ।
भद्रैश्चतुर्भिः सा यक्षी त्र्यंशद्व्यंशैस्तु रत्नजा ॥३९ ॥

उत्पलांशं प्रतिभद्रैर्भूषयेत्ताः सुतोरणैः ।
निर्यूहमदला[१२]लूपवितानाढ्यैः सुरूपकैः ॥४० ॥

नक्रैः करिहरिव्यालशाल[१३]भञ्जीगणादिभिः ॥४१ ॥

अथ मण्डपाः ।

स्तम्भान्तरं तु सार्धं त्रिहस्तात्सप्तकरावधिः ।
एक द्वि-त्रि-चतुः पञ्चभागे भित्त्यन्तरे कृते ॥४२ ॥

तदेकभाग आयामो विस्తारादधिको भवेत् ।
सार्धत्रिहस्तात्सप्तान्तं मण्डपस्योदयो मतः ॥४३ ॥

षण्मात्राात्करपर्यन्तं [१४]मण्डपे स्तम्भविस्तरः ॥४४ ॥

---

१२. लूमा in BD
१३. स्तम्भ in B, D
१४. मंडरूपेकोभविस्तरः in B

35-36. These royal palaces should be decorated with latticed window ornamented ceilings, images of lions, bells, ramparts, flagstaffs, pitchers, banners, *Siṁhakarṇa*, roll cornices, battlements.

Now the Council Hall

37. If the land is to be divided into 16 parts, the *centre* will consist of four segments, and one outer part will form the *Alinda*. That type of hall is known as *Nandā*.

38. Two parts of the *Bhadrā* type of hall will have central offset (*Bhadrā*) and the *Jayā* variety is adorned with 4 mouldings (*Bhadrā*). There will be two *Alindas* each on the four sides of *Pūrṇā* and it is also adorned with mouldings.

39. The *Divyā* type of hall will have sixteen pillars on the 9th part of the area. The hall known as *Yakṣī* is adorned with four mouldings while the one known as *Ratnajā* will have mouldings on the third or second part.

40-41. The *Utpalā* type of hall will be decorated with *Pratibhadra*, an elegant arched gateway, small towers (*Niryuha*), sloping roof (*Madalā*), continued pent, roof (*Lūpā*), canopy (*Vitāna*) of beautiful forms aquatic animals, elephants, lions, snakes, and wooden dolls.

Now the pavilion

42. The pillars will have gaps ranging from three and half hands to seven hands. Their division will be made serially from one, two, three, four, five parts.

43. One of its constituent parts will have a length greater than the breadth. The height of the pavilion will be from $3\frac{1}{2}$ hands to seven hands.

44. In a pavilion the extent of a pillar will be from six relative units to one hand.

अथ गृहमण्डपाः ।

युगास्त्रः षोडशस्तम्भः समर्थो नाम मण्डपः ।
द्वि द्वि स्तम्भविवृद्धया तु भद्रभेदेन संयुताः ॥४५ ॥

भूधरो दक्षसंज्ञश्च देवार्क्षः क्षितिभूषणः ।
कार्या द्विजातिवर्णानां पञ्चैते गृहमण्डपाः ॥४६ ॥

अथ वेदिका ॥

चतुष्कोणा तु या वेदी स्वस्तिका सा शुभाप्तये ।
विवाहेष्वासने यज्ञे राज्ञां देवार्चनादिषु ॥४७ ॥

चतुर्भद्रैर्युता भद्रा लिङ्गादिस्थापने हिता ।
श्रीधरो कोणविंशत्या देवतास्थापनेऽर्चने ॥४८ ॥

वेदी पद्मदलाकारा वसुकोणा तु पद्मिनी ।
[१५]देवपूजाप्रतिष्ठाभिषेकनीराजनादिषु ॥४९ ॥

विप्रादीनां क्रमात्सप्तषट्पञ्चयुगहस्तकः ।
त्रिद्व्येकहस्तहीनानां [१६]व्यास त्र्यंशोन्नता शुभा ॥५० ॥

विवाहेऽब्धिकरा वेदी गृहस्यैस्शेऽथ वामतः ॥५१ ॥

अथ सिंहासनम् ।

दैर्घ्ये सिंहासनं कुर्या[१७]दुन्नतं षष्ठिमातृकम् ।
पञ्चाशदङ्गुलं मध्यान्तैश्चत्वारिंशता परम् ॥५२ ॥

---

१५. देवी in A

१६. न्यास in B

१७. उत्तमं in A

Now the pavilion of a house

The pavilion known as *Samartha* is a square one with sixteen pillars. With the addition of two more pillars and different types of mouldings (called) *Bhūdhara, Dakṣasaṁjñga, Devārkṣa, Kṣitibhūṣaṇa Maṇḍapas* are built. These five types of house pavilions are to be built for Brahmins and others. 45- 46.

Now the altars

A quadrilateral altar known as *Svastikā* is auspicious for marriage, as a seat, in a sacrifice and for the worship of the King. 47.

Attached with four *Bhadrās*, the *Bhadrā* type of altar is auspicious for the consecration of *Liṅgas*. The *Śrīdhara* with 20 corners is suitable for the consecration for praying to the Gods. 48.

The *Padminī* type of altar is eight cornered, and shaped like the petals of a lotus and auspicious for the worship of Gods, consecration, coronation, lustration of arms and so on. 49.

The length of the altar of the Brahmin and others will be 7, 6, 5, 4 hands respectively. The breadth will be three, two, one hands short and if the height is 1/3rd of the breadth then it is regarded as auspicious. 50.

For a marriage, the altar will be of 7 hands and it will be placed either towards the North-East corner or to the left side of a house. 51.

Now the Royal Throne

For the measurement of the length of a royal throne the height will be up to 60 relative units. The medium one will be up to 50 *Aṅgulas* and the smaller one begins from 40 *Aṅgulas* onwards. 52.

[१८]व्यासे दशाङ्कवस्वंशहीनं [१९]दैर्घ्यार्धमुन्नतम्।
व्यासे शरांशे वा सप्तभागे भद्रं त्रिभागिकम्॥५३॥

षडशीत्योदये भक्ते तत्र भिट्टं युगांशकम्।
जाड्यंकुम्भं तु सप्तांशं कन्दमंशेन कारयेत्॥५४॥

कणपालीं तु वेदांशां [शी] द्व्यंशमन्तरपत्रकम्।
कर्णे द्विभागिकं कुर्याद् ग्रासपट्टी युगांशकम्॥५५॥

गजाः शिवैर्हया नन्दैर्नराः सप्तभिरंशकैः।
वेदी शक्रे रसैः छाद्यं तिथिभिर्मत्तवारणम्॥५६

विधेयास्तु नरा वेद्या एकांशेन विनिर्गताः।
द्वाभ्यां हयास्त्रिभिर्नागा ग्रासपट्टीयुगांशकैः॥५७॥

ततः कर्णो द्विभागेन कन्दो ग्रासवती समः।
कन्दात्षडंशैः कणकं कंदाच्च खुरकं शिवैः॥५८॥

[२०]भिट्टमेकांशकं तस्माच्चतुस्तम्भं सतोरणम्।
समाडं घण्टाकलशं ज्येष्ठं स्तम्भैर्विनापि वा॥५९॥

गजाश्वोनं तत्र सिंहैर्युतं तत्कीर्त्तिवर्धनम्।
ज्येष्ठं गजहयैर्हीनं तोरणाढ्यं सुखासनम्॥६०॥

अथ गवाक्षः।

गवाक्षो लुम्बिकाहीनस्त्रिपताकः स केवलः।
द्विलुम्बिकः स्यादुभयो र्नन्द्यावर्त्तश्चतुर्युगः॥६१॥

---

१८. ब्यासै/ब्यासं in ACDE

१९. दैर्ध्यार्थ in B C, दैर्ध्याश्च in DE

२०. एकहस्ते तु प्रासादे भिट्टं वेदाङ्गुलं स्मृतम्
एकतः पञ्चहस्तान्तं हस्तेचैकैकमङ्गुलम् अ पृ ch १२३ v १९

53. The breadth will be less by 10, 9, 8, and the height will be half of the length. Of the 5th part or of the 7th part of the breadth, *Bhadra* will cover three parts.

54. Of the height measuring 86 units, the ridge will be about 4 parts (*Yugāṁśa*). *Jāḍyakumbha* (a prominent mould of a *Jagatī*) will occupy 7 parts and a knot should also form a part.

55-56. The iron rod (*Kaṇapālī*) will occupy 4 parts and the recess between mouldings will be of two parts. The helm (*Karṇa*) will occupy two parts and the horizontal band known as *Grāsapaṭṭī* will occupy 4 parts, the elephant by 11th part, horses by 9th part, the nymph are by 7th part, the platform by 14th part, the *Chādya* by 6th part, the *Mattavāraṇa* by 15th part.

56-57. *Narā* (nymphs) are to be extended by one part of the royal throne, the horse will be on the second part, the elephant on the third, and the horizontal band (*Grāsapaṭṭī*) will be on the fourth part.

58. Then the helm in the two parts will correspond to the knot fixed in the metal part. The *Kaṇaka* will be measured from the sixth part of the knot *(Kanda)*. The heel will be measured by the eleventh(*Śiva*) part from the knot.

59. The rafter will be erected on the first part and the gate will comprise of 4 pillars. The largest type of throne will be adorned with *Māḍa,* bells, pitchers, and with or without pillars.

60. That throne which is bereft of elephants and horses but marked by lions is conducive to fame. The best one is also short of horses and elephants but adorned with a gate and that type of throne is comfortable for use.

Now the latticed window

61. A latticed window is devoid of *Lumbikā* and it is adorned with three *Patākās* only. It may have two *Lumbikās* on both the sides and if four *Lumbikās* are on the four sides, it is known as *Nandyāvarta.*

अष्टलुम्बि प्रियमुखो रविलुम्बिस्तु सन्मुखः।
छाद्येनैकमुखः छाद्यपंक्तियुग्मे प्रियाङ्गकः ॥६२॥

पद्मनाभस्त्रिभिः छाद्यैर्दीपचित्रस्तु तैर्युगैः।
विचित्रः पञ्चभिः छाद्यैः पञ्च भेदा [२१]इति पृथक् ॥६३॥

आयामेऽभ्यधिकः सिंहो हंसः स्याद्विस्तरेऽधिकः।
बुद्धिदश्चतुरस्त्रो सौमभद्रो बुद्धिसागरः ॥६४॥

गरुडः पक्षसहितो वामे दक्षे सजालकः।
राजसेनासनछाद्यवेदिकामत्तवारणैः ॥६५॥

गवाक्षाः शोभिता राज्ञां सिंहजालैलकादिभिः।
अनेकाकारविन्यासरन्ध्रैरभिविराजितम् ॥६६॥

विदध्याज्जालकं धीमांस्तथा चन्द्रावलोकनम् ॥६७॥

अथ छाद्यम्।

गृहोदयार्धनिष्क्रान्तं छाद्यं पट्टसमं शुभम्।
करालं कुमुदाकारं कलापं [२२]सूर्प्पसन्निभम् ॥६८॥

प्रलम्बं काकपक्षाभं तत् षोढाकारभेदतः।
जलपट्टी तु पादांशा पिण्डे व्यासे गुणाङ्गुला ॥६९॥

२१. सूर्य in B
२२. सूर्य in B

62. With 8 *Lumbis* it is known as *Priyamukha* and with 12 *Lumbis,* it is known as *Sanmukha.* With one *Chādya* it is known as *Ekamukha* and with two *Chādyas* in a row it is known as *Priyāṅgaka.*

63. With three *Chādyas,* it is known as *Padmanābha* and with four *Chādyas* it is known as *Dīpacitra.* It is known as *Vicitra* if adorned with five *Chādyas.* These are the five different types.

64. If the length is greater it is known as *Siṁha* and if the breadth is greater it is known as *Haṁsa.* The square one is known as *Buddhida* and the *Buddhisāgara* is having *Bhadra* in the North.

65. The *Garuḍa* will have wings on the right and left sides and it will be a latticed one. It will be adorned with *Rājasena* seats, *Chādya* platform and *Mattavāraṇa.*

66. For a King's house the latticed windows are decorated with lion-like nets(*Siṁhajāla*), Elaka and others. The latticed windows will be displayed in different shapes and arrangements.

67. A wise person will arrange trellis as well as *Candrāvalokana* properly.

Now the Chādyam

A *Chādya* is regarded as auspicious if it is projected from half of the height of a house and equal to the *Paṭṭa* (slab).

According to the different shapes, they are of six varieties– *Karāla,Kumuda* (shape of a lotus), *Kalāpa* (moon), shape of a *Sūrppa, Pralamba* (prolonged) and *Kākapakṣābha* (like the wings of a crow).

68-69. The water- band (*Jalapaṭṭī*) will be 1/4th of the whole dimension, and its width will be of 3 *Aṅgulas.*

मुखपट्टी तदग्रे तु पिण्डे सार्धद्विमात्रिका।
[२३]त्र्यङ्गुला विस्तरे श्रेष्ठा ततश्छाद्यं युगाङ्गुलम् ॥७० ॥

अङ्गुला विस्तरे दण्डाः सपादद्व्यङ्गुलोदयाः ॥७१ ॥

अथ छत्रः ॥

छत्रं व्यासे त्रिधा सार्धं द्वित्रिसार्धं त्रिभिः करैः।
पञ्चाशदङ्गुलं दैवं दण्डो हेमचतुष्करः ॥७२ ॥

रत्नैः सार्धकरं यावत्काष्ठकाञ्चनरुप्पजः।
विश्वातैर्विषमैर्दण्डश्चामरः पर्वभिर्युतः ॥७३ ॥

[२४]**अथ अर्चापीठम् ॥**

अर्चापीठं तु षण्मात्रात्करावधिशुभद्रुमैः।
वेदास्त्रमायतं वृत्तं व्यासपादान्तमुन्नतम् ॥ ७४ ॥

मणिमुक्ताप्रवालार्कः रुप्यस्फटिकहेमजाम्।
एकाङ्गुलाद्वितस्त्यन्तं प्रतिमां पूजयेद्गृहे ॥ ७५ ॥

दीपस्तम्भः कराद्रामहस्तान्त धातुदारुजः।
सपीठकुम्भकलशःसकङ्कण [२५]फलः शुभः ॥ ७६ ॥

अथ शय्या ॥

स्व-स्व व्याससमायामा शय्या दैर्घ्यार्धे विस्तरा।
स्व-स्व हस्तसमोत्सेधा पादव्यासः षडङ्गुलः ॥७७ ॥

---

२३. अङ्गुला in ACDE

२४. omittled in BCDE

२५. कणः in A

70-71. In front of these there will be *Mukhapaṭṭī* and its dimension will be $2\frac{1}{2}$ *Aṅgulas*. It is regarded best if the width is three *Aṅgulas* and then the *Chādya* is of four *Aṅgulas*. The pillarets is $2\frac{1}{2}$ *Aṅgulas* in width if counted by the *Aṅgulamāna*.

Now the Umbrella

The circumference of the umbrella will be of three sizes : it is measured by $2\frac{1}{2}$ or $3\frac{1}{2}$ and 3 hands.

72. The divine scepter will be of 50 *Aṅgulas* and made of gold and quadrangular in shape.

The divine scepter can be made of wood, gold or silver and up to half the *Kara* it will be adorned with gems.

73. The scepter will be uneven on all sides and the chowrie will be added with knots.

Now the Pedestal of Worship

74. The pedestal of worship is to be measured from six *Mātrās* to one hand and it will be made of good quality wood. It may be square, rectangular, or round in shape. The height will be one *Pāda* of the circumference.

75. The idol is to be made of gems, pearls, corals, crystals, silver, quartz, gold. In a house the idol measuring from one *Aṅgula* to *Vitasti* (9 *Aṅgulas*) is to be worshipped.

76. The lamp-stand will be from one hand to three hands and it will be made of metal or wood. That will be adorned with pedestal, pot, and pitcher and bangles and such a lamp-stand augurs well.

Now the Beds

77. The cot will be made according to one's own length and breadth and the width will be half of the length. The elevation of the bed will be according to one's own hand, and one fourth part of the width will be six *Aṅgulas*.

स्व-स्ववेदाङ्गुला व्यासे इष्टे पिण्डे गुणाङ्गुला ॥७८ ॥

वराहः ॥

हस्तात्सपादात् युग्मान्तं शय्या स्याद्द्विगुणायता।
उच्चाद्दैर्घ्यं तृतीयांशे पादे वा विविधाकृतिः ॥७९ ॥

प्रदक्षिणाग्रं काष्ठं स्याद्दीषायोगे शुभप्रदम्।
शिरीषशिंशपाशाकचन्दनाञ्जनधन्वनाः ॥८० ॥

देवद्रुमो[२६]ऽम्बुहारिद्रास्तिनिसः पनसोऽशनः।
शालः कालार्जुनो निम्बः श्रीपर्णी तिन्दुकस्तथा ॥८१ ॥

मधुकः पद्मकः श्रेष्ठा यानशय्या[२७]सनेष्वपि।
एकद्विदारुजा शय्या कार्या न बहुदारुजाः ॥८२ ॥

यवमध्याण्डपर्वा भाविकर्णा पितृत[२८]र्पिणी।
स्वामिमानादत्यधिका ह्रस्वा शय्या न शोभना ॥८३ ॥

अथ शिविका ॥

शिविका सार्धहस्तादित्र्यङ्गुलर्धा त्रिधा [२९]पृथुः।
दैर्घ्ये सपादा सार्धा वा व्यासकर्णमितापि वा ॥८४ ॥

दृढालोहे भदन्ताद्यैर्योग्येऽथ श्रीमतां नृणाम् ॥८५ ॥

अथ गृह[३०]प्रवेशः।

निष्पन्ने न विशेच्छीघ्रं चिरं नापि विलम्बयेत्।
गृहे श्रयन्ति भूताद्याः प्रवेशरहितं चिरम् ॥८६ ॥

२६. Reference of this Ambu tree is found in बृहत्संहिता Vol II, ch 79. V17.

२७. सनेष्विमे in A

२८. तर्प्पणी in A

२९. पुष्पु in A

३०. निवेशः in ACDE

78. The width will be one's own 4 *Aṅgulas* (or *Hastas*) and the desired circumference will be 3 *Aṅgulas.*

Varāha

79. The bed will be twice in breadth. From the height, the third or fourth part of the length should be of different shapes.

80-81. The square wooden frame of four corners, if added with elephant tusks, is auspicious.

82. *Śirīṣa, Śiṁśapa, Śāka, Candana, Añjana, Dhanvana, Devadruma, Ambu, Haridrā, Tinisa, Panasa, Aśana, Śāla, Kāla, Arjuna, Nimba, Śrīparṇī, Tinduka, Madhuka, Padmaka* are considered the most useful for vehicles, beds and seats. The bedstead should be made of one or two varieties of wood, not with many varieties of wood together. 80-

83. A bed with *Yava* in the centre or with (*Aṇḍa*) oval shaped joints, *Bhāvikarṇa* or *Pitṛtarpiṇī* and being too big or too little in respect of the owner is not pleasant (*Śobhana*).

Now the Palanquin

The breadth of a palanquin will be of three varieties, the size may be from one and half hands and two or three *Aṅgulas.*

84-85. Its length will be one-fourth or half or equal to the width of the corner division. It should be made strong with iron, which will be suitable for monks (*Bhadanta*) and prosperous men.

Now the entry into the house

86. After the completion of a house the owner should not wait too long and should try to enter the house as early as possible. The spirits enter therein if it remains unoccupied for long.

सौम्यायने दिने शुद्धे रिक्ता भौमार्कवर्जिते।
रोहिण्यां [३१]शतभे पुष्ये चित्रास्वात्युत्तरामृगे ॥८७॥

धनिष्ठापौष्णमैत्रेषु प्रवेशः शुभदो गृहे।
प्रवेशे सूर्य[३२]सद्मानि स्ततो वेदेषु तूद्वसम् ॥८८॥

चतुर्थोऽर्थोऽब्धिषु श्रेयश्चतुर्थ कलहोऽन्वहम्।
युगेषु गर्भनाशः स्यात् त्रिषु वासश्चिरं भवेत् ॥८९॥

सुखं कलशचक्रे स्यात्त्रिषु भेषु प्रवेशने।
शुभे निमित्ते शकुने स्थिरे लग्ने स्थिरांशके ॥९०॥

[३३]मूर्त्तादुपचये स्वीये राशौ लग्ने विधोर्बले।
सौम्यै स्त्रिकोणकेन्द्रस्थैः केन्द्राष्टान्त्यं विना परैः ॥९१॥

त्रिषडायगतैर्वा तैः प्रवेशः शुभदो गृहे।
माङ्गल्यैरङ्कुरैदीपैः स्त्रग्भिः कदलिभिर्युते ॥९२॥

अश्वत्थ[३४]चूत[३५]पत्राद्ये सकन्यातोरणे गृहे।
वासयित्वा दिने पूर्वे ब्राह्मणान्सुरभीर्वृषान् ॥९३॥

तत्र होमं जपं कुर्यात् स्वाध्यायं स्वस्तिवाचनम्।
तगरागरुकुष्टाग्रा निशाभिस्तत्प्रलेपयेत् ॥९४॥

चन्दनादैर्भुवं सिक्त्वा निशायामधिवासनम्।
गृहे पूर्वोत्तरे सूर्यदशाष्टकरमण्डपे ॥९५॥

---

३१. श्रवणे in A
३२. भेद्मानि in BC
३३. मूर्त्तावुपचये in A
३४. कृत in C
३५. पत्राये in CD पत्रथि in B

87-88ab.In the *Uttarāyaṇa* (*Saumyāyana*) month, on a favourable day except in the *Rikt, tithī,* Tuesday and Sunday, it is auspicious to enter one's house in the assemblage of *Rohiṇī, Śatabha, Puṣyā, Citrā, Svātī, Uttarā, Mṛgaśirā, Dhaniṣṭhā, Pauṣṇa* and *Maitra* stars.

88cd-89. The fourth solar position is regarded as inauspicious for the inaugural entry to the house. Amongst the fourth, fifth (*artha*) and seventh inauspicious solar positions, the fourth brings enmity and quarrelling day after day. If entry to the house is made in the fourth solar position, the base of the house will collapse or be destroyed, whereas in the third solar position the house gets stabilized and becomes permanent.

90. Three stars out of twenty-seven *nakṣatra* entering into *kalaśacakra,* good omens, fixed *lagna* and *aṁsa* are all auspicious and entrance to the house at those times and moments gives much pleasure to the owner.

91-92ab. It is auspicious to enter into one's house by the owner on his third, sixth, tenth and eleventh planetary position(*mūrta*), when *lagnas* of his birth chart and lunar position are favourable, the *āyas* are in third and sixth position and when in the center of the *trikoṇa* there are auspicious planets, while inauspicious planets are in places other than his 8th and 12th planetary position.* (vide note below) With auspicious materials, sprouts, lamps, garlands, and plantains, and with the twigs of *Aśvattha* and mango, one should enter the house through the portals with his daughter.

92cd-94.On the previous day, with *Brahmins* incense and a bull, one should perform oblations, utter prayers, chanting of Vedas and auspicious spells. He should smear the place with *Tagara, Agaru, Kuṣṭa, Agra* on the previous night.

95. The land is to be moistened with sandal wood, water etc and they should start staying there at night in the *Maṇḍapa* which are measuring twelve, ten or eight hands and set up in the N.E. corner of the house.

* Note:
In this section the time and moment for inaugural entrance into one's house for residing has been laid down. Some particular constellation of stars are auspicious, others are not congenial. This concerns the Astronomy known in those days.

सूत्रधारः सोपवीतः सालङ्कारः सिताम्बरः।
शालिभिर्दण्डमाने तु स्थण्डिले गृहमध्यगे ॥९६ ॥

[३६]विन्यस्य वास्तुं वस्त्रोर्ध्वे कलशांस्तत्समन्ततः।
स्थापयेन्नव वा पञ्च नववस्त्र[३७]समावृतान् ॥९७ ॥

सुगन्धोदकसम्पूर्णान्मणिहेमसमन्वितान्।
वास्तुदेवान्समाबाह्य सम्पूज्याथ बलिं हरेत् ॥९८ ॥

इन्द्रादिभ्यो दिगीशेभ्यो दद्यात्स्व स्व दिशि क्रमात्।
दिग्विदिक् स्तम्भमूलेषु दिवारात्र्यम्बुचारिणाम् ॥९९ ॥

[३८]नागेभ्यो भुवि सर्वेभ्यो देवेभ्यस्तु बलिं [३९]दिवि।।
श्रियैस्तु शयने मन्त्रैः प्रणवादिनमोऽन्तकै ॥१०० ॥

[४०]पृष्ठतः पूजयेद्वास्तुं सर्वं तक्षकसाधनम्।
ततो मन्दिरमध्यस्थः स्थपतिः प्रवदेदिदम् ॥१०१ ॥

ब्रह्मा विष्णुः शङ्करः सर्वदेवाः क्षोणिर्लक्ष्मीवाग्वधूः सिंहकेतुः।
ज्येष्ठा विश्वेदेवताश्च प्रजानां श्रीसौभाग्यारोग्यभोग्यं सृजन्तु ॥१०२ ॥

निरुजामुदितासघनाप्रथिता यशसामहताद्भुतवीर्ययुता।
सततं निरुपद्रवकर्मयुता पृथिवीपति जीवतु धर्मविधेः ॥१०३ ॥

धारानिपातात्सलिलप्रकोपाद्दंष्ट्रानिपातात्पवनप्रकोपात्।
अग्नेश्च दाहान्मुखिताच्च चोराद्रक्षत्विदं सद्म शिवं च मेऽस्तु ॥१०४ ॥

गृहं सम्मार्ज्य तत् सिञ्चेत्सुगन्धिकलशोदकैः।
धान्यान्यगृहवस्तूनि स्वे स्वे स्थाने प्रविन्यसेत् ॥१०५ ॥

---

३६. गृहस्य in DE वान्यस्य in B
३७. समादृतान् in A
३८. छागेभ्यो in A
३९. ददेत् in E
४०. षष्ठतः in B

96. The thread holder (*Śutradhāra*) wearing the sacred thread (*Upavīta*), ornaments and dressed in white cloths will enter the measured ground prepared for sacrifice at the center of the house with corns(*Śāli*).

97. In that plot of land, one will place pitchers on the cloth. The pitchers, numbering nine or five, will be covered with new clothes.

98. The pitchers will be filled up with scented water, gems, gold. He will invoke a worship to the presiding deities *Vāstudeva* and then offer the oblation.

99. He will present offerings to *Indra* and other (eight) *Dikpālas* of their own directions serially. Then he will also offer worship to the deities residing at the foundation of the pillars and deities residing in the water throughout day and night.

100. He will also worship the serpents and all other deities living on the Earth. At the time of entry into the resting chambers, spells starting with auspicious letters *Śrī* and ending in *Om* should be uttered.

101. Afterwards, the *Vāstu* will be worshipped in all respects by the carpenter. Then the chief architect residing in the temple will utter these mantras.

Mantras

102. *Brahmā, Viṣṇu, Śaṅkara,* all the deities, the mother earth, *Lakṣmī, Sarasvatī* (*Vāgvadhū*), *Simhaketu*(Goddess *Durgā*), the prominent among the Goddess, *(Jyeṣṭhā)* and universal deities may confer prosperity, good luck, health and enjoyment to everybody.

103. Let the Lord of the Earth thrive in good health (*Niruja*), in happiness, with riches, celebrity, fame, having great and extraordinary valour. He should be always engaged in undisturbed works according to the precepts of religion.

104. Let the house be made secure from torrential rain, from inundation, from canine attacks, from violent storms, from burning and encroachment of fire, from thieves and let happiness come to us.

105. After cleansing the house, it is to be sprinkled with perfumed water from the pitcher. Paddy and other household goods are to be kept in their proper place.

ततो गृहेशगेहिन्यो स्वजनाद्यैः समन्वितौ।
विचिन्त्य जगदीशं स्वं विशेतां वस्तुमद्गृहम् ॥१०६॥

गृहिणी गृहदेवेभ्यो बलिं सव्यञ्जनो[४१]दकम्।
ओं गृहदेवताभ्यो नम इत्युक्त्वा वितरेत्ततः ॥१०७॥

गृहाधिपः सुरान्विप्रान् स्थपतिं तक्षकानपि।
रत्नैधनाम्बरैर्धान्यैः पशुभिश्चापि तोषयेत्।
ततः स्वजनमित्राद्यैर्भोजनीयं गृहे श्रिये ॥१०८॥

सुतेन देवसिंहेन प्रार्थितः क्षेत्रनन्दनः।
स्थपतिः सृजति स्मेदं मण्डनो वास्तुमण्डनम् ॥१०९॥

इति श्रीसूत्रधारमण्डनविरचिते वास्तुशास्त्रे वास्तुमण्डने प्रकीर्णकाध्यायोऽष्टमः। श्लोकाः ।१०९॥

वास्तुमण्डनश्च सम्पूर्णः। सहयेद्वेशते आद्ये २०७, सप्ताशीति द्वितीयके ८७, तृतीये पञ्चनवति ९५, रूपाग्न्येकास्तुरीयके। १३१, द्वात्रिंशत्पञ्चमे श्लोकाः ॥ ३२॥ भूद्वयेका रससंमिते १२१, सप्तमे पञ्चनवतिः, सादित्यं शतमष्टमे ॥११२॥

श्रीवास्तुमण्डने तन्त्रे अध्याये तु प्रकीर्णके
एक्ये पुनः शतान्यष्टश्लोकाश्चाशीतिसम्मिताः ।८८२॥
सम्वत् (१६७५) वर्षे श्रीसूत्रधारमण्डनविरचिते
वास्तुशास्त्रे वास्तुमण्डने प्रकीर्णकाध्यायोऽष्टमः लिपिकृतः।
यादृशं पुस्तके दृष्टं तादृशं ल (लि) खितं मया ॥[४३]

---

४१. दनम् in B

४२ ग्रंथसंख्या ८८० in B, D, in Ch ९८०

४३ Colophon in Ms B सम्वत् १७९७ माघवदि १२ गुरौ श्री उदयपुरत्राजधान्यां श्री पुराणा श्री जगत्सिंह विजयराज्ये भट्टभाई रामसुतो भट्ट नीलकण्ठोदम लेखि श्री रामो जयति।
० in Ms C सम्बत् १८१९ मिति माघवदि २ मंगल वासरायां लीपिकृतम्
० in Ms E सम्बत् १८९० शके १७५५ फाल्गुनशत्कउवस्व वै, श्रीरामो जयति,

106. Then the master and mistress of the house with their relatives will enter the house with riches and meditate on the great Lord of the Earth.

107. The mistress will make offerings of rice with curry to the presiding deity of the house, chanting '*Om*, salute to the lord of the house' and then distribute the offering.

108. Then the sages, Brahmins, architects, carpenters are to be greeted with gems, wealth, clothing, rice and cattle by the owner of the house.

108. The inmates of the house will dine with relatives and friends for the prosperity of the house.

109. Being requested by the son of *Devasiṁha*, the son of *Kṣetra*, the architect *Maṇḍana* composed this work.

Thus ends the 8th chapter named Prakīrṇakādhyāya of Vāstumaṇḍana, the book on Vāstuśāstra written by Maṇḍana Sūtradhāra.

Vāstumaṇḍana is complete. The first chapter consists of 207 *Ślokas.* the second chapter contains 85 *Ślokas.* There are 94 *Ślokas* in the third chapter. The fourth chapter contains 130 *Ślokas,* the fifth chapter consists of 32 *Ślokas,* while sixth chapter contains 119 *Ślokas,* the seventh chapter consists of 96 *Ślokas,* and the last one, the eighth chapter contains 109 *Ślokas.*

In the *Vāstumaṇḍanatantra,* the total number of *Ślokas* of all chapters is 872.

In the *Saṁvat* 1675 the eighth chapter of *Vāstumaṇḍana* of *Vāstuśāstra* written by *Maṇḍaṇasūtradhāra* has been copied down.

As seen in the book, so is copied by me.

Appendices

I. NAMES OF THE PLANTS MENTIONED IN Vāstumaṇḍana

Ajakarṇa	Shorea robusta Gaertn.
Añjana	Hardwickia pinnata Roxb. or Memecylon edule Roxb.
Arjuna	Terminalia arjuna W. & A.
Aśoka	Saraca indica L.
Asana	Pterocarpus marsupium Roxb.
Ākāśha	Terminalia belerica Roxb.
Ākāsavela/ Ākāsāvara	
Ākāsavalli	Cassytha filiformis L.
Āmra	Mangifera indica L.
Āmrātaka	Spondias pinnata Kurz.
Badari	Ziziphus jujuba Lamk.
Bāna	Barberia strigosa Wall.
Bhurja	Betula utilis D. Don
Bibhītaka	Terminalia belerica Roxb.
Bijapurikā	Citrus medica L.
Bikañkata	Flacourtia tamontehi L Heritic or Flacourtia jangomas (Lour.) Raeusch.
Bimba	Coccinia indica W. & A.
Campaka	Michelia champaca L.
Candana	Santalum album L.
Ciñcā	Tamarindus indica L.
Cira	Ficus benghalensis L.
Darbha	Desmostachya bipinnata
Dāḍimi	Punica granatum L.
Dhanvana	Grewia tiliaefolia Vahl. or Grewia asiatica L.

Dhattura	Datura metel L. var. alba L.
Dhava	Anogeissus latifolia Wall.
Drākṣā	Vitis vinifera L.
Gavākṣa/	Glycosmis pentaphylla Corr.
Gavākṣi	Citrullus colocynthis (L.) Schrad.
	or Jasminum sambac L.
	or Streblus asper Lour.
Hāridraka	Adina cordifolia Hook f.
Hintāla	Phoenix paludosa Roxb. or Cycas circinalis Roxb.
Homa	Acacia catechu Willd.
Ikṣava/	Tribulus terestris
lkṣavāku	Lagenaria siceraria Standl.
Jāti	Jasminum grandiflorum L.
Kadamba	Anthocephalus cadamba A. Reich
Kadara	Acacia ferruginea D.C. or Acacia suma Buck-Ham.
Kalidruma	Terminalia belerica Roxb.
Kanṭa	Aglaia elacagnoidea (Juss.) Bents or Amomum subulatum Roxb. or Callicarpa macrophylla Vahl. or Cedrela toona Roxb.
Kapittha	Limonia acidissima L. Feronia limonja L. Swingle
Karañja	Pongamia glabra Vent.
Karavīra	Nerium indicum Mill.
Karcura	Circuma Zedoaria (Christon) Rosc
Karṇikāra	Cassia fistula L. or Pterospermum acerifolium Willd.
Kālaskandha	Garciria morella (Gacrtn) Desr.
Kālāgaru	A kind of black alae wood or Agallochum
Kārpāsa	Gossypium barbadens Linn.
Kāśa	Saccharum spontaneum L.
Ketaki	Pandanus fascicularis Lamk.
Khadira	Acacia catechu Willd.

Kharjuri	Phoenix sylvestris Roxb.
Kiñgśuka	Butea monosperma Taub.
Kovidāra	Bauhinia acuminata L.
Kramuka	Areca catechu L.
Kuśa	Desmostachya bipinnata
Kusuma	Schleichera trijuga Willd. Carthamus tinctorius L. Michelia champaca L. Sesbania grandiflora Pers.
Lañkuca	Artocarpus lakoocha Roxb.
Madhūka	Glycyrrhiza glabra L. or Bassia latifolia Roxb. (Mayamata)
Madhudruma/ vṛkṣa	Madhuca longifolia (Krenig) Macbr.
Mañjistha	Rubia cordifolia L.
Muni/ Munidruma	Sesbania grandiflora Pers.
Muñja	Saccharum munja
Nārikela	Cocos nucifera L.
Nimba	Azadirachta indica. A. Juss.
Nīpa	Anthocephalus chinensis (Lamk.) Rich ex Walp
Padmaka	Prunus cerasoides L. or Saussurea lappa Clarke.
Palāśa	Butea monosperma Taub.
Panasa	Artocarpus heterophylla Lamk.
Patanga	Caesalpinia sappan L. or Eclipta prostrata L.
Pathyā	Terminalia chebula Retz. Haematoxylon campechianum L.
Pārijāta	Erythrina variegata L.
Pātala	Stereospermum suaveolens DC.
Peepala	Ficus religiosa L.
Pikapriya	Mangifera indica L.
Pilu	Salvadora olleaides Dene or Salvadora persica L.
Piñdi/Piñdin	Rungia parviflora Nees.

	Vangueria spinosa Roxb.
Piśita	Nardostachys grandiflora DC.
Plakṣa	Ficus virens Ait. var Wightiana (Miq) Chithra Ficus infectoria Roxb.
Punnāga	Calophyllum inophyllum L.
Puruṣa/ Paruṣa	Grewia asiatica L.
Pūga	Arica catechu L.
Putrajiva/ Putranjiva	Putranjiva roxburghii Wall.
Raktacandana	Pterocarpus santalinus L.
Rambhā	Musa balbisiana Colla.
Rājādana	Manilkara hexandra (Roxb.) Dubard or Buchanania lanzan Spreng.
Rodhra/ Lodhra	Symplocos racemosa Roxb.
Rohini	Soymida febrifuga Roxb. or Terminalia chebula Retz. or Gmelina arborea Roxb.
Sakatphala/ Shakata	Ougeinia oojeinensis (Roxb.) Hochr.
Sallaki	Boswellia serrata Roxb.
Saptaparṇi	Echites scholaris L. or Alstonia scholaris R. Br.
Sarala	Pinus longifolia Roxb.
Sarja	Shorea robusta Gaertn. or Terminalia tomentosa W. & A.
Sarpamāra	Arimeda
Sauvarṇaka	Cassia fistula L.
Śami	Prosopis spicigera L. Mimosa suma Roxb.
Śāka	Tectona grandis L.f.
Śālakālā/ Śāla	Shorea robusta
Śālmali	Bombax malabaricum D.C. or Salmalia malabarica (DC) Schott &Exdl

Śilindhra	Fructification of fungus
Simha (Vāska)	Adhatoda vasica Nees.
Śimśapā	Dalbergia sissoo Roxb.
Śirīṣa	Albizzia lebbeck Benth.
Śleṣmāntaka	Cordia dichotoma Forst. f. Cordia obliqua Willd.
Śriparṇi	Gmelina arborea Roxb. or Aegle marmelos Corr.
Śroṇi	N.A.
Stamba	N.A.
Sūrya (Ākanda)	Calotropis gigantea R. Br.
Suradruma	Cedrus deodara (Roxb.) Loud or Lobelia nicotianifolia Roth ex Schult
Śveta/ Girikarnikā	Alhagi pseudalhagi (Birb.) Desv. or Careya arborea Roxb. or Clitoria ternatea L.
Tagara	Tabernaemontana coronaria Br.
Tamāla	Cinnamomum tamala Nees. or Nicotiana tabacum L.
Tāla	Borassus flabellifer L.
Tāliśa	jangemas raeuch or Abies pindrow Royle or Abies webbiana Lindle
Tilaka	Wendlandia heynei (Roem. & Schult.) Symplocos racemosa Roxb.
Timira	Lawsonia inermis L.
Tinduka	Diospyros embryopteris Pers.
Tinisa	Ougeinia dalbergioides Benth.
Udumvara	Ficus glomerata Roxb. Ficus racemosa L.
Vakula	Mimusops elengii L.
Vallātaka	Semecarpus anacardium L.
Vaṁśa	Bambusa arundinacea Willd.
Vaṭa	Ficus benghalensis L.
Vilva	Aegle marmelos (L.) Coree ex Schultz

II. Names of Planets Mentioned in Vāstumaṇḍana

Ravi	–	Sun
Soma (Candra)	–	Moon
Maṅgala (Bhauma)	–	Mars
Budha ga	–	Mercury
Bhṛaspati;	–	Jupiter
Śukra	–	Venus
Śani	–	Saturn
Rāhu –		
Ketu –		

III. Effect of Moon in Each Zodiac Sign

1.	Meṣa (Aries)	–	Pravāsa
2.	Vṛṣa (Taurus)	–	Nāśinī
3.	Mithuna (Gemini)	–	Mṛtyu
4.	Karkaṛa (Cancer)	–	Jayā
5.	Simha (Leo)	–	Hāsyā
6.	Kanyā (Virgo)	–	Rati
7.	Tulā (Librā)	–	Krīḍitā
8.	Vṛścika (Scorpio)	–	Nidritā
9.	Dhanu (Sagitarius)	–	Bhuktā
10.	Makara (Capricorn)	–	Jvarita
11.	Kumbha (aquirius)	–	Kampitā
12.	Mīna (Pisces)	–	Sthitā

IV. Stars Mentioned in Vāstumaṇḍana

Stars		Presiding Deity
Aśvinī	Aries	Aśvidvaya- Nasatyā, Dabhra
Bharaṇī	Aries	Yama
Kṛittikā	Pleiades (Taurus)	Agni
Rohiṇī	Taurus	Prajāpati Brahmā
Mṛgaśirā	Orion	Yajñasoma
ārdrā	Orion	Rudra
Punarvasu	Gemini	Aditi
Puṣya	Cancer	Brahmaṇaspati
Āśleṣā	Hydra	Rudra (Ahi)
Maghā	Leo	Maghavan,pitṛ
Pūrvāphālgunī	Leo	Bhaga
Uttarāphālgunī	Leo	Āditya, Aryamā
Hasta	Corvus	Savitā
Citrā	Virgo	Tvaṣṭā
Svāti	Alpha Bootes	Marutmān
Viśākhā	Corona Borealis, Libra	Indrāgnī
Anurādhā	Scorpius	Mitra
Jyeṣṭhā	Scorpius	Indra
Mālā	Scorpius	Nirṛti
Pūrvāṣāḍhā	Sagittarius	Āpa
Uttarāṣāḍhā	Sagittarius	Viśvedevā
Śravaṇa	Alpha aquarius	Viṣṇu
Dhaniṣṭhā	Delphinus	Aṣṭāvasu
Śatabhiṣā	Aquarius	Varuṇa
Pūrvābhādrapada	The square of Pegasus	Ajaikapāda
Uttarābhādrapada	Pegasus	Ahirbudhyarudra
Revatī	Pisces	Puṣan
Abhijit	Vega	

CHARTS

Śalyoddhāraḥ

Ch. - 1, Sl. 156-60

Svāti	Citrā	Hasta	Uttarā-Phālgunī
Viśākhā	Punarvasu	Puṣyā	Pūrva Phālgunī
Anurādhā	Ārdrā	Āśleṣa	Aryamā
Jyeṣṭhā	Mṛgaśirā	Rohiṇi	Kṛttikā
Maghā	Dhaniṣṭha	Śatabhiṣā	Bharaṇī
Purva-Āṣāḍha	Śravaṇa	Pūrva-Bhādrapada	Aśvinī
Uttar-Āṣāḍha	Abhijit	Uttara-Bhādrapada	Revatī

Marmavāstuḥ

Ch. I Sl. - 139 - 144

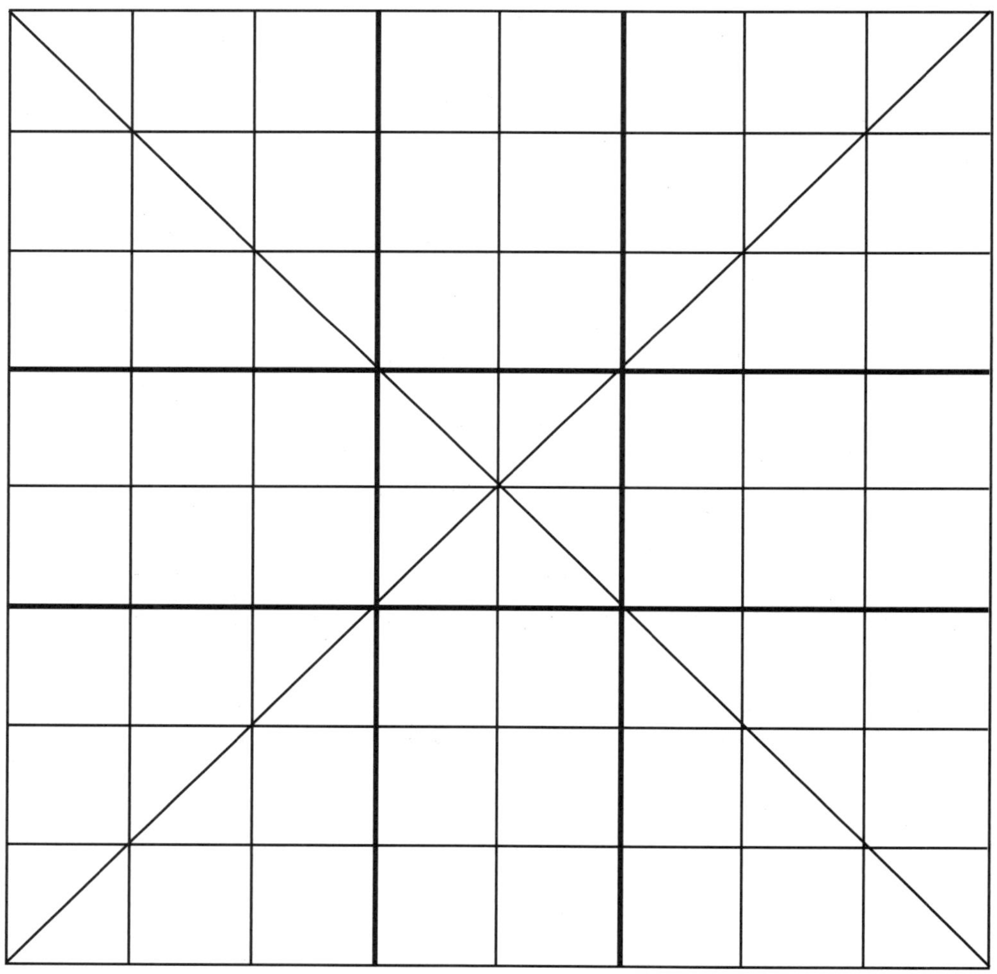

Plan of an Ordinary House

Ch. - 5

N

Storage for rice, oil etc.	Treasury, garden	Temple
Ponds or pools	Main rooms and master bed room	Door courtyard
Both room for children Sick room	Water reservoir, dinning place, dancing court	Kitchen, cowshed, etc.

S

Plan of a King's Palace
Ch. 5 Sl. - 10-32

In a city king's palace is to be erected on the 3/4th part or from Western or Northern direction, but for a palace in the fort, it will depend on the availability of place.

1. Brahmapada (open place) 2. Gate way, council hall 3. Coronation hall 4. Main rooms 5. Halls 6. Treasury 7. Sky gazing place 8. Dinning place 9. Community kitchen 10.-11. Room for king and Royal mother 12 - 13. Room for queen and other royal female 14. Temple facing south or west 15. Royal court 16. Clerical community, practice hall, pavilion and water tank 17. Painting gallery, room for teaching 18. Place for disbursement 19. Schools and legal courts 20 Storage for rice etc. 21. Main kitchen 22. Room for storing cooked food 23. Meeting room 24. Room for weapons (Armoury) dinning place 25. Painting room, place for guards and sentinels 26. Watch tower 27. Pleasure room 28. Road 29. sick room 30. Bath room 31. Place for water sports 32. Place for wrestling 33. Place for parade 34. Prince's parade 35. Granary and anjanalaya 36. Storage for weapon and poison in emergency 37. Room for the keeper 38. Stable for donkey and camel 39. Ponds for Dhatri and Sairandhri 40. Chamber for girls 41. Storage for medicinals herbs 42. Place for massage 43. Toilets, confinement room 44. Bathing place for children 45. Place for hot bath massage.

List of PĀDA

1. BRAHMAPĀDA
2. ARYAMĀ
3. VIVAŚVATA
4. MITRA
5. PṚTHVIDHARA
6. ĀPA
7. APAVATSA
8. SĀVITRI
9. SAVITARI
10. INDRA
11. INDRAJAYA
12. RUDRA
13. RUDRAJAYA
14. IŚA
15. PARJANYA
16. JAYA
17. ŚAKRA
18. SŪRYA
19. ŚATYA
20. BHŪṢA
21. VYOMNI
22. VAHNI
23. PUṢNI
24. VITATHA
25. GṚHAKṢATA
26. YAMA
27. GANDHARVA
28. BHṬḶGA
29. MṚGA
30. PITRĪ
31. DAUVāRIKA
32. SUGRĪVA
33. PUSPADANTA
34. VARUṆA
35. ASURA
36. ŚOSA
37. ROGA
38. VĀYU
39. NAGA
40. MUKHYA
41. BHALLĀṬA
42. SOMA
43. SAJLA
44. ADITI
45. DITI

Plan of a King's Palace
Ch. 5 Sl. - 10-32

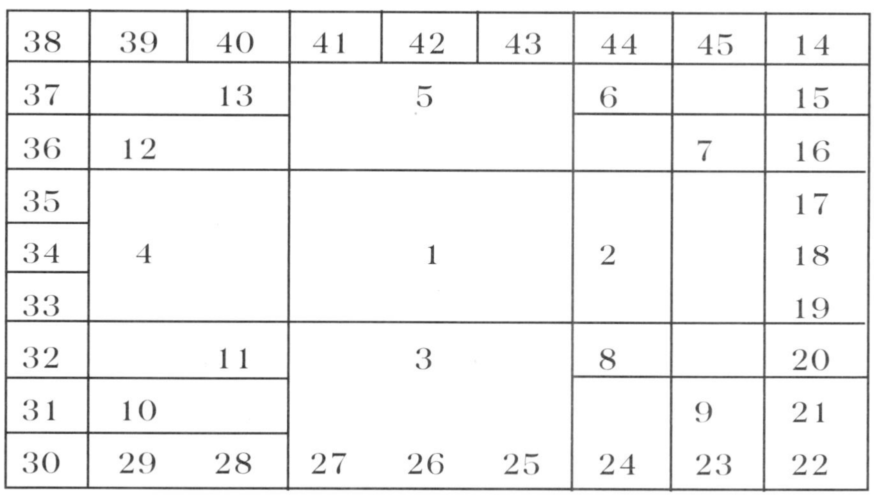

PLATE - 1

Prākāraka Ch. 3, (VM)

From the book *Kumbhalgarh : The Pride of Maharanas of Mewar.*
(Ch. - III VM)

PLATE - 2

A Panoramic view of Kumbhalgarh Fort

From the book *Kumbhalgarh : The Pride of Maharanas of Mewar.*

PLATE - 3

Kumbhalgarh Fort and Wall

Courtesy : Dr. Mitali Roy

PLATE - 4

Ambarāgāra Ch. 5, Verse 4, (VM)

Courtesy : Dr. Mitali Roy

Select Bibliography

Author	Work
Acharya P.K.	*Encyclopaedia of Hindu Architecture,* Treatise of Sanskrit Architectural terms with illustrative quotations from Silpaśāstra & archaeological record, Cosmos Publica-tions, Delhi-1994
	Illustration of Architectural & Sculptural objects with a synopsis, Oxford University Press, London-1927
Agarwala V.S.	*India as known to Panini; Study of the cultural material in the Aṣṭādhyāyī,* University of Lucknow-1953
	Evolution of the Hindu temple and other essays, Prithvi Prakashan, Varanasi-1965
Begde, V. Prabhakar	*Forts and Palaces of India,* New Delhi-1982
Bharadwaj, H.C.	*Aspects of Ancient Indian Technology and research based on scientific methods,* Motilal Banarasidas, Delhi-1979
Bhat, M. Ramkrishna	*Bṛhatsaṁhitā of Varāhamihira,* Vol. I, New Delhi-1992
Bhatt. S.C.	*The Encyclopaedic District Gazetteers of India in two volumes,* Gyan Publishing House, New Delhi-1997
Bhattacharya, Arupratan	*Ancient Indian Astronomical Terms and their Interpretations in the light of modern Astronomy,* Subarnarekha, Kolkata-1987
Bhattacharya, Tarapada	*A study of Vāstuvidya or Cannons of Indian architecture.,* 3rd revised enlarged edition, Cal - K.L.M. 1986, First published-1947

Chakravarty Jayanta & Bhattacharya D.C. — *Aspects of Indian art & culture,* Calcutta - 1983, (S.K. Saraswati commemoration volume).

Chouhan Dr. T.S. — *Encyclopaedia of Rajasthan* in Vol. I & II, Vigyan Prakasan, Jodhpur - 1996

Coomaraswamy Ananda K. — *Essays in Early Indian Architecture,* Edited & with an Introduction by Michael W.Meister, IGNCA, Oxford University Press, - 1992

Cousen H. — *The architectural antiquites of western India,* India Society, London - 1926

Dhaky M.A. & Meister Michael (Jt. Ed.) — *Encyclopaedia of Indian Temple Architecture : South India lower Drāviḍadeśa* 200 B.C. - A.D. 1324. A.I.O.S. & Oxford University Press, Delhi -1983

Dorje.C and Dimri D.N — *Kumbhalgarh - the pride of Maharanas of Mewar,* New Delhi-2008

Dutta B.B. — *Town Planning in Ancient India; Thacker,* Spink & Co. , Calcutta-1925

Ghurye G.S. — *Rajput Architecture Popular Prakasan Bombay*-1968

Gode P.K. — *Studies in Indian Cultural History* - Vol. I, V.V.R.I. Hoshiarpur-1961

Gode P.K. — *The manufacture and use of firearms in India between* 1450 - 1850, Bharatiya Vidya Bhawan, Vol. IX, Bombay-1948

Gulati S.P. — *Encyclopaedia of Rajasthan (VM),* Rima Publishing house, New Delhi - 1992

Harle J.C. — *The art and architecture of the Indian subcontinent,* Harmends worth, Penguin books - 1986

Joshi S.K. — *Defence Architecture in early Karnataka;* Sundeep Prakashan, New Delhi - 1985

Kane P.V. — *History of Dharmasastra* Vol. III (Ancient & Mediaeval Religion & Civil Law.)B.O.R.I., Poona - 1946

Kapoor Subodh — *The Indian Encyclopaedia* Vol II, Cosmos Publications, New Delhi-2002

Kramrisch Stella — *The Hindu Temple,* Calcutta University, Calcutta-1946

Kulkarni Raghunath Purushottam — *Prāsāda Maṇḍana of Sūtradhāra Maṇḍana* (Ed.) (Sanskrit text and English translation with notes and glossary), Munshiram Manoharlal, New Delhi-2005

Lahiri Kanak Lall — *West Bengal Forest,* Centenary commemoration volume, Kolkata - 1964

Mallaya N.V., (B.A.) — *Studies in Sanskrit treaties on Temple Architecture with special reference to Tantra samuccaya,* Annamalai University Publication - 1949

Martinelli Antonio, Michell George — *The Royal Palaces of India,* Thomas & Hudson Ltd., London - 1994

Michell George — *The Hindu Temple,* An Introduction to its meaning and forms, B.I. Publications, Janpath, New Delhi - 1977

Mukherjee Girindranath — *History of Indian medicine from the earliest ages to the present time,* Vol. III, Calcutta-1929

Raz Ram — *Essays on the architecture of the Hindus,* John Williams Parker, London 1834

Roy A.K. — *History of the Jaipur City,* New Delhi - 1978

Roy Amita — *Villages towns & secular buildings in ancient India,* Calcutta - 1964

Sarkar Jadunath — *A History of Jaipur Orient Longman* - 1984

Satyamurty K. — *Handbook of Indian Architecture;* Ashish Publishing home, New Delhi

Seal Brajendranath — *The positive sciences of the ancient Hindus,* Delhi - 1985

Shukla D.N. — *Vāstuśāstra (Hindu Science of Architecture) Vol. - I ,* Munshiram Monoharlal Publishers Pvt. Ltd. N. Delhi - 1993

Shukla Lalit Kr. — *A study of Hindu art and architecture with special reference to terminology,* Chowkh-amba publication, Varanasi-1972, (Chowkhamba Skt. Studies Vol. - LXXXII)

Srivastava A.L. — *Śilpaśrī:- Studies in Indian art & culture,* Sundeep Prakashan, New Delhi-1990

Tillaton, G.H.R. — *The Rajput palaces,* New Havel & Cenn London-1987

Torr Gray — *The architecture of the early western Calukyas,* (Ph.D. Dissertation), University of California., Los Angeles - 1969

Turner R.L. — *A Comparative Dictionary of the Indo Aryan Language,* Oxford University Press, London, 1966

William Gattbried Joanna — *The art of Gupta India, Empire & Province,* Heritage Publishers, New Delhi - 1983

Bengali

Guha Velavasini and Ahana — *Ṛgved O Naksatra. Gopa,* Kolkata - 1967

Biswas Kalipada & Ghosh E. Kari — *Bhāratiya Banauṣadhi - 1 - 6 Volume,* New edition, Calcutta University-1973

Sanskrit

Agni Purāṇa (with Bengali *translation)* — *Ed. By Pancanan Tarkaratna revised by Śrijiva Nyayathirta,* Navabharata Publisher, Kolkata (B.S. 1389) 1982-83

Amarakośa of Amarasinha with the commentary - Namachandrika — *Ed. by Pandit Visnu Dutta Sharma,* Benkateshwar Steam Press, Bombay-1929

Aparājita Pṛchhā by Bhuvandeva — *Ed. by P.A. Mankad, General editor B. Bhattacharya,* Oriental Institute, Baroda - 1950

Matsyapurāṇa (with Bengali translation) — *Ed. By Pancanan Tarkaratna,* Calcutta, 1910

Prāsādamaṇḍana and Rājavallabhamaṇḍana — *Calcutta Sanskrit Series,* Metropolitan Publishing house, Calcutta - 1948

Devata Mūtri Prakaraṇa and Rupamaṇḍana (Critically edited with notes and commentary) — *Ed. by Upendra Mohan Sāṅkhya tirtha with introduction by Haridas Mitra,* Calcutta Sanskrit Series, No. 12,

	Metropolitan Printing and Publishing house, Calcutta - 1936
Prāsādamaṇḍanam of Sūtradhāra Maṇḍana	(An Indian treatise on the construction of temple Building.) with text translation and commentaries, ed. Dr. Shri Krishan Jugnu, Parimal Publications, Delhi-2005
Rājavallabhavāstuśāstram	Ed. by Dr. Shri Krishan Jugnu, Parimal Publications, Delhi-2005
Samarāgaṇa Sūtradhāra by Maharajadhiraja of Dhāra or Bhoja, the Paramara ruler	Ed. by Vasudev Saran Agarwal, Baroda, 1966
Sangitaraja by Rana Kumbha, Vol. I	Ed. by Premlata Sharma, Benaras Hindu University Press, Benaras - 1963

Journals and articles

- Indian Historical quarterly, 1957, Vol. - XXX - III, (Some famous sculptors & architects of Mewar 15th Cent. A.D.), P. C. Agarwal

- Astrological Magazine, Vol. 87, no. 1 - 5, Jan. - May, 1998 ed. By B.V. Raman, Raman Publications, Bangalore

- Journal of American Oriental Society, Vol. 48-1928, pp. 250 - 275

- "Learning from old Jaipur", an article written by Balkrishna Doshi and Muktirajsinhji Chauhan from VidyadharNagar Study cell, Ahmadabad-1987.

- "Some architectural conventions of Kerala", an article written by K.R. Pishaorati in 'The Cultural Heritage of India', Volume VII, Part-I, Kolkata -2006

- Rupam (an illustrated quarterly journal of oriental art) ; ed. O.C. Ganguly.

a. No. 5, 1921.

b. No. 17-20, 1924

c. No. 25-28, 1926

d. No. 29-32, 1927

e. No. 35-36, 1928

Dictionary

Śabdakalpadruma	*Ed. by Sri Raja Radhakanta Dev Bahadur,* Kolkata - 1822 - 58 A.D.
Sanskrit to Bengali Dictionary	*Bandopadhyaya Haricaran Bangiya Śavdakosa,* 2nd ed., Sahitya Academy, New Delhi - 1978
Sanskrit to English Dictionary	*Bhide Vaman Vidyadhara,* A Concise Sanskrit English Dictionary, Gyan Publishing House, Delhi
Comparative Dictionary	*A Comparative Dictionary of the Indo Aryan Language by R.L. Turner,* Oxford University Press, London-1966

Index-Glossary

A

Abdhi	–	Number seven, 3.49; 8.89
Adri	–	Mountain, Number seven ; 4.48
Agnau	–	South east corner, 5.3
Akrama	–	want of order, confusion, not happening successively, 7.69
Alinda	–	*Balabhī* in front of the *śālā*, gallery, portico, veranda, aisle, 4.8, 24, 29; 8.2 3, 5,6,8
Ambara	–	Circumference, sky, 5.14
Aṅganam	–	courtyard, 5.3
Aṅgulam	–	Finger, 1.174, 175, 176, 184, 188, 190
Aṅka	–	Number nine, 4.24; 8.53
Annālaya	–	Principal main building in *catuśśālā* meant for kṣatriya (*Mayamatm*), 4.35
Antarapatraka	–	Inner leaves, 8.55
Antarvaṁśika	–	Keeper of the seraglia, 5.24
Anuvaṁśa	–	Geneological list or table, collateral branch of a family, 7.69
Aṣṭapatra	–	Eight leaved, 3.31
Aṣṭāstra	–	Eight cornered, 3.31
Aṣṭaśālā	–	A house with combination of 1–4 śālās, 6.32
Aṣṭavarga	–	eight divisions, 4.13
Apakrāma	–	To go away, retreat, glide away, 4.101
Apasavya	–	Not to the left, on the right side, from right to left, moving to the left, 4.68

Apavarka	–	Small structure i.e., *catuskuḍya,* an inner apartment, lying in chamber, *Koṣṭhaka,* 6.3, 49, 51, 53, 56; 8.4, 8
Arka	–	Sun, Number twelve, 2.64, 4.44, 97; 8.75
Arkahasta	–	Twelve hands, 3.41
Aśasta	–	Inauspicious, 7.11
Aśṃa/Aśmarī	–	Strangury, stone or gravel, 3.69
Avāk	–	South, 8.15, 16
Āgama	–	A tradition doctrine, or precept, sacred knowledge of learning, 4.17
Āgāra	–	Building edifice, 5.14
Āgneya	–	Southeast, 7.27
Agniyantra	–	firearms, 3.39, 69
Ākāra	–	Shape, 4.10
Āmalasāraka	–	crowning part of a temple, 7.6
Āmnāya	–	Sacred law or tradition, 4.15
Āpya/Āpa	–	West, 5.13
Ārāma	–	Pleasure garden, 1.4, 3.91
Āsana	–	seat, 4.30, 47, 49; 7.93, 72; 8.47, 82
Āsthāna	–	Place, site, ground, an assembly, 5.3
Āsya	–	Face, 5.11
Āya	–	Āyādiṣaḍvarga, āya, vyaya, ṛkṣa, tārā, yoni, aṁśa, 2.1, 2, 3, 4, 5, 8, 23, 24, 28, 30, 42, 43
Āyāma	–	Length, 3.17, 60, 74; 4.6; 8.43, 64, 77
Āyata	–	stretched, length, 4.18, 21, 23; 8.74, 79

B

Bha	–	Nakṣatra, 8.90
Bhadrā[1]	–	Auspicious quaters, south; Tithi Dvitīyā Saptamī, Dvāsami), 1.68
Bhadrā[2]	–	Projected moulding forepart, a type of building, 8.22,

23, 24, 26, 29, 30, 32, 45, 48, 53

Bhadrā - (for Kuṇḍa) a square water reservoir, 3.89

Bhīṣaṇa - Dreadful, frighful, terrible, 7.11, 13

Bhalla - A kind of arrow or missle, 3.69

Bhāṇḍāgāra - Store house, 5.13

Bhaṭa - Warrior, 3.16

Bharaṇa - Supporting components A kapāṭa also called bharaṇa, inner court, Entrance, porch, 4.82, 87, 90; 7.18

Bhauma - Tuesday, the plantt Mars, 1.6, 7, 20, 32, 35

Bhavana - house, 3.20, 33; 4.12, 123

Bhramaṇa - Circumabulatory, 4.60

Bhūmikā - Floor of a house, site, a storey, space between two adjecenct floors 4.63

Bheṣajālayam - Room for medicine, 5.8

Bheṣaja - medicine, medicament, 3.82

Bhitti - wall, 4.7, 41, 42, 48, 75, 88, 89, 90, 92; 7.63; 8.21, 26, 31

Bhojanamandiram - Dining room, 5.4

Brahmasthāna - Central part of the square, ground plan. 4.128

C

Caitya - A place for religious worship, A Buddhist temple, 4.107

Cakravellanī - Round disc, 3.53, 54

Cāmara - Chowrie, 8.73

Catuṣkara - Square or quadrangular, 4.72

Catuṣki - Four pillared porch or pavillion, 8.12

Catura - A house with forur doors, 8.10

Caturastra - Four corners of square, 8.64

Catuśśālā - Four halled house 4.28, 29; 6.14

Catvara	–	Courtyard, 3.13, 14
Chādya	–	Parapet, 7.11; 8.56, 62, 63, 65, 68
Chanda	–	An arrangement, disposition, 7.4
Chatra	–	Umbrella, 8.72

D

Dīpālaya	–	Room for lamps, 4.85
Dīpāmnāya	–	Sacred tradition of lighting lamps, 4.15
Dīpastambha	–	Lampstand, 8.76
Dīrghikā	–	Long lake, 5.10
Dīrghikāsthāna	–	Place for a long lake or tank, 5.5
Daṇḍa	–	Stick, rod, 8.71, 72, 73
Dairghya	–	Length, 3.47, 48, 52, 60, 61, 63, 65, 66, 70, 77; 8.52, 53, 77, 79, 84
Dakṣa	–	Right side, 3.55, 63, 93; 8.65
Dakṣiṇa	–	South, 3.28, 29; 5.8, 11; 8.17
Dara	–	Cave, hall in the ground, 4.71
Dāru	–	Wood, 8.82
Daśaśālā	–	A house with combination of one to four *śālās*, 4.19
Davāliḍha	–	Wood burnt by fire, 3.108
Devadoṣa	–	Providential disturbance, 7.29
Devagṛha	–	Abode of gods, temple, 3.2
Dhanālaya	–	treasury, 4.35
Dhanurdhara	–	archer, 3.6
Dharā	–	Scale, 3.66; 8.28, 32
Dhārāgṛha	–	a bathroom with flowing water, shower bath, 3.94
Dhvaja	–	Flag, 4.70
Dikśālā	–	A house with ten halls, 4.20
Dṛḍha	–	Strong, sturdy, 4.10

Druma – Tree, 3.94

Dușța – Damaged, defective, corrupted, worthless, 7.11

Durga – Fort, 3.1, 2, 5, 6, 20, 22, 31, 36; 4.34

Dvīpi – Leopard, panther, 7.15

Dvāra – Door, 3.90; 4.40, 45, 46, 47, 51, 52, 54

Dvārapaṭṭa – Panel of a door, 3.71

Dviśālā – A house with two halls, 4.60, 72, 73, 75, 77; 6.99, 100, 101

E

Ekaśālā – A house with one hall, 4.44, 59

G

Ga – Mercury, 1.27

Gaṇādhipa – Gaṇeśa, 3.27

Gaireyam – Bitumen, 3.82

Gandha – Sulphur, 3.81, 82

Gaḍha – Ditch, moat, impediment, 3.22; 4.34; 6.34

Garbha – the foundation, the adytum, 4.39; 8.28

Garbhādhāna – Sanctum, foundation deposit, 7.34

Gaurīyantra – A type of weapon, 3.62

Gavākṣa – Latticed window, 4.31, 59, 73; 8.61, 66

Ghaṇṭā – Bell, 8.59

Ghaṭīyantra – The bucket of a well or any machine for raising water, 3.94

Gṛdhra – Vulture, 7.11

Gṛha, Geha – House, 3.15, 23, 26, 93, 4.1, 3, 6, 9, 10, 12, 47, 53, 94, 107, 116

Gola – Small ball, 3.73, 74

Gophaṇā – Stone or dart thrower, 3.47

Gopura – Gateway of temple, town, palace, 3.33; 5.11; 8.19

Grāma - Village, 3.26, 33, 34, 35, 71

Grāsapaṭṭī - Metal base, Fillet, clasp, socket, clutch, 8.55, 57

Guhyaka - Demon, 4.101

Guṇāṅgulā - Three aṅgulas, 7.8; 8.69

H

Hīra - An architectural ornament employed below the neck of the column, bead. A Moulding of the column, 4.85

Haṭṭa - Market place, 3.14, 33

Haṭṭamārga - Market road, 3.19, 20

Hasta - Hand measurement 24 añgulas, the bigger standard than aṅgula, 3.9, 10, 52, 54, 60, 61, 90; 8.50, 76

Havyavāhā - Fire, 3.76, 83

Haya - House number 7, 8.37, 56, 66

I

Īśa - Northeast, 3.25, 27; 5.1, 5; 7.29; 8.37, 51

Īśāna - Northeast, 4.106

Indrajāla - Magical tricks, cheating, deception, 7.13

Iṣu - arrow, numberfive, 3.50

J

Jīva - Jupiter, 1.27

Jalagṛha - Room for water storage, 5.4

Jālaka - Latticed window, 8.65, 67

Jalapaṭṭi - Waterband, 8.69

Jalāśaya - Water reservoir, 3.20, 33

Jaṁbuka - Jackle, 7.15

Jāḍyakumbha - ?? 8.54

Jayantī - A column, a post moulding, flag or banner, 4.86

Jina - Arhat of the Jainas No. 24., no. 10. According to Rūpamaṇḍana, 4.23

Jyotikā	-	Fire container, 3.56

K

Kīrtistambha	-	Pillars of fame, 3.33
Kaṇapālī	-	??, 8.55
Kalā	-	Denotes number 64, 16 or 2 (1/16th part of a thing, unit of measurement of angle), 2.33; 3.29, 48; 4.42, 78
Kāla, Kīlaka, Kīlikī	-	A stake, pin, nail, 1.46; 3.50, 51, 53
Kalāṅgulas	-	2 aṅgulas, 3.44, 47
Kalaśa	-	Pitcher, 7.3; 8.59, 76
Kalpa	-	A-day and night of Brahma, a period of 432 millions years of mortals, 1.137
Kaṁvikā	-	shoot, branch, 1.112 (measuring point)
kanda	-	A lump, knot, 8.54, 58
kandogrāsavatī	-	Bulbous shape, 8.58
kaṅka	-	Heron, 7.11
Kaṭaka	-	Serpent, 3.70
Kapāṭa	-	The leaf or panel of a door 3.13; 4.64, 65
Kapi	-	Monkey, 7.11
Kapiśīrṣa	-	Battlement, upper part or coping of a wall, 3.8, 10; 8.36
Kapota	-	Pigeon, 7.11
Kapotāli	-	cornice, rail cornices or overhanging cornice, 7.5; 8.36
Kara	-	Regular cubit; hasta, 3.52; 8.44, 51, 76
Karaṇa	-	A house with three doors, 8.9
Karāla	-	Dreadful, frightful, 7.12
Karṇa	-	Corner projecting part, corner, angle, corner division of plan and elevation, 7.2, 5; 8.55
Karvaṭa	-	It is half the size of kuṭa and exactly similar to a

kheṭa and is also defended with a girdle of wall and located in the countryside. According to Kauṭilya it is situated in the certre of 200 villges, 4.7, 12

Khalūrikā – Parade place for military enclosure, 5.23

Khaṭaki – A side door, window, 3.16

Khara – Ass, mule, 7.16

Kheṭaka – A village, small town or hamlet. It is a small town situated on the plain near a river or in the forest by the side of hillocks and with mud wall. Its main population consists of śūdras or labour class, 3.34; 8.29

Khuraka – Heel, legs, 8.58

Krīḍāsthāna – Playground, 3.94

Kravya – carnivorous/Kravyādaya – Comprises the lion, tiger, wild dog class. They are also termed as vyala, 7.14

Koṭa – Fort, 4.7, 12

Koṭaram – The hollow of a tree, 4.107

Koṣṭha – Elongated aedicula (an entablature) nice, equivalent to śālā an attic room,

Koṣṭhaka – granary, a surrounding wall, 3.8; 4.45

Kovida – Learned, wise person, 4.17

Kṣaṇa – Designation, 6.99

Kṣaṇamukha – Towards the centre, 6.20

Kṣetraphala – The area of a land, 2.76

Kūṭa – Any prominence of projection, summit peak, corner, 3.83; 5.11

Kūṭa[1] – Small town, half of kheṭa, type of town, 3.53

Kūpa – Small well, an well with its mechanism of water wheels, 3.24, 83, 87; 4.70

Kuṇḍa – A pool, 3.89

Kuja – Mercury, 2.3

Kukṣidanta - Middle pin, 7.24

Kukṣidvāra - Central door, 7.23

Kulāla - A potter, 2.21

Kumbha - A pitcher, 7.1, 2; 8.76

Kumbhī - Base of a column, water jar, a moulding plinth, 4.49, 52, 83

Kumbhikā/Kumbhaka - The base of a column a moulding, plinth, 4.82, 84

Kuṭṭima - Base, 4.98

Kuḍya - Wall, 7.35

Kuḍyadvāra - An wall with door, 8.18

L

Latā - Creeper, 3.94

Lubdhaka - Hunter, 3.25

Lumbikā, Lambikā - Is it wire grill? 8.61

Lupā/Lumā - Rafter, continued pent roof, Lupa is a small plank which is added on the part or in between Gavākṣa says Viśvakarmā Vāstuśāstra, 8.40

Maddhya bhiṭta - partition wall, 3.89, 90

Mātrāṅgula - A measure equal to the middle digit of the middle finger in the right hand of the architect or priest, employed in measuring the sacrificial objects like the kuśa grass or seat, 1.174

Mattavāraṇa - Projecting wall of a palace, a small gate type found in the Nātyasastra, parapet, witness gate, 4.30, 81; 8.56, 65

Mukha - Front, facade, gable the triangular part of a wall at the end of a ridged roof. The face of a building, 3.71, 73, 78

Mukhabhadra - A portico, a porch the middle niche, the front room corresponding to modern drawing room or reception hall, staircase room, 8.23

Mukhapaṭṭī	–	gable, pediment, 8.70
Mūla	–	bottom, base, 3.72
Marma	–	Vital parts of the ground plan, 4.74
Maṇi	–	Gems, 8.75
Māna	–	The measurement of height or length, 3.54; 4.25; 8.83
Muśala	–	A type of yoga, 1.9
Markaṭī	–	a type of ear weapon, 3.43, 45, 49, 63, 65
Manohara	–	Pleasing, attractive, 4.10
Mahānasa	–	Kitchen, 4.34, 53, 57
Manvaṅgula	–	14 aṅgulas, 3.60; 4.47
Mukhyagṛha	–	Main Building, 5.6, 13
Maṇḍapa	–	pavillion, covered gallery, portico, 4.26, 29; 5.12; 8.44, 45, 46
Mandira	–	dwelling house temple, 4.5, 16, 17, 79
Mithyākṛtāni	–	falsify, contradictory, 7.13
Māyā	–	Illusion witchcraft, phantom, 7.14
Mārjāra	–	Cat, 7.15
Māḍa	–	Raised balcony white washed upper storeyed house, 8.20, 22, 24, 27, 30, 59
Madalā	–	Sloping roof, 8.40
Manu	–	Here it denoteds no. 14, 3.9
Mārga	–	Street, Corridoor, 3.18, 22, 23, 35

N

Nāga	–	Serpents, number eight, 8.57
Nāgadanta	–	Any overhanging member projecting from a wall or other body to support a weight, a peg or bracket, 4.49, 49, 50, 73; 7.16, 48
Nagara	–	town, city, 3.11, 28, 33
Nairṛta	–	Southeast, 3.25, 27, 30

Stambhapaṭṭa - Plinth of the column, 4.75, 88

Sura - *Devas*, 3.92

Surālayam - Temple, 5.5, 16

T

Takṣaka - Carpenter, 8.101

Tanikā - Cord, 3.56

Tantrika - extended, 4.85

Tapasvī - Ascetic, 7.14

Tārā - star, 3.83

Tarakṣu - Hyena, 7.15

Tithi - Lunar day, 4.32, 79; 5.31; 8.56

Tithihasta - 15 aṅgulas, 3.61

Toraṇa - Gate, 8.59, 60

Toyāśaya - Water reservoir, 3.94

Tripuṭa - Triangular, Three fold, a measure fo length, 4.62

Triśālā - A house with three halls, 4.30, 6.102, 103, 114, 115, 117

Trivarga - Three qualities of nature – Dharma, Artha and Kāma, 4.1

Tulā - Scale, beam, architrave, 4.49, 54, 71, 83; 7.34

Tulāstambha - Scale, beam of a balance, 7.16

Tulāśreṇi - A row of beam, 4.88

U

Ucca - Height, 8.79

Uccāṭa - ruin, causing to quit his occupation by means of magical incarnation, 1.177

Udak - South, 5.11; 8.88

Uddyāna - Garden, 3.33; 5.5, 10

Udumvara - Lintel, door sill, the lintel under which the door is placed, 4.49, 83

Udvasa	–	Uninhabited empty, solitude, 8.88
Unnata	–	Height, 3.3; 8.52, 53, 74
Upadvāra	–	Secondary door, 4.56
Ūrdhvavellanī	–	Upper disc., 3.53, 55
Utkaraṭa	–	Anything dug out, a pilestack, 3.71
Utpala	–	a broad knife or lancet, a nail print, emaciated, 3.52
Utsañga	–	the roof of a house, vault, 4.63
Utsedha	–	Elevation, the height of a building is stated to be measured from the basement to the top of the dome, 4.30, 81, 84, 8.7
Uttara	–	North, 3.24, 28

V

Vahni	–	Fire, Southeast, 3.25, 27
Vahniyantra	–	fire arms, 3.75
Vajrapaṭṭa	–	A club fillet,
Vana	–	Forest, 3.84
Vāṭabhitta	–	enclosure wall, 4.26
Vāpī	–	Tank, stepped well, 3.24, 4.70, 110
Varāha	–	Boar, 7.15
Varaṇḍī	–	A rampart separating two combatant elephants. A divisio within the boarder or cubical portio of the temple, 4.82
Vāruṇya	–	West, 3.24
Vāstu	–	Site of a house, 3.3, 4.110
Vāstukṣetra	–	Area of a land, 4.18
Vasu (Aṣṭavasu)	–	Here it denotes number eight, 2.66; 3.10; 8.49, 53
Vasygasta	–	8 hands, 3.47
Vāyu	–	Air, North west corner, 3.25, 5.5
Veda	–	It denotes No. 4 here, 3.11

Yuddhāsana - Seats for the warriors, 3.21

Yuga - number four, 3.8; 8.61, 63

Yugāṅgulam - Four aṅgulas, 3.53; 8.70

Yugāṁśaka - One fourth or part of four, 3.64; 8.54, 55, 57

Yugāstra - Four cornered, 3.8, 89, 8.45

Yugma - Two or twin, 8.62

Nāka - Heave, 3.92

Nāla - Tube, 3.69, 72, 73

Nandā - A title, number nine. pratipadā, ṣaṣthī, ekādaśī these three are known as Nandā

Nāḍi - Chord, 2.74

Narālaya - human abode, 4.122

Nilaya - A house with two doors on east and west, 7.9

Nindita - Prohibited, forbidden, 7.10

Nirvāṇaṅgāra cūrṇakam - burnt coal dust, 3.79

Niryūha - Cross circle, a small tower, a large pin or bracket projecting from wall, 8.39, 40

Nṛtyaśālā - dancing hall, 5.4

P

Pāda - Foot, quarter, fourth part, 8.79

Padāṁśa - a quarter, 3.12

Pādavyāsa - 1/4th of the breadth or diameter, 8.77

Pīṭha - A seat, pedestal, 8.76

Pañcaśālā - a house with combination of 1 to 4 śālās, 4.29

Pañjara - A cage, 3.48, 50, 51, 60

Pāṣaṇḍī - Buddha, Jaina heretics, 7.9

Paṭṭa/Bhūmikā - The floor of a house, a spot, site or storey, rectangular fillet

Paṭṭaśālā - a religious establishment, lobby hall, 3.27, 28

Paṭṭī - Strap, band, 3.5

Parigha - big door bolt used in great gates of the towns and their gopuras, Crossbars fasten the door, a beam, metal bolts. For kumdas abode of bakas i.e., doves, 3.89

Parikhā - Moat, 5.11

Parivṛtti - change, alteration, 7.58

Paryaye	–	deviation from customery observances, 4.68
Paścima	–	West, 5.5, 6, 7, 9; 8.17
Pūrva	–	East, 4.106
Phalaka	–	Plank, part of a column or a moulding, 4.22, 56; 7.4
Piṇḍa	–	Bodily frame, perimeter of a thing joined main buildings (Ref. house), 3.10, 44, 45, 53; 4.64, 65; 8.69, 70, 78
Pṛthu	–	broad, wide, 3.49; 8.84
Pitṛtarpiṇī	–	The part of the hand between forefinger and thumb, 8.83
Piśāca	–	Goblin, 7.14
Prācī	–	East, 2.24, 25; 3.24; 5.1
Pradakṣiṇā	–	circumambulation, walking round a person or idol with the right side kept towards it as a reverential salutation, 8.80
Prahara	–	A period of roughly three hours, 1.57
Praṇāla	–	water channel, drainage system, 4.70, 93
Prāk	–	East, 5.7; 8.25
Prākāra	–	Rampart, enclosure of a temple, town or palace, 3.6, 7, 8, 33, 74; 4.75; 5.11
Prakāśa	–	appearnce, 4.28
Prakṛti	–	Nature but here it means no. 21, 4.79
Pramāṇa	–	Dimension, 4.7
Prāsāda	–	Palace, 3.20, 33; 4.47, 70, 107
Prasravaṇa	–	Spring or fountain, 4.70
Prastāra	–	A chhanda which is used here to build various types of houses according to laghu(alinda) guru(wall), 6.102, 119
Pratibhadra	–	type of scale, plain, low rectangular block for supporting statue vasu etc., 3.89; 8.24

Pratikāya	-	One of the main entrance, 4.36
Pratimā	-	idol, 4.70, 8.75
Pratirūpaka	-	corresponding picture, 7.10
Pratolī	-	Main entrance, a gateway sometimes provided with flight of steps, a small turret, the mainroad of a town, 3.16, 4.61, 62
Pratyak	-	West, 5.11, 8.15, 16
Pravāla	-	coral, 8.75
Priyamukha	-	A type of Gavākṣa with 8 lumbis, 8.62
Pura	-	City, type of a town, 3.15, 26, 34, 35, 40, 63, 74; 4.33; 5.1, 57, 59

R

Racanā	-	Arrangement, 4.63
Rītimayī	-	Brass or bell metal, 3.69
Rājagṛha	-	King's palace, 3.14; 5.10
Rājamandira	-	Kings palace, 5.9
Rājamārga	-	A royal or main road, 4.75
Rājaveśma	-	Royal palace, 4.37; 7.10
Rāmahasta	-	Three hands, 8.76
Raṅgabhūphalaka	-	the stage, play house, 4.22
Rasa	-	here it denotes no six, 4.31; 8.56
Rathyā	-	A road for carriages, a highway, ; a place where many roads meet, 3.70
Raudra	-	Violent, fierce, 7.11
Rudra	-	no eleven, 4.35
Rudrakara	-	eleven hands, 3.41
Rujāyutam	-	Diseased tree, 4.110

S

Śakra	-	Indra, number four, 8.86

Śālā	–	A hall, elongated house, 3.90; 4.44, 53, 88, 91, 97; 8.1, 2, 5, 6
Śara	–	Arrow, no. 5, 8.53
Śayanam	–	Bed, 4.47; 7.93
Śṛṅgāṭa	–	Where four roads meet, 4.70
Śilājatu	–	Bitumen, 3.80
Śiva	–	A vāstudeva, Iśa, number eleven, 4.31; 8.56
Śmaśāna	–	Crematorium, 4.107
Ṣaṭdāru	–	Wooden frame, made out of six pieces of woods, generally used for floor, 4.44, 47, 51; 6.103; 7.5
Sabhā	–	Hall, square, outward roo, 5.13
Savya	–	Left, 4.36
Sadma	–	A house, a temple, 4.69
Sambhrama	–	Agitation, confusion, 7.1
Saṁgrāmayantra	–	War Machinery, 3.16
Saṁkīrṇa	–	Mixed, 4.66
Saṁvaraṇa	–	Rampart, construction of a belled stepped roof for the halls, 8.35
Saṁvardhana	–	Extension, 7.58
saṁvarta	–	A kind of yoga, 1.18
Sarit	–	A river, 4.108
Satantrika	–	Extended, 4.83
Saumyāyana (Uttarāyaṇa)	–	winter solstar to summar solstar, the period i.e., 23rd Dec. to 23rd June, 8.87
Siṁhāsana	–	Royal throne, 8.52, 53
Soumya	–	North, 4.106; 5.9
Soumyaśālā	–	A hall without having a hall in he north, 6.115
Stambha	–	Column, 3.52, 61, 62, 65; 4.40, 84, 86, 87, 128; 7.1, 2, 4, 6, 8; 8.24, 25, 27, 30, 32, 33, 44, 59
Stambhakābali	–	Row or group of pillars, 4.88